The United States and China

The United States and China

Into the Twenty-First Century

THIRD EDITION

Michael Schaller

University of Arizona

New York Oxford
OXFORD UNIVERSITY PRESS
2002

Oxford University Press

Oxford New York
Athens Auckland Bangkok Bogotá Buenos Aires Cape Town
Chennai Dar es Salaam Delhi Florence Hong Kong Istanbul Karachi
Kolkata Kuala Lumpur Madrid Melbourne Mexico City Mumbai Nairobi
Paris São Paulo Shanghai Singapore Taipei Tokyo Toronto Warsaw

and associated companies in
Berlin Ibadan

Published by Oxford University Press, Inc.
198 Madison Avenue, New York, New York, 10016
http://www.oup-usa.org

Library of Congress Cataloging-in-Publication Data

Schaller, Michael, 1947–
The United States and China : into the twenty-first century / by Michael Schaller.—3rd ed.
p. cm.
Rev. ed. of: The United States and China in the twentieth century. 2nd ed. 1990.
Includes bibliographical references and index.
ISBN 0-19-513758-2 (alk. paper)—ISBN 0-19-513759-0 (pbk. : alk. paper)
1. United States—Foreign relations—China. 2. China—Foreign relations—United States. 3. United States—Foreign realtions—20th century. 4. United States—Foreign realtions—2001—Forecasting. I. Schaller, Michael, 1947– United States and China in the twentieth century. II. Title.

E183.8.C5 S323 2002
327.73051—dc21

2001036128

Printing number: 9 8 7 6 5 4 3 2 1

Printed in the United States of America
on acid-free paper

To my children, Nick, Gabe, and Daniel

Contents

Preface

Since the appearance of the first edition of this book two decades ago, China has experienced a "second" and perhaps a "third" revolution. The pace and direction of its economic and political transformation have been startling, even to seasoned "China watchers." For example, when I completed writing the second edition of this text in 1989, trade between China and the United States had increased from nearly nothing in the early 1970s to a modest $13 billion per year. Most economists predicted steady but small increases in trade over the next decade. By the start of the twenty-first century, however, annual two-way trade between China and the United States had increased eightfold, to over $100 billion. Tourism, cultural interaction, educational exchanges, and other forms of unofficial contact grew equally rapidly.

Until the early 1990s, the strategic foundation of Chinese–American cooperation continued to be a mutual interest in containing the Soviet Union. The collapse of the Soviet empire in 1991 eliminated the strategic matrix that bound together Washington and Beijing since the early 1970s. Since 1989, in fact, the American public and many political figures have voiced mounting concern over China's internal policies and external goals. Although some of these misgivings, such as disapproval of China's treatment of dissidents, export of military technology, and trade practices, reflect serious and principled disagreement, others appear based on old cultural stereotypes. At the beginning of the twenty-first century, some politicians and journalists even revived the lurid "yellow peril" notions of the nineteenth century, which portrayed most Chinese as criminals lurking in the shadows and conspiring against the "white" race.

Since the second edition of this book appeared in 1990, the political geography of Asia has changed dramatically. A more democratic Russia and several independent central Asian republics now exist along the old China–Soviet border. China regained sovereignty over Hong Kong and Macao. Japan's economic predominance in Asia declined, both in absolute and relative terms. The two Koreas remain divided, although tensions between these two cold war states have recently declined. Against most expectations, Taiwan has thrived economically and matured into a democracy. Its status, as de facto independent nation or renegade Chinese province, remains one of the most vexing problems in East Asia and a continuing source of tension between China and the United States.

In this edition, I have benefited from the substantial new scholarship on Sino–American relations in the past century, much of it written by a younger generation of historians active in both China and the United States. This has greatly enriched my understanding of the period, especially since the 1940s. As a result, the first half of the volume has been largely rewritten and the second half completely so.

Over the years, many colleagues and students have suggested corrections and improvements to the text. I thank them all, and especially Chris Jespersen, who critiqued the new manuscript carefully, and Bill Stueck. Since historians are no better at predicting the future than anyone else, I have avoided prognosticating. I hope that my "predictions of the past" will help readers understand the complexities of Chinese–American relations in the last century and into the next.

0
500
1000 Miles
R U S
Yenisey R.
Irtysh R.
Lake Balkhash
ALTAI MTS.
MONGOLIA
Alma Ata
Urumchi
TIEN SHAN
Hami
PAMIR MTS.
Tarim R.
SINKIANG
Yarkand
Lop Nor
KANSU
KASHMIR
Koko Nor
Sining
KUNLUN MTS.
TSINGHAI
HIMALAYA MTS.
TIBET
NEPAL
CHAMDO
Shigatse
Lhasa
BHUTAN
SIKKIM
Ganges R.
Brahmaputra R.
INDIA
Mekong R.
E. PAKISTAN
Kunming
YUNNAN
BURMA
PEOPLE'S REPUBLIC OF CHINA
Autonomous Regions
Main railways (in China and Russia)
THAILAND

Lake Baikal
Nerchinsk
Komsomolsk
Khabarovsk
Amur R.
Manchouli
HEILUNGKIANG
Tsitsihar
Sungari R.
Harbin
GREATER KHINGAN MTS
KIRIN
Ch'ang-ch'un
Vladivostok
Mukden
LIAONING
Yalu R.
NORTH KOREA
Pyongyang
Seoul
SOUTH KOREA
Huhehot
Paotow
Beijing
Port Arthur
Dairen
Tientsin
Chefoo
GREAT WALL
HOPEH
Taiyuan
SHANSI
Tsinan
SHANTUNG
Tsingtao
Yellow R.
Kaifeng
SHENSI
Sian
HONAN
KIANGSU
Nanking
ANHWEI
Shanghai
HUPEH
Wuhan
Ningpo
Hangchow
Yangtze R.
CHEKIANG
Nanchang
Wenchow
Changsha
HUNAN
KIANGSI
OKINAWA
RYUKYU IS.
FUKIEN
Foochow
Taipei
Pacific
Ocean
Kweilin
Amoy
TAIWAN (FORMOSA)
Republic of China
KWANGTUNG
West R.
Canton
Swatow
PESCADO
Nanning
Hong Kong
Macao
HAINAN
PHILIPPINE IS.
South China Sea
Vaughn Gray

The United States and China

ONE

The Gate of Heavenly Peace

For half a century, Americans have perceived the massive Gate of Heavenly Peace (Tiananmen), the portal separating the imperial "Forbidden City" in Beijing from the ordinary world, as a backdrop for the drama of modern China. Here, in the tradition of earlier insurgents, a triumphant Mao Zedong proclaimed creation of the People's Republic of China (PRC) on October 1, 1949. Mao had already declared that the new China would "no longer be a nation subject to insult and humiliation." The Chinese people had "stood up" and were sweeping out the remnants of Chiang Kai-shek's (Jiang Jieshi) Nationalist army, as well as the Western missionaries and merchants who had flocked to China during the past century. In the cold war between the Soviet Union and the "imperialist" United States, Mao explained, China would "lean" toward the socialist camp.

Prominent Americans condemned this new "Red China." In an official "white paper," or government report, released in August, the Department of State disparaged Mao's government as a Soviet puppet regime that "could not even pass the first test of legitimacy . . . it is not Chinese." *The New York Times* condemned the Chinese Communist movement as a "nauseous force," a "compact little oligarchy dominated by Moscow's nominees." *Life* magazine, whose publisher, Henry Luce, was the child of Christian missionaries to China, proclaimed that Mao's anti-American tirade "shattered the illusion cherished by many Americans—the illusion that

China's Communists are different." By the end of 1950, American and Chinese soldiers were killing each other on the Korean peninsula while Republican politicians, led by Senator Joseph McCarthy of Wisconsin, condemned "treasonous" diplomats and others in the Truman administration who had allegedly "lost China."

Twenty-one years later, on October 1, 1970, Communist party Chairman Mao Zedong still had the United States on his mind as he reviewed a national day parade from atop Tiananmen. An old friend, American journalist Edgar Snow, stood beside the aging Chairman. Mao hoped Snow's presence would signal President Nixon—who began his career chasing real and imagined Communists in the State Department—as well as China's masses that he wanted to end the bitter hostility between Beijing and Washington and get help in restraining the Soviet Union. Barely two years and one presidential trip to Beijing later, Nixon's national security adviser, Henry Kissinger, described a stunning policy reversal. Among all nations "with the possible exception of the United Kingdom, the PRC might well be closest to us in its global perceptions." By 1973, Kissinger boasted that the United States and China had become "tacit allies."

In June 1989, events in front of Tiananmen once more riveted American attention. For weeks, tens of thousands of student activists and other government critics demanding democratic reform had challenged Communist oligarchs by occupying the massive square before the gate. They erected a replica of the Statue of Liberty (dubbed the Goddess of Democracy) to stare down the giant portrait of the now-deceased Mao that still hung on Tiananmen. On June 4, Chinese soldiers smashed the statue and killed many students as they fled into surrounding streets. Grainy videos of a lone protestor defying a tank column and of the subsequent violence flashed via satellite to millions of television viewers around the world.

For many Americans, the "Tiananmen Massacre," as it became known, revived images of ruthless Chinese "hordes." Some feared reversal of the steady improvement of Sino–American relations begun in 1971. U.S. officials condemned the crackdown, and the PRC denounced outside interference in its internal affairs. Although Washington and Beijing restored contacts, both nations remained wary of the other's intentions.

A decade later, when U.S. warplanes accidentally bombed the Chinese embassy in Belgrade during the 1999 Balkan war, police in Beijing could not or would not restrain a vengeful mob from partially sacking the U.S. embassy. Meanwhile, in Washington, Republicans in Congress spent four years investigating questionable campaign contributions made to President Clinton's 1996 reelection campaign by groups linked to China. Some Republicans charged that the donations were actually part of a Chinese conspiracy that included stealing U.S. nuclear secrets. Their thinly veiled racial epithets echoed century-old talk of a "yellow peril" poised to overrun America and the rants of Senator Joseph McCarthy who, in 1950, accused President Truman and his diplomatic advisers of betraying America by "losing China" to communism. Even though China had become America's fourth largest trading partner (after Canada, Mexico, and Japan), journalists reported fears of a revived cold war. The new Bush administration in 2001 took to describing China as a "strategic competitor" or rival.

The turbulence in Chinese–American relations since the Second World War has roots in two cultures that barely understood each other. In 1937, only twelve years before Mao first stood on Tiananmen, another Chinese ruler commanded American headlines. Japan had just invaded China and threatened to subjugate it, and perhaps the rest of Asia. *Time* magazine proclaimed Generalissimo and Madame Chiang Kai-shek "Man and Wife of the Year" for their courageous but probably doomed effort to resist the onslaught. Japanese soldiers were described by the magazine as an avalanche of warlike "ants" driven by a primal urge to conquer. In contrast, the Chinese people, under "one supreme ruler and his remarkable wife," fought in defense of values common to Western civilization. If Chiang prevailed, *Time* speculated, he might become "Asia's Man of the Century."

Many of the 1,500 American missionaries in China echoed these sentiments. Appalled by brutal Japanese mistreatment of both Christian and non-Christian Chinese, they lauded the generalissimo and his wife as the "most enlightened, patriotic, and able rulers" in China's 3,000-year history. Such hyperbolic language encouraged a U.S. alliance with China after Japan attacked Pearl Harbor and helps explain why so many Americans saw the Communist victory in China as such a fearsome event. In less than a decade, China had gone from victim to ally to Communist enemy—or had it?

China, one scholar remarked, has long served as a kind of "national Rorschach test [a psychological exam in which subjects are asked to describe a series of irregularly shaped ink blots] for the United States onto which we project our hopes and fears" of the moment. It has been perceived, often simultaneously, as a vast export market, an economic rival, a society reaching out for Western ideas, a culture fearful of and hostile to outsiders, an emerging democracy, a repressive dictatorship, a military threat, and a strategic ally. At different times and to different degrees, all these perceptions were accurate.

The dramatic reversals of 1949 and after were not nearly so startling when seen in the perspective of the past two centuries. From their initial contacts in the 1780s, Americans and Chinese have misunderstood one another, reflecting their radically different cultures and histories. The relative trickle of Chinese immigrants to the United States all but ended in 1882. Until changes in the immigration law in 1965, a trip to New York or San Francisco's "Chinatown" was about the only contact European-Americans had with Chinese, their history, or culture. Between 1949 until 1971, travel between the two countries was virtually impossible. Each interpreted virtue, justice, and progress in terms of their own norms and experience. What was different was, by definition, inferior.

In the 1780s, the new United States was overwhelmingly Christian and dominated by European-Americans who saw themselves as leading a bold experiment in representative government and progress. Americans considered exports of agricultural and manufactured goods as keys to prosperity and, in the colonial period, they had developed a taste for imported Chinese luxury goods, such as silk and porcelain. Tea was especially coveted by American colonists who, in 1773, vented their fury at British taxation of the product by dumping a shipload of it from China's Amoy province into Boston harbor. Following independence, the U.S. government encouraged business initiative at home and abroad, especially after the Civil War solved the problem of slavery and assured rapid transcontinental development. By the late nineteenth century, the United States was quickly becoming the world's most populous and productive industrial democracy.

Traditional China presented a radically different picture from modern America. Not only had China developed in relative isolation, but it sputtered into an era of steep decline exactly when the United States began its ascent to global power. A large, geographically diverse, overwhelmingly rural society, China often seemed more a concept than a country. A tiny literate elite shared a written language, but most Chinese spoke mutually unintelligible regional dialects. China's agriculture and technology compared quite favorably to that of eighteenth century Europe and America, but the industrial, commercial, and scientific revolutions of the nineteenth century that transformed the West largely passed China by. Between 1700 and 1900, China's population swelled to about 400 million, straining food supplies. In addition, misrule by a decaying government, several large domestic rebellions, and frequent foreign assaults placed heavy burdens on the mass of peasants who tilled the soil. Producing sufficient food to feed themselves and pay the rising rents and taxes levied on them by landlords and all layers of government became increasingly difficult. By the beginning of the twentieth century, one historian concluded, "poverty, abuse, and early death were the only prospects for nearly half a billion people" in China.

A rigid political hierarchy governed traditional China. The hereditary emperor, known as the "Son of Heaven," stood at the apex of the system, and power radiated downward into the many provinces through an imperial bureaucracy. Most of those who administered local affairs were chosen by competitive civil service examination. In theory, anyone could qualify for government service and the path to wealth and power it opened. In reality, however, passing the examinations required long, rigorous training in Chinese classics. To master the thousands of characters that comprised written Chinese required many years of arduous study. The complexity of language and the arcane nature of the imperial examination system kept most Chinese illiterate and unqualified for government service. High culture was a privilege of the ruling class and more a barrier to mobility than an agent of enlightenment.

Most of those who took and passed the civil service exams and entered government service were the sons of wealthy landowners, the so-called gentry, who dominated rural life. Because provincial officials came from the gentry class, and since there were too few bureaucrats to administer the country, a strong bond of mutual interest developed between government officials and big property owners. With official encouragement, the gentry assumed responsibility for local security, the collection of taxes and rents, and public roads and irrigation systems. In return, the government recognized the gentry's unofficial domination of rural life. This symbiotic arrangement secured the well-being of both groups.

A highly structured social philosophy, known as Confucianism, justified the organization of Chinese society. Confucianism was not a religion in the Western sense, but a system of norms and obligations premised on subordination to one's "natural superiors." For example, Confucian ideology established the hierarchy of men over women, age over youth, mental over physical labor, and gentry over peasant. At the head of the human family reigned the Son of Heaven, who commanded that obedience to local and central authority be as complete as that given one's own father.

The wealth extracted from peasants by landowners and tax collectors subsidized creation of magnificent buildings and objects of art, none more impressive than the Forbidden City which flourished from the Ming Dynasty in the 1400s until the collapse of the Qing (Ch'ing) in 1911. But only a tiny proportion of China's population, which numbered between 400 and 500 million by the dawn of the twentieth century enjoyed these luxuries. High land rent and taxes periodically provoked local or regional uprisings. Some revolts even succeeded in toppling reigning dynasties. Reshuffling emperors and the ruling class, however, had little impact on the underlying order or quality of life for ordinary Chinese. Without a fundamental change in political, social, and economic values, new leaders quickly adopted the institutions and methods of their predecessors.

Even foreign conquerors, such as the Mongols led by Genghis Khan in the thirteenth century or the Manchus, who established China's final dynasty, the Qing, from 1644–1912, soon accommodated themselves to the prevailing system and ruled through Chinese Confucian-trained officials and their gentry allies. Real change awaited a collapse of the old order and the appearance of an alternative vision of society. The assault on China by Western nations, including the United States, set this transformation in motion and shattered the cycle of one dynasty decaying only to be replaced by another.

THE WESTERN IMPACT

Before the late 1700s, China had little routine contact with Western cultures. Arab trading caravans occasionally braved the desert route through inner Asia, carrying exotic luxury goods to and from Europe. In the thirteenth century, merchant and writer Marco Polo followed this route (although some scholars suggest he merely chronicled accounts by other travelers) to "Cathay." In the fifteenth century, a daring Chinese admiral led naval expeditions to Africa and Southeast Asia, bringing back exotic products and animals, including a hapless giraffe, before the Ming court lost interest. The most sustained Western contact begin in the early 1600s, when a small group of Jesuit missionaries got permission from a Ming emperor to take up residence in Beijing. They assisted court astronomers and mathematicians in improving their calculating methods and helped produce better weapons. Many of the elaborate, bronze astronomical devices they constructed remain on exhibit in China. The Jesuits maintained good relations with the "Son of Heaven" and his court by not directly challenging the notion that the emperor was God's representative on earth and by soft-pedaling efforts to convert ordinary Chinese to Catholicism.

These tactics unsettled the Church hierarchy in Rome. By the late 1600s, rival religious orders, such as the Franciscans, turned the papacy against the Jesuits. The collapse of the Ming Dynasty and the advent of the Qing in 1644 strained relations with the small number of remaining priests, and by the end of the century most were gone.

China had more routine contact with its Asian neighbors than with Western cultures. Many of the smaller states in East and Southeast Asia, including Burma, Vietnam, Thailand, Korea, and Japan, borrowed heavily from Chinese culture and sent periodic "tribute missions" to China, carrying trade goods and offering pledges of loyalty. The emperor rewarded these delegations by exchanging gifts and pledges of friendship. In practice, the tribute system served as a sort of Asian trade and alliance network with China at its center. In fact, the Chinese word for their country, *Zhong guo* (central, or middle, kingdom), embodied this ideal. The middle kingdom represented the center of human achievement, while those outside were barbarians or, less charitably, "foreign devils." Even tribute bearers were made to acknowledge Chinese superiority by performing the *ke tou* ("kowtow" in the West), a ritual "knocking the head on the floor" before Chinese officials. Possessing the dominant economy, culture, and military power in East Asia, Chinese had reason to believe that their society was the center of the world.

This arrogance, though striking, was hardly unique to China. Europeans and North Americans felt much the same about less powerful people they encountered during the successive waves of exploration and colonization of the New World, Africa, Southeast Asia, and the Middle East. Buddhists, Hindus, Muslims, and other non-Christians were dubbed heathens whose earthly and eternal salvation depended on their acceptance of Christianity and Western culture.

A century elapsed between the departure of the Jesuits from China and the large-scale return of Westerners. In the interim, the European world experienced a technological and commercial revolution that soon made Western Europe the center of global power. New and better ships, weapons, industrial techniques, and economic organization gave European explorers the ability to push their empires further into Asia.

China, with its huge population of potential consumers and desirable exports, such as tea, silk, and porcelain, lured Western merchants who followed in the wake of explorers. In 1783, almost immediately after winning independence from Britain, American merchants sent a ship to China that bore the evocative name "Empress of China." Americans initially admired what they encountered. China impressed them as an orderly, cultured "meritocracy," where government officials were selected by examination, not heredity. One of the first Americans to reach China, Amasa Delano, remarked that it was "the first for greatness, riches, and grandeur, of any country every known." Delano passed his enthusiasm, as well as a sizeable fortune, to his grandson, Franklin Delano Roosevelt.

European and American merchants soon experienced impediments that changed their attitudes. Concerned that foreign trade and contacts would unsettle society, Chinese officials confined commerce. In a version of the tribute system, a small number of European and American merchants were permitted seasonal residence in Whampoa, then a village near the port city of Canton (Guangzhou). There they were required to conduct all business through thirteen authorized Chinese merchant associations, or hongs. These conditions restricted Western merchants' personal and business contacts, as well as their profit. While Western merchants bought luxury products such as tea, silk, and porcelain for export to the United States and Europe, the Chinese purchased from the Westerners furs, sandalwood, and ginseng (used in folk medicine and as an aphrodisiac). The cost of goods bought by Western merchants far exceeded the value of goods sold by them to Chinese. To keep trade moving, the foreign merchants had to import large amounts of silver, which Chinese used as a currency.

Western merchants and governments hoped to persuade the Chinese government to modify these practices. They wanted treaties setting down formal rules governing trade and contracts, permission to move around freely, and normal diplomatic contact with the emperor's court. These proposals, which implied that barbarians were entitled to equal rights and privileges, horrified Chinese officials.

In 1793, the British king, George III, sent an envoy, Lord McCartney, to China in hope of convincing the emperor to sign agreements expanding commercial and diplomatic ties. The Qing court would have none of it. McCartney was permitted to visit Beijing as a tribute bearer, not an equal, but his refusal to perform the "kowtow" offended court officials, who denied him an audience with Emperor Ch'ien Lung. Instead, through the envoy, the emperor sent a condescending letter to the British monarch in which he sympathized with but rejected England's desire to acquire the "rudiments of our civilization . . . for your alien soil." After dismissing British calls for establishing diplomatic relations, Ch'ien Lung addressed the trade issue. China, he declared, "possesses all things . . . and has no use for your country's manufactures." McCartney was sent home with instructions that King George should respect China's sentiments and "display even greater devotion and loyalty in the future, so that by perpetual submission to our Throne, you many secure peace and prosperity for your country thereafter."

Because China's relative wealth and power remained so strong in Asia, Britain could not challenge this edict. The Qing rulers did, however, agree to some informal trade concessions. They permitted Western merchants to expand somewhat the highly regulated commerce in Canton. For the next four decades, the stalemate continued. The British and occasionally American governments requested formal trade and diplomatic agreements, and Chinese officials routinely rebuffed them.

The growth of the world's first great international narcotics trade ultimately broke down China's isolation and pushed it into the global economy. Although Chinese had long used opium, the refined sap of the poppy, as a painkiller, it had not been widely utilized as an intoxicant. For reasons that remain unclear, after 1802, "recreational" use of opium increased rapidly. Almost immediately, this drug trade transformed Western commerce with China, as well as the Asian balance of power.

British merchants sold most of the opium that went to Chinese addicts. This proved a double bounty, as most of the product came from India, under the control of the British East India Company. The company licensed opium cultivation and processed the sap into the smokable drug. It then auctioned chests of opium, which private vessels carried to China. Opium exports accounted for about one-seventh of the revenues of British India and helped defray the costs of the immense British appetite for Indian and Chinese tea. American merchants carried Turkish opium to China and managed to capture about 10 percent of the Chinese drug trade.

The scale of the trade grew so rapidly that in 1839 alone, 40,000 chests of opium, each weighing 133 pounds, entered China. This reversed the flow of silver, which now streamed out of China and into the hands of British and American merchants. The economic and social impact of the trade devastated China. The increasingly corrupt Qing government tried, half-heartedly, to ban the import of the drug, but smuggling continued virtually unabated. Justifying drug sales, one Westerner commented that "it is my business to make a fortune with the least possible loss of time. . . . Our business is to make money, as much and as fast as we can—and for this end all modes or means are good." Another trader noted in his diary one Sunday, "opium sales brisk . . . no time to read my Bible."

In 1839, in the face of growing financial, legal, and health problems, the Chinese emperor dispatched a special commissioner to Canton, Lin Tse-hsu, with broad powers to suppress the opium trade. Lin closed opium dens, arrested dealers, and opened treatment centers for addicts. He then blockaded the foreign warehouses or "factories" in Canton and demanded the surrender of 20,000 opium chests stored there. Before turning the chests over for destruction, British merchants consigned them to a British government representative in Canton. Technically, therefore, the Chinese had seized official British property. To explain his action, Lin sent a letter to Queen Victoria. He noted that importation of opium was illegal in Britain. How, Lin asked, could the queen allow "it to be passed on to the harm of other countries? Let us ask, where is your conscience?"

An artist's depiction from the 1820s of the European and American warehouses near Canton from which opium and other goods were traded. (Metropolitan Museum of Art)

The Chinese appeal to the Golden Rule collided with the Western fixation on the rule of gold. The destruction of British and American opium at Canton sparked a war that broke down China's isolation and power. To avenge the wrong to its citizens and property, the British government launched a punitive expedition against China. The so-called Opium War (1839–42) sought far more than compensation or even the legalization of the opium trade. Britain, cheered on by America, had decided to force China to open itself to Western economic and cultural penetration. British military power would be a wedge to "civilize" the "Chinese barbarians."

Even though Lin had confiscated some American-owned opium, the U.S. government took no part in the hostilities. But many influential political and economic leaders weighed in rhetorically. Former president John Quincy Adams, a valiant opponent of slavery and fervent critic of both opium and tobacco, spoke openly in support of Britain's cause. Adams condemned China's arrogant insistence on the "kowtow" and its trade restrictions as an "enormous outrage upon the rights of human nature." British troops advanced "Christian precepts" against China's "insulting and degrading" refusal to adopt Western-style trade and diplomatic treaties.

Following three years of sporadic coastal raids against Chinese ports, the Qing court agreed to a settlement largely on British terms. The Treaty of Nanking (Nanjing) in 1842 ushered in a 100 year period of disgrace known to the Chinese as the era of the "unequal treaties" or the "century of dishonor." Britain, and then other foreign powers, treated China as a benighted country in need of stern discipline. Over the next twenty years, following two more European attacks and a brief Anglo–French occupation of Beijing, Western nations imposed an intricate system of indirect foreign control on a weak China. Many of the provisions were common to treaties among European states. What made this and later pacts so unequal was that China made all the concessions while the Western nations received all the benefits. The system outlasted the Qing Dynasty by almost half a century.

Although the Treaty of Nanking did not mention opium (which the British took as a license to carry on), it gave the victors nearly everything they wanted except the right to station an ambassador in Beijing. The Chinese agreed to pay an indemnity, give Britain the island of Hong Kong near Canton as a permanent trade and military outpost, and permit regular commercial and consular access to Canton and five additional "treaty ports" along the China coast. A supplementary agreement in 1843 granted British citizens in China "extraterritoriality," an exemption from Chinese law. A British subject accused of, say, murdering a Chinese was tried in a British, not Chinese, court. The British government insisted on this clause because they considered China's legal system corrupt and brutal. Chinese officials agreed to this exemption (later applied to Americans and others in China) in the misguided belief that it would minimize contact with the troublesome barbarians. Instead, it became a source of tremendous resentment among ordinary Chinese, who saw foreigners living privileged lives, flouting local customs, and their own government unwilling or unable to defend their interests. This was especially true in cases of accidental killings of Chinese by foreigners, often during bird hunting season around treaty ports, when hunters shot peasants whose land they crossed. Typically, the Westerners considered the case resolved by paying the equivalent of a few dollars to the family of the deceased.

The treaty ports, which eventually numbered almost eighty along China's coasts and rivers, followed a pattern. Each resembled a small European port city, generally walled and on the outskirts of a larger Chinese city. Shanghai was the prototype. The special foreign zone contained warehouses, shops, restaurants, churches, homes, clubs, racetracks, and parks. Social segregation was enforced, sometimes with signs in parks that proclaimed "no Chinese or dogs allowed." Physical labor on the docks and in factories was often directed by a Chinese middleman or "compradore," who mediated between the foreigners and local laborers.

As John Quincy Adams's words revealed, the American government and merchants were cheerleaders to the British war with China. In 1843, President John Tyler sent diplomat Caleb Cushing to China to secure by treaty commercial privileges (but no territory) like those given the British. Qing negotiators were prepared to give the Americans most of what they wanted, partly out of the misguided belief they could gain advantage by playing off rival barbarian states against each other, and also because they hoped to minimize contact and complications with another Western power. Even before Cushing reached Macao (a tiny Portuguese enclave near Hong Kong) in 1844, Emperor Hsuan-tsung decided unilaterally to give the Americans what they most desired: equal privileges with the British. "Now that the English barbarians are allowed to trade," the emperor wrote in 1843, "the United States and others should naturally be permitted to trade without discrimination, in order to show Our tranquilizing purpose."

With the help of Peter Parker, an American medical missionary who spoke Chinese and had befriended Chinese negotiator Ch'i-ying, Cushing got the Chinese to agree to the Treaty of Wang-hsia (named for a small village near Macao) in 1844. The pact included a "most favored nation clause," which assured that the United States would receive future benefits given by China to any other nation. Thus, whenever Britain, France,

Germany, Japan, or Russia extracted new privileges from China by force or threat, the benefit passed automatically to the United States. This meant achieving the gains of war and intimidation without the material costs or moral compromise of violence. Americans assured themselves that this proved their moral superiority over other foreign powers in dealing with China. Most Chinese deplored the U.S. approach as "jackal diplomacy."

In the 1850s, as the weakened Qing rulers confronted the massive Taiping Rebellion in central China, all the Western powers demanded additional concessions. In 1858, fed up with Chinese stalling, an Anglo–French naval squadron bombarded the China coast. The Qing emperor quickly agreed to the Treaty of Tientsin, which limited taxes on foreign goods to no more than 5 percent and granted missionaries and merchants rights to proselytize and trade in China's interior. Some missionaries even tried to extend extraterritoriality beyond themselves and their churches to Chinese converts as well. In 1860, when the Chinese balked at implementing the 1858 pact, British and French troops marched overland to Beijing and sacked the emperor's Summer Palace, destroying an artistic masterpiece. The foreign forces stayed until the Qing court honored the treaty. Over the following decades, the British and American navies enforced their treaty rights by permanently deploying armed vessels in China's rivers, giving birth to the term "gunboat diplomacy." Thus, by the late nineteenth century, while nominally independent, China had lost a large measure of economic, legal, military, and social control over its own destiny.

Pressed on all sides by Western power, ideas, and culture, Chinese officials initially found it difficult to distinguish the United States and Americans as a distinct country and group. British and American merchants who spoke the same language, fraternized, and made similar demands were often lumped together as part of the same band of "hairy barbarians" or "big noses." After the Cushing treaty, Chinese writers and officials began to distinguish the two nations and even voiced some hope of playing them off against each other. Publicly, the Chinese called the United States "Mei Guo," or beautiful country. Privately, Ch'i-ying, who negotiated with Cushing, informed the emperor that Americans were among the least civilized barbarians, coming from an "isolated place, outside the pale, solitary and ignorant."

Prominent Americans returned the sentiment. Unlike the early observers who praised China's sophistication, by the 1850s, Americans perceived it as an archaic and decadent society. Philosopher Ralph Waldo Emerson voiced a common thought when he remarked that "as for China, all she can say at the convocation of nations must be . . . I made the tea."

By the 1860s and 1870s, Qing officials concluded they must "understand the Barbarians in order to control them." The dynasty created a special bureau for handling relations with the United States and Europe. In 1861, Prince Kung, the emperor's chief adviser on foreign affairs, voiced hope that a more sophisticated knowledge of Westerners would "help control them and make them exploitable by us." In the 1870s, reformers promoting the "Self-Strengthening Movement" sent Chinese students abroad to study and began importing Western technology for local use. In 1872, two of the reformers, Zeng Guofan and Li Hongzhang, sponsored an educational mission to the United States that included 120 students. However, by the 1880s, anti-Chinese sentiment in the United States drove out most Chinese students, travelers, and new immigrants. Within China, conservatives who feared losing power to a Westernized elite bitterly contested reform efforts.

Of course, not all China's problems were caused by foreign exploitation. A population explosion along with a steep decline in the quality of Qing administration created massive difficulties. But the growing foreign presence and unequal treaties added to the burden. Privileges granted foreigners undermined Chinese confidence in their own government. The foreigners, moreover, carried radically new religious, political, and economic ideas that gnawed away at traditional Chinese beliefs and provoked a crisis of cultural confidence. Chinese lost faith in the old ways but hesitated to adopt new ways. Christian missionaries, including a large number of Americans, played an especially large role in promoting the erosion of the traditional order.

THE MISSIONARY MOVEMENT

Following Senate ratification of the Cushing treaty in 1845, and well into the 1890s, the U.S. government played a limited role in China. It stationed no troops in the region, fought no wars, and let Britain, France, and other powers set the pace for extracting new privileges from the Chinese government. Since private U.S. trade with and investment in China remained quite small in the nineteenth and early twentieth centuries, Christian missionaries comprised the largest and most influential group of Americans in China from the 1850s through the outbreak of the Second World War.

Some of the early missionaries and the boards sponsoring them exuded intolerance. As S. Wells Williams remarked in 1843, "God's plan of mercy" for Chinese included "harsh measures to bring them out of their ignorance, conceit and idolatry." But most later missionaries were neither intolerant Bible thumpers nor naïve do-gooders. Typically, they were idealists motivated by the dual desires to spread the gospel of Jesus and the American way of life. Charles Denby, the American minister (chief diplomat) in China in 1895 saw this clearly. "Missionaries," he informed Secretary of State Walter Gresham, "are the pioneers of trade and commerce. Civilization, learning, instruction breed new wants which commerce supplies." In the 1960s, a similar, secular drive to remake the world manifested itself in the enthusiastic response among young Americans who joined the Peace Corps created by President John F. Kennedy.

Missionaries came to China with the opium merchants early in the nineteenth century, but enjoyed little security outside the treaty ports until 1858. Then, new treaty rights opened all China to an evangelical crusade. Catholic and Protestant missionaries, from Europe as well as the United States, formed something like an invading army. The "enemy" was the "pagan" mass of Chinese as well as the disease and superstition that Westerners saw wherever they looked. Victory could be measured by a body count: how many of China's 450 million souls could be won for Christ? This crusade relied on donations raised each Sunday at American church services.

Without question, most missionaries were dedicated men and women. They hoped not only to convert the heathen, but to build schools, open hospitals, and improve agriculture. Missionaries pioneered the study of Chinese language in the West and often developed admiration for Chinese culture. By its nature, however, the Christian missionary movement was subversive. Christian faith pulled the convert away from ancestor worship—a key social value—and often from deference to local political and social leaders. For the traditional Chinese peasant, the local gentry and bureaucrat were the paragon of virtue; for the Christian convert, the minister or priest held pride of place. By most estimates, only 2 or 3 percent of Chinese became Christians. The bulk of the population remained indifferent or hostile, seeing missionaries as imperialists of righteousness.

The massive Taiping Rebellion, which rocked central China during the 1850s and 1860s, appeared to confirm the threat to order posed by Christianity. The leader of the revolt, Hung Hsiu-ch'uan, was a failed Confucian scholar who had studied briefly with a missionary. For over a decade, Hung led a peasant army in rebellion against the Qing dynasty, promising to establish a utopian system with Christian overtones. To the discomfort of his early tutor, Hung proclaimed himself the younger brother of Jesus. By the time the rebellion collapsed, between 20 and 40 million Chinese had perished and entire provinces were laid waste.

British and American diplomats initially voiced sympathy for the Taiping rebels. After all, the insurgents professed support for Christianity and might prove far more pliable than the weak but obstinate Qing court. Eventually, however, the Western powers grew suspicious of the Taiping movement and its call to abolish private property. They decided that their interests would be better served by the continuation of a weak Qing dynasty, which had become dependent on their good will for its survival.

After the 1860s, the number of missionaries grew steadily. By 1920, they totaled about 3,000, perhaps half of them Americans. Among Protestant couples, often only men were officially counted as missionaries. Yet, wives played critical roles in all aspects of mission schools, hospitals, and other institutions. Groups such as the Y.M.C.A. saw their goal as spreading Christianity, civilization, and an "American way of life." In 1895, the group's annual report on missionary activity bore the evocative title "Strategic Points in World Conquest."

Equally important as the message carried to China was the lesson brought to American churchgoers through religious newspapers, magazines, and sermons. By the 1920s, church films became a popular format with which to reach those at home. They carried titles such as "The Cross and the Dragon," "The Conquest of Cathay," and the "Missioner's Cross." Typically, these films showed dedicated missionaries carrying the gospel to throngs of eager Chinese converts.

Almost from the beginning, however, the missionary movement provoked a countermovement in China. Isolated acts of violence against church property, missionaries, and Chinese Christians were common. Occasionally, the violence escalated into major riots. Attacking a missionary or Chinese Christian was about the only way an ordinary Chinese could lash out against foreign domination. Sometimes even elite Chinese voiced contempt for religious imperialism. In1889, for example, a Chinese official told a Philadelphia audience that true civilization meant more than using overwhelming force to get one's way. "A truly civilized nation should respect the rights of other societies, and refrain from stealing other men's property, or imposing upon others unwelcome beliefs."

But just as Commissioner Lin's plea to Queen Victoria to stop the opium trade went unheeded, most Americans accepted as axiomatic the justice of actively trying to convert Chinese to Christianity. The missionary movement remained a source of great tension in Chinese–American relations right up until the Communist revolution. In 1949, China's acceptance of communism, expulsion of missionaries, and persecution of Christians seemed an act of cruel ingratitude. To many Chinese, these actions marked a reassertion of pride.

THE MYTH OF THE CHINA MARKET

The impulse to "uplift and civilize" and win souls was one of two compulsions Americans felt toward China. The prospect of a lucrative trans-Pacific trade quickened the pulse of U.S. business and political leaders since the American Revolution and the exploration of the West. Bursts of U.S. expansion in 1819 and 1846, the drive to complete the transcontinental railroad and to acquire Alaska, Hawaii, and then Panama were all partly motivated by the desire to speed passage to China.

Opium began to decline in importance as a trade good after the 1850s. Many Chinese continued to use the drug, but they now bought mostly locally produced supplies. Western merchants hoped to find new markets for agricultural and manufactured exports. The very phrase "China Market" conjured up an image of 450 million consumers, enough to buy endless amounts of food and textiles. Even at the beginning of the twenty-first century, the phrase still tingles the spine of American exporters.

The facts of the China trade scarcely warranted such optimism. From the mid-nineteenth through mid-twentieth centuries, China remained a poor, overwhelmingly rural land of near subsistence farmers who either could not or would not buy most Western products. China lacked a credit and distribution system as well as a transportation infrastructure, making it nearly impossible to move most goods from the treaty ports into the interior. During the 1890s and the early years of the twentieth century, the value of U.S. exports to China hovered at around 1 percent of total foreign sales, and two-way trade totaled a paltry $42 million in 1900. Nevertheless, hope sprang eternal, and prominent Americans became concerned when it appeared some other power, such as Germany, Japan, or Russia, might monopolize China.

Talk of the China Market peaked whenever China appeared to be slipping under foreign control, such as in the 1890s and 1930s. For example, as Japan's legions swept over China after 1937, popular books and films alerted Americans to the economic danger this posed. A best-selling book by Carl Crow bore the blunt title, *400 Million Customers*. The 1935 film *Oil for the Lamps of China*, contained a climactic scene in which a petroleum executive tells a group of starry-eyed salesmen: "The Company is sending you out to China to dispel the darkness of centuries with the light of a new era. Oil for the lamps of China. American oil. Helping to build a great corporation, helping to expand the frontier of civilization is a great ideal, gentleman. But you have the youth, the vision, and the courage to follow that ideal and with the unbounded faith of Galahads going into a strange land." With minor changes, this pep talk has been recycled regularly since 1971.

THE CHINESE IN AMERICA

Before the mid-1860s, nearly all contacts between the United States and China flowed in one direction. Perhaps a few thousand Americans, mostly merchant seamen, had even superficial familiarity with the Chinese. The industrial boom that followed the Civil War pulled into the United States millions of immigrant workers, mainly from Eastern and Southern Europe, but many from China. In fact, Chinese migration to the United States from 1848–82 was part of global working-class migration to the Western hemisphere by displaced peasants, in this case from South China.

Secretary of State William Seward played a key role in bringing Chinese to the United States. Seward promoted both the purchase of Alaska and completion of the transcontinental railroad as ways of expanding American commerce across the Pacific. In 1868, Seward signed a treaty with China (negotiated by Anson Burlingame, a retired American diplomat working for the Chinese) that allowed Chinese immigrants to be recruited as contract laborers to lay railroad track and dig minerals in the western United States. About 100,000 Chinese had already sailed from Canton to "Old Gold Mountain" (San Francisco) in the wake of the gold rush, and their number grew three or four times over the next decade. They were considered ideally suited for hard labor since, as a prominent medical text of the period explained, the primitive Chinese nervous system made them immune to ordinary pain.

After 1868, as many as 300,000 "coolies" (a derogatory term derived from the Chinese word for bitter labor) were recruited, mostly from the vicinity of Canton, to work in America—either temporarily or permanently. The migration to the United States was part of a much larger exodus of Chinese to Southeast Asia. Besides their alleged ability to ignore pain, they worked cheap and hard. Construction bosses on the western railroad admitted they never could have laid track across the Sierra Nevada without Chinese crews who blasted tunnels and laid track under extremely hazardous conditions.

Although many immigrant groups encountered discrimination in the nineteenth century, the hostility that greeted Chinese surpassed the norm. They were even less like white, Anglo-Saxon Protestants than were the Irish, Slavs, Italians, and Jews. The fact that most Chinese were single males and many were "sojourners" who intended to earn what they could and return home, outraged many Americans. The Chinese, forced by discrimination and language problems to live in small enclaves or "Chinatowns," found some solace in gambling, opium use, and prostitution. At one point, nearly half the Chinese women in California worked as prostitutes, servicing Chinese males. This confirmed the view of both working- and middle-class whites that the Chinese community threatened wage rates, white women, and public morals.

During the 1870s and 1880s, waves of anti-Chinese violence swept the western states. Attacking the "heathen Chinee" became a popular sport in many cities and mining towns. Generally these assaults went unpunished, even when twenty-eight Chinese were brutally murdered in Rock Springs, Wyoming, in 1885. The American satirist Bret Harte captured the pathos of these racist attacks in an obituary he wrote for "Wan Lee:" "Dead, my reverend friends, dead. Stoned to death in the streets of San Francisco in the year of grace 1869 by a mob of half-grown boys and Christian school children." Cartoonist Thomas Nast, best known for his scathing attacks on urban political corruption, summed up how many Americans viewed the "Chinese problem" in 1880. Nast sketched a terrified Chinese man cowering before a crazed lynch mob. Pinned to the shirt of the "coolie" were the labels "slave, pauper, and rat eater." The outrages depicted by Harte and Nast added a vivid phrase to American slang: "Not a Chinaman's chance." Hostility toward Chinese also found expression in minstrel shows, which, like those directed against African Americans, featured white actors in "yellow face."

For decades, Western powers had justified armed intervention in China and the imposition of extraterritoriality on the grounds that lawless mobs threatened foreigners. Yet Chinese in America, who typically came at the invitation of business interests, routinely experienced discrimination and violence. China's representatives in the United States protested mob violence and discriminatory actions by the state and federal governments, but lacked the power to assist their nationals abroad. Meanwhile Britain, France, and the United States did not hesitate to send gunboats up Chinese rivers to pummel cities where attacks on foreigners occurred.

California politicians demanded, in the words of Senator Aaron A. Sargent, an end to the "great and growing evil of Mongolian immigration,"

"Columbia protecting John Chinaman from a lynch mob." In this 1871 cartoon, Thomas Nast turned his attention from his usual target, urban political corruption, to depict the plight of Chinese immigrants in the American West. After torching a "colored orphan asylum," the mob sets out after "John Chinaman."

which threatened "Republican institutions" and "Christian civilization" on the Pacific coast. Business leaders who valued cheap labor and eastern Republicans generally resisted western demands to stop Chinese immigration. Despite this, western states enacted several methods to discourage new migrants and drive out resident Chinese. These included a variety of taxes on foreign miners and laundries that fell most heavily on Chinese as well as vigilante attacks in which white mobs, in a sort of symbolic scalping, cut off the queues (pigtails) worn by Chinese men. Federal laws passed during the 1870s began to make it more difficult for Chinese to become naturalized citizens. In an effort to hinder the creation of viable families and communities, the Page Act of 1870 banned most immigration by Chinese women.

In 1879 Congress took its boldest action yet by enacting a law limiting to fifteen the number of Chinese laborers permitted to enter the country on one ship. Although President Rutherford B. Hayes vetoed the bill, its legislative passage showed a change in national sentiment. By 1880, both the Republican and Democratic party platforms endorsed strict curbs on Chinese immigration. In 1881 the Senate ratified a treaty the State Department had pressed on China that permitted the United States to "suspend" (but not ban outright) the "coolie trade." Congress promptly enacted the Chinese Exclusion Act of 1882, suspending immigration by all Chinese—not just unskilled laborers—for ten years. This placed Chinese in the same category as imbeciles, paupers, and prostitutes. Increasingly harsh refinements of this law remained in place for over a half century

From the 1890s through the 1920s, state and federal laws, as well as court decisions, stripped Chinese and other Asians of many legal and property rights. In 1913, California barred persons ineligible for citizenship (in effect, Asians) from owning land. The National Origins Act passed in 1924 barred all new Asian immigration. The Supreme Court ruled that Asians already in the United States, but not born there, could be refused the right of naturalization.

In 1943, with China and the United states allied against the avowedly racist Germany and Japan, Chinese exclusion became an embarrassment. Congress, with some misgivings, bowed to pressure from President Roosevelt to replace exclusion with a token quota of 105 immigrants per year. A decade later, the McCarran–Walter Act dropped the principal of Asian exclusion but set a miniscule immigration quote of one hundred annually for each Asian nation. This virtual ban remained in effect until 1965, when President Lyndon Johnson persuaded Congress to pass the landmark, colorblind, Immigration Reform Act.

By the end of the 1880s, the worst anti-Chinese violence had subsided. But racial prejudice had a much longer shelf life. American religious and reform groups described Chinese living in China with a measure of empathy. For example, the Salvation Army's official journal, *War Cry*, referred to such people in stories by their formal names or as "Chinese men and women." But *War Cry* routinely condemned most "Chinamen" living in this country as drug dealers and white slavers, corrupting Americans. President Theodore Roosevelt probably spoke for many Americans when he characterized Chinese as an "immoral, degraded, and worthless race."

In the late nineteenth and first decades of the twentieth centuries, the most common image of China came from popular culture, including comic strips and pulp magazines. The "pulps," which sold as many as 20 million copies per month, serialized tales, such as the saga of "Mr. Wu Fang" who continuously lusted after the "blonde maiden, Tanya."

Hollywood films and radio dramas eventually replaced pulp magazines as the conveyor of ideas. On film, Chinese characters were generally portrayed as menial workers, criminals, and even fiends. In Britain and then America, this "yellow peril" took form in the stories, novels, and films created by Sax Rohmer, the pen name of Arthur Sarsfield Ward, who was raised in England and moved to American in 1931. "Imagine," Rohmer wrote, "a person tall, lean and feline, high shouldered, with a brow like Shakespeare, and a face like Satan, a close shaven skull and long magnetic eyes of a true cat green." Then "invest him with all the cruel cunning of an entire eastern race, accumulated in one giant intellect with all the resources of a wealthy government. Imagine that awful being an you have a mental picture of Dr. Fu Manchu, the yellow peril incarnate in one man."

Between 1913, when he unveiled *The Insidious Dr. Fu Manchu*, through his last publication in 1959, Rohmer produced thirteen novels and numerous short stories, comic books, radio plays, movie scripts and even television shows that features the "fiendish yellow dragon of death." During this span of nearly a half century, Rohmer's fictional hero, Nayland Smith, tutored millions of readers about things Chinese. The "swamping of the white world by the Yellow hordes might well be the price of our failure," Smith warned.

After Frankenstein's monster, Fu Manchu became the movie villain Americans most loved to hate. As first portrayed by Boris Karloff, who also played Frankenstein's monster, Fu Manchu personified the term "Chinese torture." In films released as late as the 1960s, a bloodthirsty Fu Manchu, depicted with Communist overtones, conspired to violate white women and conquer the world.

A Police Gazette comic book of the 1880s warns of girls lured into Chinese opium dens in American cities.

To be sure, Hollywood occasionally showed heroic Chinese such as the peasants of the "Good Earth" (discussed in the next chapter) or the Honolulu-based detective, Charlie Chan. In several dozen films released over four decades, a half-dozen actors, none Chinese, played Chan. All spoke as if they learned English from a fortune cookie. ("Motive like end of string, tied in many knots.") Nothing in the series had much to do with Chinese realities. Yet, in 1971, when President Richard Nixon startled the public with his opening to China, American television stations tried to ride the wave by showing old Charlie Chan and Fu Manchu movies in late-night time slots.

Americans took genuine pride in their eagerness to educate Chinese. After 1900, several prominent American universities established branches in China and others brought thousands of Chinese scholarship students to the United States. (This phenomenon would recur at the end of the twentieth century, when Chinese again comprised the largest number of foreign students at American universities.) But whether a Chinese attended Yale-in-China or Yale in New Haven, Connecticut, the underlying goal was to make him or her more like an American. Both on film and in real life, a "good Chinese" meant one who converted to Christianity and worked to make over Chinese culture in the American image.

SELECTED ADDITIONAL READINGS

Among the best studies of China during the nineteenth and twentieth centuries are: Four studies by Jonathan D. Spence, including, *The Gate of Heavenly Peace: The Chinese and Their Revolution, 1895–1980* (New York, 1981); *The Chan's Great Continent: China in Western Minds* (New York, 1998); *God's Chinese Son: The Chinese Heavenly Kingdom of Hong Xiuquan* (New York, 1996); *The Chinese Century: A Photographic History of the Last 100 Years* (New York, 1996); John K. Fairbank and Merle Goldman, *China: A New History*; Mary C. Wright, *The Last Stand of Chinese Conservatism: The T'ung-Chih Restoration, 1862–1874* (Stanford, Calif., 1957); Philip Kuhn, *Rebellion and Its Enemies in Late Imperial China* (Cambridge, Mass., 1974); Orville Schell and Franz Schurman, eds., *Imperial China: The Decline of the Last Dynasty and the Origin of Modern China, the 18th and 19th Centuries* (New York, 1967); Studies of the Western impact on China, trade, missionaries, and immigration through the 1890s include: John K. Fairbank, *Trade and Diplomacy on the China Coast: The Opening of the Treaty Ports* (Cambridge, Mass., 1953); Peter Fay, *The Opium War, 1839–42* (Chapel Hill, N.C., 1975); Jacques M. Downs, *The*

Golden Ghetto: The American Commercial Community at Canton and the Shaping of American China Policy, 1784–1844 (Bethlehem, Pa., 1997); Michael Hunt, *The Making of a Special Relationship: The United States and China to 1914* (New York, 1983); Akira Iriye, *Across the Pacific* (New York, 1967); James C. Thomson, Peter W. Stanley, and John. C. Perry, *Sentimental Imperialists: The American Experience in East Asia* (New York, 1981); Harold Isaacs, *Scratches on Our Mind: American Images of India and China* (New York, 1958); John K. Fairbank, ed., *The Missionary Enterprise in China and America* (Cambridge, Mass., 1974); Paul Varg, *Missionaries, Chinese, and Diplomats: The American Protestant Missionary Movement in China, 1890–1952* (Princeton, N.J., 1958); Jane Hunter, *The Gospel of Gentility: American Women Missionaries in Turn-of-the-Century China* (New Haven, Conn., 1984); Jonathan D. Spence, *To Change China: Western Advisers in China, 1920–1960* (New York, 1980); Ronald Takaki, *Strangers from a Different Shore: A History of Asian Americans* (New York, 1989); Stewart Miller, *Unwelcome Immigrant: American Images of the Chinese, 1875–1882* (Berkeley, Calif., 1969); Robert Mc Clellan, *The Heathen Chinee: A Study of American Attitude Toward China, 1890–1905* (Columbus, Ohio, 1971); Maxine Hong Kingston, *China Men* (New York, 1980); David L. Anderson, *Imperialism and Idealism: American Diplomats in China, 1861–1898* (Bloomington, Ind., 1985); Jonathan Goldstein, *Philadelphia and the China Trade* (Philadelphia, Pa., 1978); Stephen Ambrose, *Nothing Like it in the World: The Men Who Built the Transcontinental Railroad, 1863–1869* (New York, 2000); Marilyn B. Young, *The Rhetoric of Empire* (Cambridge, Mass., 1969); Ernest R. May and John K. Fairbank, eds., *America's China Trade in Historical Perspective: The Chinese and American Performance* (Cambridge, Mass., 1986); Robert G. Lee, *Orientals: Asian-Americans in Popular Culture* (Philadelphia, 1999); Eileen Scully, *Bargaining with the State from Afar* (New York, 2001).

TWO

Asia in Disorder, 1890s–1936

In the three-quarters of a century that elapsed between the end of the American Civil War and the outbreak of the Second World War, few nations had more varied experiences than did the United States and China. While the United States began a period of accelerated economic expansion that culminated in a rise to world power, China continued its slide into poverty, rebellion, and foreign domination. The increasingly feeble Qing dynasty survived largely because the Great Powers found it more convenient to leave the Manchus on the throne than to assume the burden of ruling China directly. Meanwhile, American missionaries and merchants, who enjoyed the full benefit of the unequal treaties imposed on China, passed through the door forced open by others. Most of the time, the U.S. government hardly bothered about China, as long as no one interfered with American commercial and religious activities.

Until 1899, the United States deferred to Great Britain on most China policy matters. Americans took a more active role elsewhere in the Pacific, gradually dominating the Hawaiian islands and acquiring Wake and Midway islands and parts of Samoa. The U.S. Navy played a key role in forcing Japan to open itself to foreign contact. In 1853–54, Commodore Matthew Perry led a naval expedition to Tokyo Bay, with orders to make the Tokugawa Shogun (a hereditary military ruler) sign a trade agreement along the lines of those imposed on China. Perry's steam-powered warships convinced the Japanese to bow to foreign pressure and sign unequal treaties with the Western powers. As a writer in the *Presbyterian Review* happily observed, "Christian civilization and commerce had closed upon the Japanese Empire on both sides." Japan, it appeared, would follow in China's unhappy wake.

For several reasons, however, Japan escaped China's fate. For almost fifteen years after Perry "opened Japan," most of the European powers and the United States were involved in wars, including the Crimean War and American Civil War, that consumed their attention. The Japanese elite, desperate to avoid becoming a semi-colony, used this interim to depose the Tokugawa military rulers and to organize a new government under the leadership of the formerly ceremonial emperor. This so-called Meiji Restoration of 1868 ushered in an era of rapid economic and social change. Japanese reformers borrowed Western technology, science, and organizational ideas in their quest to build a powerful and independent Japan. By the 1890s, Japan had transformed itself into a regional military power, rid itself of unequal treaties, and begun to compete with Western nations to dominate Asia.

THE COLLAPSE OF THE ASIAN POWER BALANCE

In the mid-1890s, the balance of forces that had preserved a rough equilibrium in East Asia since the 1840s began to break. Inside China, popular resentment against foreign domination and the inept Qing dynasty grew more intense. At the same time, the European nations, the United States, and Japan intensified their rivalries to dominate the less developed areas of the world. Between the 1860s and about 1910, nearly 25 percent of the globe was seized as new colonies. This included most of Africa, large parts of Southeast Asia, outlying provinces of China, areas in the Middle East, and numerous Pacific islands. Late industrializing nations, such as Japan, Germany, and Czarist Russia, in addition to England and France, were especially motivated to achieve greatness by building new empires. Before 1898, U.S. overseas expansion was limited to a few small Pacific islands and Alaska. But among American opinion leaders, including key politicians, businessmen, religious thinkers, and popular writers, the idea grew more appealing in the 1880s and 1890s that national power, purpose, and prosperity required the United States to play a more active global role. A naval building program, begun in the late 1880s, reflected this concern.

Japan's surprisingly quick victory over China in the Sino–Japanese War of 1894–95, which was fought for influence over Korea, precipitated a race to divide China into "spheres of influence." Since the 1860s, Qing internal affairs were dominated by the Empress Dowager Tz'u-hsi, concubine of the Emperor Wen-tsung who died in 1861. Gradually, she extended her meddling to foreign policy and soon managed to undermine China's international position. For example, Tz'u-hsi diverted tax money intended to build a modern navy into the construction of elaborate marble ships that decorated the lake at her summer palace.

Following the thrashing of China's army in 1895, Japan overreached when it demanded that China give it control of several provinces. France, Germany, and Russia intervened to block this. Instead, the Europeans and Japanese began informally dividing among themselves China's railroad lines, ports, and mines. In the United States, which suffered from a severe economic depression that had started in 1893, many political and economic leaders worried about the consequences of being frozen out of China by the creation of these "spheres of influence." In January 1898, a group of business leaders founded a lobbying group eventually known as the American Asiatic Association to press the government to protect their commercial interests in China. Policymakers increasingly sympathized with the idea that the government should defend the rights of the American business community to operate in China. The outbreak of the Spanish–American war in April 1898 thrust the United States into playing a more active role throughout the Asia-Pacific region.

Cuba, Spain's last major New World colony, had been fighting for independence for almost a decade. The Spanish army's brutal antiguerrilla campaign had provoked widespread revulsion among Americans. President William McKinley demanded an end to human rights violations in Cuba and urged Spain to accept U.S. mediation. Madrid's rejection of this proposal, followed by the mysterious destruction of the U.S. naval cruiser *Maine* while on a "goodwill" visit to Havana, prompted McKinley and Congress to go to war on Cuba's behalf. The defeat of Spanish forces on the island during the summer of 1898 proved only a small part of a larger drama.

It took several months for the largely volunteer army to organize an invasion of Cuba. But the U.S. Navy also quickly struck and subdued Spanish outposts scattered around the Pacific, such as the Philippine Islands. The small American Asiatic squadron, under Commodore George Dewey, sank a decrepit Spanish fleet in Manila Bay and then cooperated with Filipino independence fighters to force a Spanish surrender of Manila. Although Dewey had promised guerrilla leader Emilio Aguinaldo that the Philippines would be set free, powerful interests in Washington decided otherwise.

McKinley first claimed he had no idea where the Philippine islands were located and had no intention of keeping them. Gradually, he came to share the views of men such as naval strategist Captain Alfred Thayer Mahan and former assistant secretary of the navy, Theodore Roosevelt, who argued that the United States needed Pacific colonies to build its manly "character" and preserve influence and commercial opportunities in and around China. After moving to annex Hawaii, which American sugar planters had seized control of in 1893, McKinley explained to a delegation of Methodist clergymen his decision to annex the entire Philippine island chain. The islanders, he explained, were incapable of self-rule. It would be "bad business" to turn them over to America's "commercial rivals" in the Orient. After much prayer, he resolved to "uplift and civilize and Christianize [the Filipinos] and by God's grace to do the very best we could by them as our fellow men for whom Christ also died."

The notion that American control and guidance meant a better life for Asian peoples found expression in commercial advertisements as well as in presidential rhetoric. For example, a full-page advertisement by the Pears Soap Company featured a likeness of then Admiral Dewey washing his hands with a bar of Pears soap. Around him were pictures of missionaries and merchants handing bars of soap to naked savages. The caption read: "The first step towards lightening the White Man's Burden is through teaching the virtues of cleanliness. Pears Soap is a potent factor in brightening the dark corners of the earth as civilization advances, while amongst the cultured of all nations its holds the highest place—it is the ideal toilet soap."

In February 1899, for a token payment, Spain ceded the Philippines, Guam, and Puerto Rico to American control and granted Cuba independence. While the Senate debated the treaty of annexation, some prominent Americans, such as Democratic presidential candidate William Jennings Bryan, writer Mark Twain, and industrialist Andrew Carnegie denounced the move to acquire the Philippines as a betrayal of democracy. Several Southern senators opposed annexation because it involved bringing more people of color under American control just as the states of the former Confederacy were reimposing rigid segregation. But in the end, two-thirds of the Senate supported the decision to create an Asian empire. Few expected the Filipinos to react by launching a guerrilla war against the United States; 70,000 American troops spent the next four years suppressing the bloody insurgency.

Until 1898, most business leaders believed that trade with China would eventually grow due to the efficiency of American industry and farms. There was also hope that a new burst of reform in China, begun in 1898 by court official K'ang Yu-wei, with the blessing of the young emperor

Kuang Hsu, would modernize and stabilize the crumbling Middle Kingdom. But after a brief flowering of reform, Empress Dowager T'zu-hsi (the Kuang Hsu emperor's aunt and the real power in the Qing hierarchy) struck back. She had her nephew imprisoned, and then killed or scattered most of the reformers. Amidst the confusion, Germany, Japan, and Russia seemed poised to divide China up into "spheres of influence," raising fear among Americans that their own enterprises would suffer discrimination in these zones.

Pressed to do something, Secretary of State John Hay turned to William Rockhill, the State Department's leading China expert. Rockhill, who had a genuine regard for China, feared that its division by the Europeans and Japanese would be a disaster for the Chinese and American business interests. The scramble for foreign control that would follow the collapse of the Qing dynasty might destabilize the whole world. For its own interests as well as those of others, Rockhill told Hay that the United States should act to preserve China's territorial integrity.

Hay and McKinley generally agreed, but were reluctant to commit the United States to protecting China directly or to opposing creation of spheres of influence. Rockhill then advocated an approach suggested to him by Alfred Hippisley, an English friend who worked for the Chinese Customs Service. Hippisley worried that within the growing number of foreign-dominated spheres, the Germans or Japanese might stifle English or U.S. trade in favor of their own and block customs payments to the central Chinese government. Since these payments were the major source of revenue sustaining the Qing dynasty, closing the spigot would quickly destroy the central government of China.

Hippisley told Rockhill that both the Chinese government and the regional balance of power could be preserved by getting all the foreign powers to pledge that even if they established special spheres, they would not discriminate against foreign trade or interfere with customs collections. Hay liked the idea and, in September 1899, set them down in the so-called Open Door Notes he sent to all the powers involved with China. He did not bother to consult with or inform the Chinese of his action. The major powers that received the American notes all gave evasive or weakly positive replies. None, however, rejected the idea outright.

Hay's apparently successful gambit to assure nondiscrimination against American trade nearly collapsed less than a year later when a mass antiforeign campaign swept over China. The so-called Boxer Rebellion was part of a broad-based antimissionary, antiforeign, anti-Christian, anti-Qing movement that had developed a large following since the mid-1890s. The

"A Fair Field and No Favor." This cartoon from Harper's Weekly *in 1899, depicts the view held by many Americans: the United States was "protecting" and helping China by blocking any one nation from dominating its trade.*

Boxers, one of several secret societies, took the lead in slaughtering hundreds of missionaries and thousands of Chinese Christians. They also denounced the Qings as incompetent lackeys of the foreign devils. The Boxers, like other insurgents who fought Western armies in Africa and Asia, claimed that magic potions and rituals made them immune to bullets and other modern weapons.

As the Boxers gathered strength, T'zu-hsi attempted to redirect their anti-Qing fanaticism by summoning them to Beijing to assist the dynasty in ridding China of the foreign devils. In June 1900, the Boxers killed Germany's chief diplomat and laid siege to the foreign diplomatic compound

President McKinley and Uncle Sam suppress Boxers, 1900. This cartoon depicts McKinley, who had led the United States into war with Spain over Cuba and then opted to annex the Philippines, as playing a leading role in the International Military Expedition that invaded China to rescue diplomats, missionaries, and merchants.

in Beijing. Although the regular Chinese army gave only half-hearted assistance to the Boxers, the Empress Dowager boldly declared war against the world.

The siege, which captured world attention, lasted two months while an international military force fought its way from the China coast to the capital. American marines from the Philippines joined the expedition, along with troops from nearly all the European nations and Japan. Germany's

U.S. troops on maneuvers near the Forbidden City, Beijing, 1900.

Kaiser Wilhelm had exhorted his troops to avenge his murdered ambassador by making sure Chinese trembled for the "next thousand years" whenever they heard German spoken. Even if few other leaders issued such fanatic orders, the expedition devastated the countryside between the coast and Beijing. The events in China also kindled images of the "yellow peril" threatening whites.

By September, the relief force had broken the siege, scattered the Boxers, and sent the terrified Qing court fleeing from the Forbidden City to the hinterlands. Concerned about saving face, T'zu-hsi called the exodus an imperial "inspection tour." A year later, in 1901, the foreign powers imposed a harsh settlement that required China to pay them huge cash indemnities and permit their stationing large numbers of troops in China. The Japanese deployed the Kwantung Army to Manchuria, while the United States retained a small force of marines and infantry in North China. These troops supplemented the naval gunboats that the British, Americans, and others used to police the treaty ports and navigable rivers.

Alarmed by the prospect that the Europeans and Japanese might also seize Chinese territory as compensation for the Boxer attacks, Secretary of

State Hay dispatched a second round of Open Door Notes in July 1900. Now he argued against using the Boxer troubles as a pretext to carve up China into formal colonies. Privately, Hay and McKinley approved contingency plans to "slice the watermelon" and grab a naval base and some territory if China did fall apart. This, fortunately, proved unnecessary. The Europeans and Japanese were too jealous of each other to agree on any division of China so, in the end, they chose to permit the Qing dynasty to continue its feeble rule.

Both sets of Open Door Notes revealed growing American interest in Chinese and Asian affairs. They also showed a determination to limit commitments to the region. China was important, but not so important to risk direct confrontation with, say, Japan or Russia. U.S. economic, strategic, and other attention remained focused primarily on Europe and Latin America. The American public, as well as policymakers, enjoyed thinking of themselves as protectors of China. They also recognized the increasing regional power of Japan and the fact that by 1900, its two-way trade with the United States of about $60 million already surpassed that of China.

Right up through the 1930s, American opinion flip-flopped on the question of whether to emphasize protection of China or cooperation with Japan. Policy sometimes changed because of the idiosyncratic mix of interests, personalities, and prejudices dominant at any given time. Americans regularly paid lip service to the Open Door, but viewed China as an abstraction. It became "real" only when Americans were threatened by Chinese or when Russian or Japanese expansion might seal it off or utilize it as a base for further imperial conquest in Asia.

In February 1904, Czarist Russia and Imperial Japan collided in northeast China, or Manchuria, in a war that lasted two years. Since suppressing the Boxers, Russian forces had occupied much of China's northeast, an area of relatively few people and immense natural wealth. Japanese expansionists, moving north from Korea, saw the Russians as a threat to their own imperial designs. China, the nominal sovereign in Manchuria, could do little to protect its own territory. President Theodore Roosevelt, who succeeded the assassinated McKinley in 1901, considered the Russians a bigger threat to American interests and privately encouraged New York bankers to provide badly needed loans to finance the Japanese war effort. By attacking Russia, he wrote his son, Japan was "playing our game in Asia." In 1905, the president mediated a settlement between the warring powers for which he received the Nobel Peace Prize.

Once more, China survived the Russo–Japanese war nominally intact, but with reduced control over its territory. Roosevelt's grudging respect for

Japan's modernization did not extend to China. The president considered China's lack of national spirit contemptible and proof that those he often called "chinks" were a "worthless, degraded race." Despite America's nominal defense of the Open Door, Congress in 1904 permanently banned most Chinese immigration, and soon the Roosevelt administration and the legislatures of several western states added measures that blatantly discriminated against Chinese as well as Japanese and Korean residents. American racism served as a catalyst for a new nationalism within China.

Students, merchants, and urban residents in China, appalled by the mistreatment of Chinese abroad—and by the imperial government's inability to do anything about it—organized an effective boycott of American products. This economic offensive of 1905 did not change American immigration policy, but it did convince many Chinese that the nation's interests could only be defended by popular, grass-roots action, not the moribund Qing dynasty.

For Roosevelt, the key issue in East Asia after 1905 was not protecting China, but avoiding conflict with an increasingly powerful and assertive Japan. Anti-Japanese agitation, especially in California during 1907, complicated this goal. Roosevelt's successor, William Howard Taft, attempted to confront rather than placate Tokyo. During much of his presidency (1909–13) Taft and Secretary of State Philander Knox hatched schemes to prevent both Russia and Japan (which had reconciled some of their disputes over Manchuria in 1907) from dominating this important area in northeast China. Influenced by junior diplomats such as Willard Straight, who overvalued the economic importance of Manchuria to the United States, Taft and Knox tried in 1911–12 to encourage major American investments in northeast China. Known popularly as "dollar diplomacy," their plan called for constructing American-owned railroads in Manchuria as a way to counterbalance Japanese and Russian influence. The idea, euphemistically called a plan to "internationalize" Manchuria's infrastructure, failed when Japan and Russia jointly objected and U.S. investors showed little enthusiasm. Taft, like several of his successors, misplayed his hand by overestimating the economic and strategic significance of China to the United States and underestimating its importance to Japan and Russia.

While Roosevelt and Taft pondered how to protect American interests in China, the Qing court surprised everyone by finally initiating major reforms, many along the lines of those adopted by Japan in the 1860s. Qing officials modernized the education system, replacing the moribund Confucian examination system with Western models. It streamlined the archaic system of internal taxes that stifled enterprise. In a bid to regain the support of local leaders, the central government created provincial assemblies. Qing reformers hoped these actions would appease domestic critics and improve China's ability to stand up to outside pressure.

The reforms, while vital, came too late. More and more Chinese believed that only the overthrow of the Qing could save China. Among these was Sun Yat-sen, a Christian partly educated in Hawaii. He and his followers were part of a large, informal network of revolutionaries plotting to overthrow the Qing and establish a modern republic.

When change came, it failed to follow the revolutionary script. For example, Sun was on a fundraising trip to the United States and missed most of what was later called the 1911 Revolution. What finally brought dynastic collapse was a groundswell of disgust at the cumulative record of Qing weakness combined with several regional military revolts and declarations of autonomy by the new provincial assemblies. General Yuan Shih-k'ai, an influential military official, engineered the abdication of the last Qing emperor in February 1912. He then proclaimed a republican form of government with himself as leader. Sun Yat-sen occupied a minor position in the new government, but was quickly forced out. He devoted his energy to reorganizing his followers as a new political force, the Kuomintang, or Nationalist party.

During the next four years, Yuan tried to unify China and win foreign support. In 1913, the new American president, Woodrow Wilson, recognized Yuan's government but withdrew U.S. support from an international banking consortium organized to lend money to China. The president considered the consortium antidemocratic. Although well intentioned, Wilson's decision left America with little ability to influence the actions of other powers toward China.

Several private American advisers counseled Yuan's regime. For example, Professor Frank Goodnow, a specialist on government, encouraged Yuan to replace the dysfunctional republic with a restored monarchy. Yuan followed the American's advice, suppressing opposition groups and, in 1916, proclaimed himself emperor.

THE IMPACT OF WORLD WAR I

China's disorderly transition to modern nationhood soon foundered on the shoals of World War I. With all the European powers engaged in warfare, and the United States struggling to remain neutral, Japan moved to dominate China. First, it seized the German-controlled Shandong Peninsula. Then, in 1915, Tokyo presented Yuan's government with a set of far-reaching "21 Demands." These included provisions giving Japan a dominant economic role in much of China and enhanced powers in Manchuria, limiting China's relations with other powers, and installing Japanese "advisers" throughout the Chinese government.

President Wilson, prompted by the strong opposition voiced by minister to Beijing Paul Reinsch and many missionaries, weighed in on China's behalf. He made it clear to Tokyo that Washington considered the 21 Demands a violation of the Open Door and a threat to Chinese sovereignty. In a bid to expand American leverage, Wilson reversed his earlier decision and agreed to support American banks lending money to China through an international consortium. In the face of American resistance, Japan backed down from implementing the 21 Demands.

This small victory was soon overshadowed by chaos within China. Yuan Shihkai died in 1916, leaving a power vacuum filled by regional military commanders. For the next twelve years, and in some regions until 1949, China had no real central government. Militarists, the so-called warlords, used their private armies to hold sway over whole provinces or regions. They sometimes formed tactical alliances and often installed figureheads to serve in Beijing. But no real national government existed. The warlords relied on onerous taxation and foreign bribes to finance their operations. Meanwhile, outlying regions such as Mongolia, Tibet, and Manchuria slipped toward quasi-independence or into foreign control.

The onset of the warlord era meant that no one really spoke for Chinese interests at the Versailles Peace Conference of 1919, at the end of World War I. Japan was pressing the Allied powers and the United States to recognize its racial equality as well as its wartime seizure of Shandong and its claim to special rights in China. Meanwhile, the Chinese public and a Chinese diplomatic mission to Versailles demanded the restoration of Chinese control in Shandong.

A growing number of Chinese students enrolled in Christian and secular universities and intellectuals had come to admire President Wilson's calls for the export of democracy and the right of all people to determine their own form of government. Wilson's support for open and fair treaties and his call for creation of a League of Nations prompted many Chinese to see the United States as its potential savior against Japan. Prominent Americans, such as philosopher John Dewey, who lectured in Beijing during 1919, were widely admired for espousing American-style democracy as the answer to China's problems.

Unfortunately for China, international political realities at the Versailles conference undermined its hope for American patronage. The refusal of the

Western powers to adopt a racial equality resolution deeply insulted the Japanese. To make amends and lure Japan into joining the League of Nations, Wilson conceded temporary control of Shandong to Japan. Chinese students, intellectuals, and patriots denounced Wilson's betrayal of their hope and condemned the decrepit warlord regime in Beijing for its powerlessness. Neither American democracy nor the League of Nations, they reasoned, would protect China. Thousands of embittered students took to the streets of Beijing on May 4, 1919 to protest the Shandong deal. Many of these activists, such as an assistant librarian at Beijing University, Mao Zedong, called for radical political and cultural reforms to make China a truly modern nation. Participants in the so-called May 4th Movement soon found their way into both the reformed Kuomintang and the new Chinese Communist party founded in 1921.

CHINESE NATIONALISM AND INTERNATIONAL DIPLOMACY: THE 1920s

The Versailles settlement only partially defused problems in East Asia, in part because the United States rejected membership in the League of Nations. From 1919 to 1921, Chinese nationalists agitated against Western and Japanese imperialism, even as central rule in China all but disappeared. Meanwhile, Americans worried about a big Japanese naval build-up that threatened to drag the United States into an armaments race. This seemed especially unfortunate since Japan's trade with the United States had grown steadily larger while China's stagnated. Also, the new Communist regime in the Soviet Union worried Japan and the Western powers alike by declaring its support for Chinese and other Asian people trying to throw off the yoke of foreign domination.

Secretary of State Charles Evans Hughes hoped to resolve these problems through an international conference. In 1921, Hughes issued invitations to the major European powers and Japan (a Chinese delegation observed the proceedings) to convene in Washington to address problems of the Asia–Pacific region. The conference, which extended into 1922, produced three major treaties that placed limits on battleships, guaranteed the status of existing Pacific colonies, and pledged the signatories not to interfere with China's political or territorial integrity. By preventing a naval arms race in the Pacific and guaranteeing existing colonies, the Washington treaties contributed to the economic boom that continued until the end of the decade.

Both the Soviets, who were barred from the Washington conference, and the Chinese, who got nothing out of it, were infuriated by the treatment meted out to them by the so-called treaty powers. As in the past, the great powers focused on preserving their own privileges, not on treating China as a sovereign nation. As a sop, the treaty powers offered China a vague promise to begin future discussions on the restoration of tariff autonomy.

Angry and frustrated at the refusal of the West and Japan to accommodate change, Chinese nationalists discovered that the Soviet Union—itself an outcast since the Bolshevik Revolution of 1917—was eager to assist their struggle. Vladimir Lenin, leader of the Bolshevik movement, had modified Marxist theory to justify revolutionary action in preindustrial, colonial societies that lacked a traditional working class. Even if countries such as China were not ripe for a true Communist revolution, Lenin argued, small groups of political activists could organize a mass movement under the banner of nationalism. The immediate goal would be to defeat the warlords and end foreign encroachment. This would weaken the capitalist countries and ally China with Russia. Creation of a Communist China could wait for a later stage. The road to power in Western Europe, Lenin reportedly declared, "ran through Beijing."

In an early show of support, a Bolshevik official in July 1919 had issued the so-called Karakhan Manifesto. Word of this unofficial pronouncement reached China early in 1920 and stunned those who heard it. The Bolsheviks promised to renounce the special privileges and territory seized by the Czarist regime under the unequal treaties. Even though the declaration was couched in generalities and, by the time it reached China had ceased to be Soviet policy, the tone marked a dramatic break with past practice and current treatment of China by the great powers. For the first time since 1842, a foreign nation said it would give something back to China, not take more away.

During the early 1920s, agents of the Communist International, or Comintern, established contacts with several nationalist groups in China. In reality an arm of Soviet foreign policy, the Moscow-based Comintern functioned as the headquarters of the world Communist movement. Soviet emissaries encouraged creation of a small Chinese Communist party, but the Comintern placed its heavy bets on Sun Yat-sen, leader of the Kuomintang (KMT), or Nationalist party. For several years, Sun had flitted between Beijing, Shanghai, and Canton (Guangzhou) in search of military and financial support. In 1923, Soviet envoy Adolf Joffe made a deal with Sun to provide support for a KMT reorganized along the lines of the Soviet Communist party.

As part of the deal, Sun sent his military aide, Chiang Kai-shek (Jiang Jieshi) to Moscow in 1923 to study Soviet military organization. When Chiang returned he established the Whampoa military academy near Canton to train a KMT army. In 1924, the KMT and infant Chinese Communist party (CCP) formed a "United Front" that allowed Communists like Zhou Enlai and Comintern agent Michael Borodin to train political organizers at Whampoa. Both parties participated in the Northern Expedition, launched in 1925 to unify the country.

The United Front began to fray in 1925, following the death of Sun Yat-sen from cancer. After seizing control of the KMT, Chiang Kai-shek moved the party in a more conservative direction than had Sun. Despite his mistrust of his Chinese Communist junior partners, Chiang's reliance on Soviet support required a continued United Front. The Soviets, who considered the KMT the more powerful Chinese ally, gave it the bulk of their aid and pressed the CCP to remain subordinate.

During 1926 and early 1927, as the Northern Expedition moved toward central China, the Europeans, Japanese, and Americans worried about the nationalist movement's impact on their trade and investments in cities like Shanghai. At various times, the foreign powers considered military intervention to stop Chiang, who nervous Americans called "the Red general." But in the spring of 1927, after his troops had reached Shanghai, Chiang struck against his Communist partners. In a brutal purge, Chiang ordered the slaughter of several thousand Communists who had helped him seize the prized cities of central China. Only a small number, including Mao Zedong and Zhou Enlai, escaped to the countryside. Mao, whose wife died in the KMT attack, never fully forgave the disastrous advice of the Russians. Meanwhile, Comintern agents either fled or were expelled.

Chiang's purge of domestic and foreign Communists secured his supremacy in the KMT. It also eased fears among wealthy Chinese and foreign diplomats that his plans for national unification might include a social revolution and expulsion of foreigners. Earlier descriptions of Chiang as a "Red general" were replaced with praise for his efficient elimination of Communist influence. During 1927–28, Chiang convinced foreign governments that violent attacks on foreigners during the Northern Expedition had been the work of the now purged CCP. In return for foreign support and recognition, he pledged to protect foreign interests and work for the peaceful revision of the unequal treaties.

In 1928, Chiang emerged from complicated power struggles within the KMT as its main, if not undisputed, leader. The treaty powers showed their appreciation by extending recognition to the newly proclaimed "Republic of China," with its capital in Nanjing. The government was, in fact, a one-party state. Although fiercely anti-Communist, the structure of the Kuomintang party and Nationalist government closely resembled the system created by Stalin in the Soviet Union. Even though Chiang faced frequent challenges from other military leaders, and bands of Communists remained active in rural areas, China appeared more unified and stable than at anytime since 1911. Foreign banks extended loans to China, and Chiang won a promise from the treaty powers to discuss giving up some foreign privileges. The United States took a lead in this, agreeing in 1928 to return tariff autonomy to China.

In addition to his firm handling of the Communists, Chiang's personal and religious behavior won plaudits from Americans. At the end of 1927, the general married American-educated Soong Mei-ling, sister-in-law of Sun Yat-sen, and sister of Harvard-educated banker T. V. Soong. The Soong family provided Chiang both political legitimacy and access to wealthy Chinese bankers from Shanghai. As part of his marriage vows, Chiang began the process of converting to Christianity, in this case Methodism. American missionaries who instructed him and heard his marriage vows portrayed the event as proof that their labors were finally achieving success and that China was becoming more like America. Chiang's marriage was featured prominently in *Time* magazine and the weekly newsreel, *The March of Time*. Publisher Henry Luce, who as a "missionary kid" lived in China, became the couple's unofficial publicist in the United States, celebrating their marriage as "made in the U.S.A."

In addition to the sympathetic coverage China received in *Time* magazine from 1927–31, the American public gained new appreciation of Chinese life through reading Pearl Buck's best-selling, Pulitzer Prize winning 1931 novel, *The Good Earth*. Buck, another child of China missionaries, based her sympathetic account of rural life on events she had witnessed. The story of the Wang clan's struggles against drought, locusts, poverty, and famine humanized nameless, faceless peasants. The impact on American opinion reached a peak after 1937 (by which time Japan and China were at war), when Hollywood released a film based on the book.

Although U.S. policymakers were generally reassured by the turn of events in China and the rapid expansion of trade with Japan in the late 1920s, Congress continued to view Asia with contempt. A revision of immigration law in 1924, the National Origins Act, codified the jerry-rigged statutes and "Gentlemen's Agreements" dating back forty years, restricting Chinese and Japanese immigration. The new law severely limited the entry of Eastern Europeans and completely excluded "Orientals," a catchall term that included Chinese, Japanese, and most Indians and Southeast Asians. Protests, especially in Japan and China, had no effect on Congress then or at any time before World War II.

THE GREAT DEPRESSION AND THE COLLAPSE OF THE WASHINGTON TREATY SYSTEM

To a considerable degree, international cooperation in Asia, especially restraints on Japanese expansion, relied on world prosperity. For example, Japan tolerated Chiang's efforts to expand his government's authority in Manchuria so long as Japan enjoyed access to other markets and sources of raw materials. Booming world trade during most of the 1920s promoted good relations between Tokyo and Washington and gave the Republic of China some breathing space after 1927. In 1929, for example, America's two-way trade with Japan totaled $692 million and that with China reached $290 million. By late 1931, however, the Great Depression that began in the United States two years earlier shattered the order imposed on Asia by the Washington treaties. The consequences to China proved devastating and soon enveloped the world.

As world trade and credit shriveled, Japanese exports were frozen out of Europe and the United States. This further impeded resource-poor Japan's ability to purchase raw materials for its industry. Unrestricted access to China, especially Manchuria, appeared to Japanese leaders as the solution to their economic problem. Since 1929, Chiang had moved gradually to re-establish Chinese authority in Manchuria—long dominated by Japan or its local puppets. The Japanese government, divided among competing civilian, military, and big business factions, had debated how best to protect its interests in China. During most the 1920s, civilians and career diplomats kept militarists in line by showing that good trade relations with the West outweighed the value of seizing Manchuria. By 1931, however, Western economies had collapsed and new trade barriers shut Japan out of many Western markets. Even if seizing Manchuria meant alienating the United States and Great Britain, the economic gain appeared to outweigh the risk.

Japan's actions were partly determined by the semi-autonomous Kwantung Army, a Japanese force stationed in Manchuria since the Boxer Rebellion. Only loosely under the control of the civilian government in Tokyo, the Kwantung Army had developed extensive economic interests in Manchuria that were threatened by the return of Chinese control. When Chiang Kai-shek struck a deal with a Manchurian warlord, Chang Hsueh-liang, to impose real Chinese authority in Manchuria, the Kwantung Army reacted violently. In September 1931, the Japanese staged a mock Chinese attack on their own forces in Manchuria and used this as a pretext for the Kwantung Army to take full control. Japan then created a puppet state called "Manchukuo" ruled by Pu Yi, the child emperor on the Qing throne when the dynasty collapsed in 1912.

Chinese troops proved no match for the Japanese army and soon fell back south of the Great Wall. For a brief time, Chiang found it expedient to retire as supreme leader. Western governments and the League of Nations criticized Japan's aggression and its violations of the Washington and Kellogg-Briand treaties (which pledged no use of force or seizure of Chinese territory), but took no retaliatory action. A headline in the influential Hearst newspaper chain put it simply: "We sympathize. But it is not our concern."

Secretary of State Henry Stimson prevailed on a reluctant President Herbert Hoover to take symbolic action. In January 1932, the secretary proclaimed the Stimson, or Non-Recognition, Doctrine, in which the United States refused to recognize the legal status of Manchukuo or other territory seized by Japan. But this remained the limit of American action against Japan until the late 1930s. Even an attack by the Japanese navy on Shanghai, which killed thousands of Chinese civilians, provoked only statements of regret from Washington. Amidst the hardships of the Depression, the rise of fascism in Europe and Japan, a broad-based American peace movement that opposed foreign military intervention, and China's glaring weakness, most Americans in and out of government saw no compelling reason to risk involvement in a Far Eastern conflict. Americans wished China well, but would not stand in Japan's way.

TO THE SINO-JAPANESE WAR

After reconciling himself to the loss of Manchuria, Chiang spent the years from 1932–36 fighting domestic rivals and creating a viable government in the parts of China controlled by the Kuomintang party which, in effect, was the Republic of China. The KMT represented a fluid alliance of militarists, bureaucrats, landlords, and business interests united mostly by their anticommunism and conservative nationalism. A "military council," headed by Chiang, controlled the KMT, and he eventually held more than eighty government posts simultaneously. American journalist Theodore White observed how this centralization of authority operated. "Any concept of China that differed from Chiang's own," White wrote, was "treated with as much hostility as any enemy division." Both in party ranks and the government bureaucracy, more than honesty, experience, or ability, Chiang demanded "complete, unconditional loyalty to himself."

The revolutionary ideals of land and social reform proclaimed by KMT founder Sun Yat-sen largely died with its founder. Even during the "golden years" of KMT rule, from 1932–37, the regime never fully governed China. It exercised complete control in only two provinces and partial control in eight. Eighteen provinces remained under the rule of semi- or fully independent provincial officials or warlords. In rural China, where most peasants lived, national policies had little impact on the routine of daily life.

Chiang maintained his authority by manipulating the competing factions within the KMT. This blocked any combination of rivals from effectively challenging him, but also kept the army and party apparatus too divided to cooperate in governing. The central government in Nanjing enacted numerous reform laws during the 1930s to reduce rents, rationalize taxation, control usury, and spur economic development. But local authorities generally ignored laws adopted in the capital. Since the KMT depended heavily on landlord support, it had little incentive to implement reforms that undermined the status of landowners.

Chiang's relatively moderate nationalism and his very public conversion to Christianity won praise among the foreign, especially missionary, community. He actively cultivated the support of American missionaries by inviting many of them to assist in government health and education campaigns. The New Life Movement, launched in 1934, typified this process. The reform program represented a hybrid of Confucian ideology and Christian dogma. To improve their own lives and the nation's well-being, peasants and workers were encouraged to "correct their posture, avoid spitting on floors, pursue right conduct," and obey existing authority exercised by both the government and landlord. To promote domestic order, Chiang created a fascist-style police force within the KMT, the so-called Blue Shirts. Led by General Dai Li (Tai Li), the group modeled itself on the private party armies created by Hitler and Mussolini to suppress dissent.

Although the new presidential administration of Franklin D. Roosevelt kept its distance from Chiang before 1937, the Chinese leader enjoyed the patronage of publisher Henry Luce. In 1931, Chiang made his first appearance on the cover of *Time*, which praised him for resisting Japanese aggression. He appeared next in 1933, fighting Communist guerrillas. Luce put the KMT leader on *Time*'s cover twice in 1936, stressing his opposition both to communism and Japanese expansion. Chiang responded to internal and external threats with "good roads, good morals, and good bombs," the magazine declared. This made him the "greatest man in the Far East."

President Roosevelt, later Chiang's champion, took a dim view of China's prospects in 1933. As president-elect, he paid lip service to the

Stimson Doctrine but, once in office, did all he could to avoid conflict with Japan. Until the late 1930s, Roosevelt focused on domestic recovery. His only sustained foreign policy initiative lay in improving relations with Latin America. In 1934, when Japan declared that its "special responsibilities" in Asia justified opposition to any foreign technical, military, or economic aid to China, the State Department issued a perfunctory response that avoided a debate with Tokyo.

Unlike Henry Luce, most public figures, business leaders, and American diplomats saw more reasons to disengage from China than expand involvement. Wall Street banker Thomas Lamont, himself deeply involved in international finance and humanitarian ventures on China's behalf, typified this view. In 1936, he told State Department Asia expert and ambassador to China, Nelson Johnson, that if China was too weak to protect itself, the United States could not do the job for it. "Certainly America is not going to court trouble by any quixotic attempt to checkmate Japan in Asia." Similarly, the Roosevelt administration generally discouraged private, unilateral economic aid to China or other actions likely to antagonize Japan.

In fact, before the outbreak of the Sino–Japanese War in July 1937, the only financial initiative undertaken by the United States that affected China proved disastrous. In 1934, under pressure from domestic silver producers to raise prices, the Treasury increased silver purchases. With more profit to be made selling silver coins to the Treasury than leaving them in circulation, millions of dollars worth of Chinese currency flowed to the United States, practically wrecking China's economy. The Chinese government appealed for relief during 1935, but Roosevelt declined to antagonize Japan by giving aid to China or to anger the domestic silver lobby by curbing purchases. The president explained he would not change his policy "merely because the Chinese were unable to protect themselves."

Despite these economic pressures, as well as Japanese military probes south of Manchuria, Chiang concentrated much of his attention and resources against his domestic rivals. Between 1931 and 1934, the Nationalist armies launched five massive "Bandit Extermination Campaigns" against Communist forces that had regrouped under Mao Zedong and had created a small "Soviet" area in the mountains of Kiangsi province. Chiang relied heavily on both political and military advice offered by German advisers, such as General Hans Von Seeckt, sent to China with Hitler's encouragement, to coordinate the strategy of encirclement that eventually forced the Communists to flee in 1934. Surrounded and outnumbered, Mao and about 100,000 Communist followers broke out of the KMT blockade and began what became known as the Long March. Only about a third of the original force survived the year-long trek of over 6,000 miles that led to poor, remote Shensi province in China's northwest. The hardships endured by the marchers became a legend in revolutionary history. American journalist Edgar Snow, who visited the Communist area in 1936 and described the Long March in his 1938 book, *Red Star Over China*, helped make the Communist movement and its leader, Mao Zedong, well known in the West.

Since 1932, the Chinese Communists had called for all Chinese to resist Japan. By the end of 1935, following the lead of the Comintern, the CCP urged creation of an anti-Japanese United Front among all Chinese factions. Mao realized that if the KMT heeded this call to redirect its hostility toward Japan, it would ease pressure on the CCP and enhance the party's stature as defender of the nation. Communist unity appeals found support among the Manchurian troops of General Chang Hsueh-liang (Zhang Xueliang) who, having been driven from China's northeast, now, as Chiang's allies, faced off against the Reds in China's northwest. They preferred to reclaim their lost province from Japan rather than kill other Chinese as Chiang demanded.

Despite mounting criticism inside and outside the KMT, Chiang doggedly pursued the Communists. He blockaded their northwestern redoubt and planned a final campaign to destroy the "Red Bandits." Frustrated by the slow pace of the campaign, Chiang flew to forward military headquarters in the city of Sian (Xi'an) in December 1936. Instead of rallying to him, however, dissatisfied KMT generals, led by Chang Hsueh-liang, placed him under house arrest on December 12.

Several of Chiang's captors in Sian favored executing him; government officials in Nanjing suggested bombing Sian, even if it endangered Chiang's life. Ultimately, the Chinese Communists, Soviet Union, and the United States all weighed in against killing the KMT chief. Both Stalin and Roosevelt feared that Chiang's death would precipitate chaos in China, easing the path for Japanese conquest. Roosevelt instructed his ambassador to China to spread the word that Chiang's survival was of grave concern to the "whole world." Stalin, who feared that a Chinese collapse would open the door to a Japanese invasion of the U.S.S.R., passed word to Communist negotiator Zhou Enlai (Chou En-lai) that only Chiang, with all as faults, could bring together a United Front. Admiral Harry Yarnell, commander of the U.S. Asiatic Fleet, described Chiang as a "Man of Destiny" who "personified Chinese resistance to Japan. While exaggerations, these concerns contained just enough truth to help save Chiang. On Christmas Day, Chiang and Zhou Enlai announced an end to the civil war and formation of a loose United Front to resist Japan. The big loser in the so-called Sian Incident was Manchurian general Chang Hsueh-liang. Arrested by Chiang, he spent the next half century in prison, first in China and later on Taiwan.

Chiang's stature, within and outside China, had grown immensely during his two-week ordeal as a prisoner. The *March of Time* newsreel, shown in thousands of American theaters at the conclusion of the incident, implied that Chiang's release from captivity (which he attributed to "reading his bible") on Christmas morning should be seen as a sign of divine grace for an indispensable leader. In the view of many Americans, China had ceased to be an abstraction. Chiang Kai-shek had become China.

SELECTED ADDITIONAL READINGS

Walter LaFeber, *The New Empire: An Interpretation of American Expansion, 1960–1898* (New York, 1963); Thomas J. McCormick, *The China Market: America's Quest for Informal Empire, 1893–1901* (New York, 1967); David S. Healy, *U.S. Expansionism: The Imperialist Urge in the 1990s* (Madison, Wisc., 1970); Marilyn B. Young, *The Rhetoric of Empire: American China Policy 1895–1901* (Cambridge, Mass., 1968); Diana Preston, *Besieged in Peking: The Story of the 1900 Boxer Rising* (London, 1999); Joseph Esherick, *The Origins of the Boxer Uprising* (Berkeley, Calif., 1987); Michael Hunt, *Frontier Defense and the Open Door: Manchuria in Chinese American Relations, 1895–1911* (New Haven, Conn., 1973); Jerry Israel, *Progressivism and the Open Door: America and China, 1905–1921* (Pittsburgh, Pa., 1971); Paul Varg, *The Making of a Myth: The United States and China, 1879–1912* (East Lansing, Mich., 1968); Michael Hunt, *The Genesis of Chinese Communist Foreign Policy* (New York, 1996); Eileen Scully, *Bargaining with the State from Afar* (New York, 2001); Emily Rosenberg, *Financial Missionaries to the World: The Politics and Culture of Dollar Diplomacy* (Cambridge, Mass., 1999); Walter LaFeber, *The Clash: A History of U.S.–Japan Relations* (New York, 1997); Lloyd Gardner, *Safe for Democracy: The Anglo-American Response to Revolution* (New York, 1984); Ernest Young, *The Presidency of Yuan Shih-K'ai: Liberalism and Dictatorship in Early Republican China* (Ann Arbor, Mich., 1977); Akira Iriye, *Pacific Estrangement: Japan and American Expansionism, 1879–1911* (Cambridge, Mass., 1972); Noel Pugach, *Paul S. Reinsch, Open Door Diplomat in Action* (Millwood, N.Y., 1979); Chou Tse-tung, *The May Fourth Movement* (Cambridge, Mass., 1960); Sherman Corchoran, *Big Business in China: Sino-American Rivalry in the Cigarette Industry* (Cambridge, Mass., 1980); Akira Iriye, *After Imperial-*

ism: The Search for a New Order in the Far East, 1921–31 (Cambridge, Mass., 1965); Roger Dingman, *Power in the Pacific: The Origins of Naval Limitations, 1914–22* (Chicago, Ill., 1976); Dorothy Borg, *American Policy and the Chinese Revolution* (New York, 1947); Warren Cohen, *Empire Without Tears* (Philadelphia, Pa., 1987); Edgar Snow, *Red Star over China* (New York, 1938); Harrison E. Salsbury, *The Long March: The Untold Story* (New York, 1985); T. Christopher Jespersen, *American Images of China, 1931–1949* (Stanford, Calif., 1996); William C. Kirby, *Germany and Republican China* (Stanford, Calif., 1974); James C. Thomson, Jr., *While China Faced West: American Reformers in Nationalist China 1927–37* (Cambridge., Mass., 1969); James Sheridan, *China in Disintegration: The Republican Era in Chinese History* (New York, 1975); Lloyd Eastman, *The Abortive Revolution: China under Nationalist Rule, 1927–37* (Cambridge, Mass., 1974); Christopher Thorne, *The Limits of Foreign Policy: The West, the League and the Far Eastern Crisis, 1931–33* (New York, 1973); Dorothy Borg, *The United States and the Far Eastern Crisis of 1933–1938* (Cambridge, Mass., 1964).

THREE

From the Marco Polo Bridge to Pearl Harbor

The year 1937 promised great things for China. Chiang Kai-shek had clutched victory out of the jaws of defeat at Sian, emerging as the symbol of national unity. The KMT and CCP had formed a new anti-Japanese United Front designed to end the civil war that had split the country for a decade. In an editorial on January 1, the *Ta Kung Pao* newspaper expressed a common hope when it declared: "China will have only the United Front, and never again will there be internal hostility."

This optimism lasted barely six months. The common purpose celebrated in China struck Japanese leaders as a threat to their goal of creating an empire across the Pacific. On July 7, 1937, Japanese troops stationed near the Marco Polo Bridge north of Beijing provoked a battle with Chinese soldiers. As the fighting escalated, Tokyo demanded greater control over north China as the price of settlement. Patriotic fervor among ordinary Chinese made it impossible for Chiang to appease Japan as he had done in Manchuria in 1932. Both sides rushed reinforcements to the battlefield and soon China and Japan were engaged in a massive, undeclared war that lasted eight years.

Japan's invasion of China, like its earlier seizure of Manchuria, aroused American anger toward the aggressor and sympathy toward the victim. It did not, however, provoke American intervention. President Roosevelt, his administration, and the public harbored many contradictory impulses concerning foreign policy. Many Americans believed that U.S. involvement in the First World War had been a tragic error. This idea fueled a powerful peace movement that promoted neutrality laws passed by Congress in the mid-1930s. These laws barred government as well as private weapons sales and loans to warring nations. At the same time as "isolationist" impulses gripped the nation, Americans gazed with alarm at mounting Japanese, Italian, and German aggression. Japan had moved from Manchuria to invading the rest of China. A rearmed Germany annexed Austria in 1938 and quickly cast its eye toward Czechoslovakia and Poland. Italy had seized Ethiopia in 1935 and a year later joined Germany in support of the General Francisco Franco's Fascist revolt against the democratic government of Spain. Japan joined Nazi Germany and Fascist Italy in an "anti-Comintern" pact in 1936, raising the specter of a coordinated effort by the three nations to dominate the world. Japan's loose alliance with Germany and Italy made many Americans more wary of confronting its aggression in Asia.

Despite a few early Chinese victories, the Japanese army quickly overran most of the major ports and cities, and cut lines of communication along China's coast. Japanese troops, encouraged by their officers, often engaged in brutal assaults on Chinese civilians, such as the notorious "rape of Nanjing," where several hundred thousand men, women, and children were raped, bayoneted, and shot in an orgy of violence. After about eighteen months, Japan controlled most of what it deemed important, roughly the eastern third of China and most of its coast. Tokyo then settled into a war of attrition in which it awaited the collapse of organized resistance.

After losing several battles and a large part of his army, Chiang opted to avoid direct resistance and began "trading space for time." The KMT government and armies withdrew southwest into China's vast interior. The isolated, provisional capital, Chungking (Chongqing), was nearly beyond the range of Japanese planes and difficult for ground forces to attack. From this relatively safe but distant bastion, Chiang began his own campaign of attrition, waiting until Japan either overextended itself or blundered into war with the United States.

Americans observed the spectacle with a sense of empathy as well as detachment. During 1937, Hollywood studios released two major films that portrayed China sympathetically. *The Good Earth*, based on Pearl Buck's best-selling 1931 novel, was the most popular film ever made about Asians. Although it did not deal with the Japanese attack, it portrayed China's peasants as facing incredible natural and human-made hardships with courage and devotion to family. *Lost Horizon*, based on the 1933 novel by James

Shelton, also appeared in 1937. This utopian fantasy about the valley of Shangri-La in the Himalaya Mountains portrayed Tibetan Buddhists who had created a sanctuary of love and reason in a violent world. Both films, however patronizing, depicted Chinese and Tibetans as sympathetic human beings. This made the slaughter in Nanjing and elsewhere all the more horrible to Americans.

Public opinion surveys from 1937 on showed a large and growing number of Americans sympathizing with China over Japan. In September 1937, 43 percent of the public voiced sympathy for China and only 2 percent for Japan in their conflict. A year later, 59 percent favored China, 1 percent Japan, and 40 percent neither side. By June 1939, the number of Americans supporting China's cause had risen to 74 percent, the undecided had declined to 24 percent, and pro-Japanese Americans comprised only 2 percent of respondents. Yet in spite of their sympathy, in mid-1939 only 6 percent of Americans favored fighting Japan in defense of China or American treaty rights there. Half of all Americans supported trade sanctions against Tokyo, and a fourth of the public favored doing nothing.

Roosevelt provided an implicit assist to China by simply not invoking the neutrality laws. In theory, this allowed China to buy munitions and receive American loans. Japan, of course, had no need for either. Unfortunately no loans or arms were forthcoming for China. In October 1937, the president condemned Japan during a speech delivered in Chicago, which decried the "epidemic of world lawlessness" that ought to be "quarantined" by a coalition of civilized nations devoted to stopping the disease of war. But Roosevelt failed to follow up on these words with action and declined to impose trade sanctions on Germany, Italy, or Japan. Even in December 1937, when Japanese planes sank the U.S. Navy gunboat *Panay* on the Yangtze River, as it escorted Standard Oil barges, and machine-gunned survivors in the water, President Roosevelt accepted apologies and compensation from an obviously insincere Japan. Opinion polls found that the public was more concerned that Americans sailors were in a war zone than outraged by the Japanese attack. Many prominent public figures argued that the most prudent course for Americans in China was withdrawal.

In the year following the sinking of the *Panay*, however, the views of the American public and government changed substantially. By the end of 1938, the idea took hold that the U.S. national interest required preservation of an "independent, democratic, and pro-American" China. Americans perceived Japan as not just a regional bully, but a global menace allied to Nazi Germany and Fascist Italy. Also, the gruesome human cost of the war in China gradually influenced American opinion. In a world still shocked

A Chinese child amidst the rubble of Japanese-bombed Shanghai, 1937. This photograph was widely circulated in the United States during the 1930s and early 1940s to raise money and support for China.

by modern air war, the bombing of defenseless Chinese cities and the deliberate rape and pillage by victorious Japanese troops seemed especially barbaric. The Japanese, as depicted by American journalists, resembled mad "warrior ants" destroying everything in their path; they were "faceless fiends" driven by violent primal urges. During the Japanese attack on Shanghai at the end of 1937, a journalist photographed a wounded, abandoned Chinese child crying amidst the twisted tracks of a bombed railway station. Among the greatest of war photographs, it was still referred to five years later when Americans sent donations to "United China Relief," an aid organization begun by Henry Luce. A woman from New Jersey sent $3.00 with a note saying "it is from my three daughters and it is for the little guy on the railroad tracks somewhere in China." A few weeks after the picture appeared, *Time* magazine placed on its cover portraits of Generalissimo and Madame Chiang Kai-shek as 1937's "Man and Wife of the Year."

American diplomats, navy personnel, and missionaries in China also spread word of Japanese cruelty and attacks on foreign interests. They insisted that the Japanese had more in mind than merely occupying China. Ambassador Nelson Johnson believed the Japanese intended to "eliminate all Western influence among the Chinese." Admiral Harry Yarnell informed President Roosevelt that the war in China was fundamentally a challenge to "Western civilization." Unless the United States stopped Japan, the "white race would have no future in Asia."

As these reports percolated through government and popular circles, another idea struck President Roosevelt and some of his advisers. Although Chinese forces had little offensive capability, their mere existence tied down millions of Japanese troops. As long as Chiang did not surrender and the Japanese remained bogged down, these troops would not be able to attack the Philippines, French Indochina, Malaya, Singapore, the Dutch East Indies, British India, Australia, or New Zealand—all targets Japan hoped to incorporate into what it called its "Greater East-Asia Co-Prosperity Sphere."

An almost certainly apocryphal but vivid story was told of a news conference in 1938 by a Chinese army commander. "General," an American journalist asked, "in the past year you lost over one million men in a series of battles, while the Japanese lost only one-hundred thousand. With losses of such magnitude, what is going to happen?" Patiently, the Chinese commander replied, "pretty soon there be no more Japanese." The view of China as a vast punching bag on which the Japanese would wear themselves out had a certain brutal, but understandable, appeal to the United States. If U.S. aid allowed Chinese resistance to continue, Japan's military expansion could be stymied.

THE ORIGINS OF THE CHINESE-AMERICAN ALLIANCE

During 1937–38, members of the Roosevelt administration, like the American public, were torn between desires to assist China and to avoid conflict with Japan. Although some presidential advisers argued as early as September 1937 that the "peace of the world is tied up with China's ability to win or prolong its resistance to Japanese aggression . . . a Japanese victory increases greatly the chances of a general world war," this remained a minority view. By late 1938, however, Hitler had gobbled up most of democratic Czechoslovakia and unleashed massive violence against Jews under his control. Japan's talk of imposing a "new order" on Asia, in part by incorporating China and Western colonies into the "Co-Prosperity Sphere," appeared to resemble Hitler's scheme to dominate Europe. As China's military and economic situation grew more desperate, the prospect of a Japanese victory on the Asian mainland became more chilling. When some of Chiang's aides began spreading rumors that he might soon be forced to end resistance or even cut a deal with Tokyo, key officials in the Roosevelt administration took action.

The most influential and active friend of China among Roosevelt's intimates was Secretary of the Treasury Henry Morgenthau, Jr. Morgenthau considered both Germany and Japan America's enemies and believed the time right to take a stand against them. He judged it critical to sustain Chinese resistance to Japan, either to deter a wider war or to buy time for the United States. Morgenthau shared the opinion that economic assistance to Chiang would enable his forces to tie down and perhaps ultimately defeat Tokyo's legions—without direct U.S. involvement.

In contrast, Secretary of State Cordell Hull shied away from supporting China. Although he disliked Japan, Hull desperately hoped to avoid involvement in any Asian war. His caution forced Morgenthau to work around, rather than with, the State Department. The Treasury secretary developed a plan to grant China commercial credits to purchase vital supplies in the United States. The proposal for a $25 million credit was quite modest in size, but much larger in symbolic value. Stanley Hornbeck, a State Department China expert who, unlike his boss, favored active measures, urged Roosevelt to approve the loan. Economic aid, he explained, was a first step in America's "diplomatic war plan" against Japan.

Hornbeck and Morgenthau made the point that the collapse of Chinese resistance was only one possible result of America's failure to provide aid. Soviet leader Josef Stalin, who also feared Japanese expansion, had approved credits for China and would soon begin providing planes and pilots for its defense. If the United States did nothing, Chiang might be driven into the "hands of Russia," expanding the reach of communism in Asia.

These warnings swayed Roosevelt. In December 1938, while Secretary of State Hull was on a visit to Latin America, the president approved a $25 million credit for China. The decision had a striking effect on sagging KMT morale. The official press hailed the loan as proof of a commitment to Chinese independence. Privately, one of the Chinese who negotiated the terms of the deal, informed Chiang that the aid was a "political loan." The United States had "thrown in her lot with China and cannot withdraw."

Although the first loan did not lead immediately to a cascade of American assistance, during the next three years, Washington gradually escalated the size and scope of aid to China. Loans to China were eventually coupled with trade restrictions on the sale of American products to Japan. In 1939, Roosevelt asked American companies to impose a "moral embargo" on sales of airplane parts to Japan. In January 1940, the State Department announced it would not renew the 1911 commercial treaty with Japan. This allowed Washington to impose selective embargoes on the sale of strategic material to Japan, including aviation gasoline, steel, and, after July 1941, petroleum.

In the three years that elapsed between the first direct aid to China and the Pearl Harbor attack, China's friends and Japan's critics faulted Roosevelt for giving China too little and being too cautious in punishing Japan. But Roosevelt and his military advisers recognized that economic warfare posed real risks to the United States. Japan was so sensitive to some strategic imports, such as petroleum, that any sudden or complete cut-off of sales might actually provoke Japan into war before the United States was prepared to fight. The president suggested it was preferable to "slip a noose around Japan's neck" and every once in a while "give a tug," rather than to attempt a hanging while the culprit was still on a rampage.

U.S. assistance to China was also complicated by competing demands to speed American rearmament and concentrate on the defense of Europe. American strategic thinking emphasized the primacy of stopping Hitler. Defending China and containing Japan were important but secondary considerations. In addition, Chinese factionalism confused the question of who should receive U.S. assistance. Chiang used foreign aid not only to fight the Japanese, but also to gain leverage against his internal rivals, including the Chinese Communists. In some ways, this was his greatest concern, and the KMT leader lobbied hard to assure that he was the exclusive recipient of American generosity.

The first U.S. trade credits of December 1938 were not actually granted to the Chinese government but, instead, to a Chinese government "front," the Universal Trading Corporation (UTC). Americans hoped this ruse would mute Japanese protests over aid to China. Chiang favored the plan because UTC (succeeded by China Defense Supplies, or CDS) was controlled by family loyalists, such as his brother-in-law T. V. Soong. Soong placed several former federal officials on his payroll, making them paid lobbyists with the job of assuring support from their old departments. Men like Thomas Corcoran, formerly a White House lawyer close to Roosevelt, were hired by the Chinese because of their close affiliation with powerful figures.

Some of the Americans involved in Soong's operation made fortunes. More importantly, they forged personal links between the Nationalist regime and a wide assortment of politicians and bureaucrats. American employees of CDS promoted anti-Communist, pro-KMT activities with an intent to influence the power contest in China. Even Treasury Secretary Morgenthau, a firm supporter of aid to China, sometimes expressed exasperation at how difficult it was to work with American employees of CDS. He never knew if they were working for "Mr. Roosevelt or T. V. Soong, because half the time they were on one payroll and the rest of the time . . . on the other."

Chiang also established personal lines of communication to supersede the roles of American diplomats and war department attaches whom he distrusted. Among the important personal conduits was James McHugh, American naval attaché in Chungking. Generalissimo and Mme. Chiang were personal friends of McHugh and often entrusted him with "secret" information to pass on directly to high navy officials or the president. Between 1939 and 1942, these included several warnings of imminent Chinese collapse unless more aid was forthcoming. These cries of panic generally succeeded in prying a bit more money from Roosevelt.

The Chiangs had little trust in their government's regular representatives in Washington or American career diplomats in Chungking. As a result, they utilized a series of American friends to pass on sensitive information or requests. U.S. officials were never certain if they had received a complete and accurate message or to whom they should respond. Because T. V. Soong "coordinated" this system, and since many of the priority messages came from his three influential sisters, Soong Mei-ling, Soong Ai-ling, and Soong Ching-ling, the Treasury Department staff composed a sarcastic tune entitled "Sing a Song of Six Soongs" to describe their dealings.

Despite confused and secretive communications, American aid to China increased substantially by the end of 1940. Early in 1941, Roosevelt proposed and Congress approved a massive Lend-Lease foreign aid program designed to give the president a nearly free hand in assisting any nation whose defense he deemed vital to America. Britain and China were among the first nations designated to receive Lend-Lease aid in the spring of 1941.

Even as the size and scope of American assistance to China grew in 1940–41, so did tensions within the United Front. As Chiang became more certain of U.S. support, he appeared less inclined to fight the Japanese and more prone to attack the Chinese Communists. The U.S. effort to keep China fighting Japan had the unintended consequence of rekindling the civil war within China.

THE COLLAPSE OF THE UNITED FRONT

At best, the United Front created in 1937 represented a limited truce between the KMT and CCP. While both parties opposed Japan, each planned to fight the enemy in a way designed to maximize its own chance eventually to emerge supreme. After 1938, Chiang generally avoided large-scale battles with the Japanese and hoarded American aid for eventual use against the Communists. According to the Generalissimo, the "Japanese were a disease of the skin; the Communists a disease of the heart."

The Chinese Communist movement, centered in the remote northwest city of Yenan after 1937, possessed a tiny military force, compared to the KMT. Beginning the war against Japan with an armed force less than a tenth as large as that fielded by the Kuomintang, the Communists used the struggle as a way to recruit new soldiers and political supporters. Mao downplayed Marxist theory in favor of nationalist resistance to Japan and practical measures of land reform and social justice aimed at relieving peasant grievances. As the size of Communist forces increased and as the Japanese threat diminished, Mao planned to redirect his followers against the Nationalist regime.

Both Chiang and Mao recognized the other's long-term strategy, but while Japan remained a common enemy, they both had an incentive to maintain the United Front. The KMT and CCP each stationed a few representatives in each other's capitals, but otherwise remained nearly as hostile as before the Sian incident. Neither party tolerated political dissent in areas it controlled. The KMT secret police, headed by Dai Li, were notoriously brutal in suppressing dissident activity. In order to limit the size and scope of Communist operations, and to prevent their receipt of outside aid, a KMT army headed by General Hu Tsung-nan blockaded Yenan.

Another facet of the KMT–CCP relationship was that through 1940, Nationalist forces received substantial military assistance from the Soviet Union. Stalin, like Roosevelt, feared Japanese expansion in Asia and looked to China as a buffer. In 1939, Soviet and Japanese troops fought a major skirmish at Nomohan, along the Mongolian–Soviet border. After Japan backed off, Stalin adopted a plan to use Chiang's forces as a proxy to restrain the Japanese. This valuable Soviet aid probably restrained Chiang from launching a direct attack on the Chinese Communists.

By the end of 1940, however, these constraints disappeared. To meet the growing German threat in Europe, Stalin signed a nonaggression pact with Japan in April and reduced aid to the Chinese Nationalists. At the same time, the level of American aid began to increase. Chiang had told several Americans, including Ambassador Johnson, that he intended to move forcefully against the Chinese Communists once he received more U.S. support. By November, Chiang told Americans that he could handle Japan, but required increased assistance from Washington to suppress the "defiant Communists."

President Roosevelt and most of his advisers were appalled by the notion of using American aid in a Chinese civil war. They believed all Chinese should concentrate on defeating Japan and building the sort of good will and cooperation that would preserve China's postwar unity. At the same time, Roosevelt felt compelled to increase aid to China. In September 1940, Japan joined Nazi Germany and Fascist Italy in the Tripartite, or Axis alliance. The three nations pledged mutual aid against an American attack. Although an avowed racist, Hitler publicly referred to Japanese as "honorary" members of his master race. In private, however, he confided that after defeating Britain and the Soviet Union, he would turn his power against the "little yellow monkeys" and take Asia for himself.

To blunt the impact of Japanese cooperation with Germany, as well as Tokyo's growing support for a Chinese puppet government headed by Wang Ching-wei, Roosevelt moved to signal an increased commitment to Chiang. Late in 1940, he approved a $100 million credit to China, the largest aid package to date. The American move had at least one unintended result.

In January 1941, shortly after receiving the new U.S. loan, the Generalissimo ordered his forces (who were still advised by a Soviet military officer) to attack and destroy the Communist New Fourth Army in disputed territory along the Yangtze River. This outbreak of civil strife threatened China's utility as an anti-Japanese bulwark. To make matters worse, ever since Germany overran France and Holland in June 1940, Japan had increased its pressure to gain control of mineral-rich French Indo-China and the Dutch East Indies. Civil war in China would free Japanese troops for service in Southeast Asia. These concerns impelled the Roosevelt administration to seek a compromise between the CCP and KMT.

American mediation efforts, destined to last until 1947, were hampered by a lack of knowledge about the Communist program and the party's relationship to Moscow. Between the break-up of the first United Front in 1927 and the mid-1930s, American diplomats in China doubted that a Communist movement, in the formal sense, even existed. They speculated that rural insurgents and bandits used Communist insignia and slogans to attack Chinese government outposts and foreign property, but these groups had few ties to Moscow and filled their ranks with angry peasants, not urban workers. Many diplomatic dispatches voiced grudging sympathy for the insurgents battling corruption and poverty. As Ambassador Johnson put it to Secretary of State Stimson in 1933, "the shadow of Bolshevism will lie over parts of China until" meaningful rural reform "has improved the lot of the masses and an efficient administration has produced a sense of security in the interior."

Following creation of the second United Front in 1937, both CCP and KMT officials downplayed their differences, stressing instead their common anti-Japanese program. American journalists, such as Edgar Snow, who traveled to Communist-controlled areas in the mid-1930s, portrayed the CCP in a favorable light. Snow's account, published in 1938 as *Red Star Over China*, contrasted Communist honesty and patriotism with rampant corruption in areas controlled by the KMT. While not denying the fact that Mao and his followers were dedicated Communists, Snow believed they were largely independent of Moscow and eager to cooperate with the United States against Japan.

In 1937–38, two U.S. army attaches in China, Joseph W. Stilwell and Evans Carlson, reported extensively on Communist military performance. Based on their personal observations, both Stilwell and Carlson (who sent many of his reports directly to Roosevelt) praised the Communists as exceptionally skilled organizers and effective guerrilla fighters. But both doubted that orthodox communism had much appeal to China's "individualistic peasants."

By the time of the New Fourth Army incident early in 1941, no consensus existed in Washington about the nature of the CCP. But Roosevelt and his aides worried that the collapse of the United Front could only help Japan. With Congress poised to approve Lend-Lease, the president hoped to expand military aid to China. If Chiang turned American weapons against his domestic foes, U.S. assistance would actually worsen China's situation. With this concern in mind, Roosevelt dispatched a personal emissary to China, Dr. Lauchlin Currie.

Before 1941, Currie had served as an influential New Deal economic planner. He helped popularize the idea of deficit spending, or "pump priming," to stimulate economic recovery. Currie, who introduced the ideas of British economist John Maynard Keynes to Americans, personally leaned toward Marxism. In the 1950s, congressional investigators accused Currie of spying for the Soviet Union during World War II. He denied the charge and left the United States. In the 1990s, after historians examined copies of Soviet communications intercepted during World War II, it seemed clear that Currie had provided at least some information to Soviet agents. Ironically, however, Currie made his most important contribution to China policy by convincing Roosevelt to expand support for Chiang Kai-shek, not Mao Zedong.

After spending several weeks in Chungking in February and March 1941, Currie returned to Washington with a plan to prevent the collapse of the United Front and to increase American assistance to Chiang. The American envoy urged the Generalissimo to follow "Roosevelt's example" of undercutting radical opposition with reform, not violence. Currie convinced the president to send Chiang a group of "liberal advisers" who would work to improve transportation, tax collection, and government efficiency in Nationalist-controlled areas. Currie hoped this would reduce CCP–KMT tension and enhance KMT popularity. Meanwhile, the U.S. government would enhance Chiang's image through "inspired stories" in the American press. If journalists "said nice things about him," Chiang's stature would grow at home and abroad. Currie assured Roosevelt that Chiang considered him the "greatest man in the world," giving the American leader tremendous leverage over the Generalissimo.

In his report, Currie laid out the broad picture of what became Roosevelt's China policy until the final stages of the Second World War. The Nationalist regime should be treated like a "great power." Chiang should be given more economic and military support and be encouraged to reform. This would promote cooperation within China and ensure a more effective struggle against Japan.

In his eagerness to help China, Currie sugar-coated his deep suspicion of the KMT leadership's willingness or ability to reform. He also exaggerated the degree of American control over Chinese affairs. Whatever one might think of Chiang, he remained an intensely proud patriot who barely concealed his contempt for Western culture and advice. He would never surrender his power to foreign civilian or military advisers or allow them to interfere with his rule. Currie also underestimated the risk of inflating Chiang's image in the U.S. press. The wildly pro-Nationalist accounts that appeared from 1941 on misled the American public and provided the Generalissimo with an exaggerated sense of his importance to the United States. Although the strategy paid some short-term dividends, such as preserving at least the skeleton of the United Front, in the long run it served neither the United States nor China very well.

At the time, few of these problems were obvious to Currie or Roosevelt. The effect of the recommendations and passage of the Lend-Lease Aid program solidified the American connection to the KMT. Of course, when Roosevelt sent a group of technical experts to advise Chiang, he ignored them. But the White House scarcely noticed. The Generalissimo now had several powerful friends around the president, and he had received a promise to equip thirty infantry divisions with American arms. Despite production and shipping bottlenecks, and the need to arm American forces and Great Britain, aid began flowing during the last half of 1941. The more aid that arrived, the greater the American stake in China's success became. The greater the stake, the more pressing the need to protect it. As one historian observed, "a silver cord attached the American to the Nationalist government. There is no more entangling alliance than aid to indigent friends." This silver cord pulled the KMT and the United States further along the road of joint military operations, to the growing alarm of Japan.

A SECRET AIR WAR PLAN AND THE PEARL HARBOR ATTACK

As the United States committed itself to the defense of Great Britain and China during 1940–41, American military planners conceived of several covert schemes to hinder the war-making abilities of Germany and Japan. Among the most elaborate of these was a plan for "private" American pilots, employed by a Chinese company, to initiate air strikes against Japanese forces in China and the Japanese home islands. The objectives included boosting Chinese morale, weakening Japan, and deterring the Japanese military from expanding the war beyond China.

Advocates of the secret air war plan claimed it could achieve great benefits at a small cost and minimal risk. The bulk of American war supplies during 1941 were destined for Britain and, after June, to the Soviet Union. Nearly all U.S. decisionmakers agreed that preventing Hitler's conquest of Britain and the Soviet Union was priority number one. Following the June 1941 German attack on the Soviet Union, American strategists also believed that aid to Stalin would deter any Japanese move against Siberia.

Supporters of the air war plan argued that deployment of a small number of fighter planes and bombers against Japan might compensate for the Europe-first aid strategy. Moreover, by attacking Japan under the cover of a Chinese flag, the United States would avoid direct responsibility, reducing the chance of provoking war with Japan before American forces in the Pacific were fully operational.

This concept originated in the mind of Claire L. Chennault, a retired army air force pilot. After his resignation from the service in 1936, Chennault worked as a private military adviser to Chiang and Mme. Chiang, whom he called "princess." With the outbreak of the Sino–Japanese war, the Nationalist leader hoped to use Chennault to win American support for an ambitious strategy of air warfare. In the summer of 1940, Chennault and T. V. Soong were sent to the United States to promote the idea of creating a secret Chinese–American air force to attack Japan.

In November 1940, they submitted to Treasury Secretary Henry Morgenthau, Jr. plans to create a 500-plane force supplied by the United States and flown by American pilots employed by a private Chinese company. Instead of just harassing Japanese forces in China, the air force would "attack Japan proper," Soong explained, destroying its war industry and undermining morale. Morgenthau, then a key figure in the China aid program, urged approval of the idea in discussions he held with the president and representatives of the State, War, and Navy departments. Encouraged by the initial response, Morgenthau told Soong that although 500 planes were not available, "what did he think of the idea of some long-range bombers with the understanding that they were to be used to bomb Tokyo and other large cities?" Both men believed this might "change the whole picture in the Far East."

By December 1940, the plan had progressed far enough for Morgenthau to discuss with Chennault and Soong specific targets and weapons. The Treasury secretary advocated use of incendiary bombs because "Japanese cities were all made of just wood and paper." Chennault agreed that "a lot of damage could be done using this method, and that, even if the Chinese lost some of the bombers, it would be well justified." Morgenthau gave little thought to how Japan's leaders would respond to such an attack. He merely hoped that the bombings would deter a wider war with Japan and relieve pressure on China and Southeast Asia.

Secretary of War Henry Stimson and Army Chief of Staff General George C. Marshall vigorously opposed the scheme. They resented any move to divert scarce bombers from American forces in the Philippines or Great Britain. They also disliked planning military operations outside the normal chain of command and were certain that any attack on Japan by American-piloted aircraft would provoke a Japanese counterattack against the United States. Roosevelt suggested a compromise. Instead of bombers, he would divert 100 fighter aircraft to China. These could attack Japanese troops and shipping in and around China, but not Japan itself.

Since China lacked the personnel to fly these aircraft, Chennault worked out a solution with Morgenthau, Currie, and Navy Secretary Frank Knox. The president issued a secret executive order permitting American military pilots to resign their commissions and sign contracts with a private company (Central Aircraft Manufacturing Corporation) whose operating funds came through Lend-Lease. The pilots, designated as the American Volunteer Group (AVG), would fly the fighter planes transferred to the Chinese government under Lend-Lease.

By May 1941, key decisions on aid to China shifted from Morgenthau's Treasury Department to the White House, which distributed Lend-Lease. Currie, who had recently returned from China, worked closely with Soong and Chennault and became a great believer in their air war scheme. He revived the plan to bomb Japan and urged Roosevelt to endorse it. The secret air war, he informed the president, would be of immense value to "our men to acquire actual combat experience." The bombardment of Japanese cities and industry would psychologically bolster China and might even scare off the Japanese from attacking the European and American colonies in Southeast Asia.

As Roosevelt mulled over Currie's proposal, the world situation deteriorated. In June 1941, Germany attacked the Soviet Union, pushing Russian armies back toward Moscow and reducing Stalin's ability either to help China or deter Japan. By July, Japan was poised to seize control of southern French Indochina and perhaps the Dutch East Indies, with its large petroleum reserves. This would threaten Britain's Southeast Asian colonies, which provided vital raw materials for the European war effort. On July 26, immediately after, Japan occupied southern Indochina. Roosevelt announced a freeze on nearly all trade with Japan, leaving Tokyo with only a 12- to-18-month petroleum stockpile. At the same time, the president signed a secret order sending American bombers to China to be flown by the AVG against Japan. Roosevelt hoped that the oil embargo and covert military pressure might persuade Japan to pull back from Southeast Asia and eventually evacuate China.

The secret American air war against Japan never took place because the Japanese attacked Pearl Harbor before Chennault's planes arrived in China. Quite likely, the Japanese picked up reports of the scheme, and it may have influenced the timing of their decision to strike on December 7, before their petroleum ran out or the American bombers in China were operational. Chennault, as discussed later, went on to play a controversial role in wartime China. After Japan's defeat, he resurrected the AVG as Civil Air Transport (CAT), a private airline that helped supply Kuomintang forces during the Chinese civil war. After 1949, CAT became Air America, with the CIA serving as Chennault's business partner. Air America played a major role during the Vietnam War, supplying the French until 1954 and working with U.S. allies throughout Southeast Asia after the French defeat.

By the time Roosevelt approved the secret bombing plan in July 1941, war between the United States and Japan had become practically inevitable. But the two countries spent almost five months going through the motions of negotiations to avert conflict.

In Washington, Secretary of State Cordell Hull and Japanese envoy Admiral Nomura discussed various plans to postpone, if not avert, a U.S.–Japan war. Tokyo insisted that before it would consider withdrawing from Indochina, Washington must first resume oil sales to Japan, cease aid to China, and press Chiang to make peace on Japanese terms. The United States replied that before it resumed oil sales, Japan must pull its troops out of Indochina, end the war in China, promise not to seize additional territory, and sever its alliance with Nazi Germany. The Japanese considered American terms a thinly veiled effort to contain and eventually crush their independence. U.S. negotiators were equally certain that Japan intended to seize control of mainland Asia and the Pacific at any cost.

Some consideration was given to reaching a short-term agreement, a so-called modus vivendi freezing action by both sides for a few months. But Chiang's supporters insisted that even a temporary deal would risk the collapse of Chinese morale. On November 25, 1941, Chiang informed Roosevelt that any softening of the oil embargo against Japan—the minimum condition for postponing war—would be a "sacrifice" of China. "The morale of the people will collapse," he warned, "the Chinese army will collapse and the Japanese will be enabled to carry out their plans." This loss "will not be to China alone," he emphasized. When members of Roosevelt's inner circle cautioned him against accepting a "sellout," the president abandoned plans for a temporary deal.

Electronic intelligence intercepts added to American wariness of Japan. During 1941, naval cryptoanalysts had "broken" several high-level Japanese diplomatic codes. They did so, in part, by creating a machine, code-named *Purple*, that exactly matched a sophisticated, automatic coding device used by the Japanese. This technological marvel resembled the British achievement of reading coded messages sent on the German Enigma machine, a close relative of the Japanese model. Given the code name *Magic*, intercepts of Japanese communications permitted American policymakers to learn the gist of what their counterparts in Tokyo were telling their own diplomats. Based on many messages, American intelligence officials concluded that Japanese diplomats were not negotiating in good faith and lacked to power to make binding decisions. Even if negotiators in Washington reached a settlement, the Japanese military might overturn the agreement and launch a military strike. This information made Roosevelt and his key advisers doubtful that war could be averted. Unfortunately, U.S. codebreakers had not yet deciphered Japanese military codes, leaving Washington in the dark about specific war plans.

On November 26, Secretary of State Hull told Japanese negotiators in Washington that the United States and its allies in Britain and the Dutch East Indies would resume oil sales only when Japan agreed to withdraw from China and Indochina and pledged no further aggression in the Pacific. From reading intercepts, Hull knew these terms were unacceptable to leaders in Tokyo. Washington notified American military and naval commanders in the Pacific that Japan might attack at any time, although no one knew the precise time or place. With their oil reserves draining away and with the American military build up in China and the Philippines growing rapidly, Japanese military leaders resolved to strike against the United States, beginning with an air attack against the Pacific fleet at Pearl Harbor.

The Japanese–American confrontation flowed in large part from the U.S. determination to resist Japanese expansion in Asia by enhancing Chinese strength. Containing Japan, Roosevelt came to believe, required a strong and stable China led by Chiang Kai-shek. More than just a military calculation, in American eyes the Generalissimo became a symbol of China's future. Already, Roosevelt's thoughts turned to building a new order in postwar Asia based on an alliance between the United States and a united, strong, and pro-American China. That vision energized and frustrated Americans as they began the bloodiest struggle in world history.

SUGGESTED ADDITIONAL READINGS

Among the important studies on the decade leading up to the Pearl Harbor attack are: Iris Chang, *Rape of Nanking: The Forgotten Holocaust of World War II* (New York, 1997); Michael Barnhart, *Japan Prepares for Total War: The Search for Economic Security, 1919–1941* (Ithaca, N.Y., 1987); Dorothy Borg and Shumpei Okamoto, eds., *Pearl Harbor as History: Japanese-American Relations, 1931–1941* (New York, 1973); Warren I. Cohen, *The Chinese Connection: Roger S. Greene, Thomas W. Lamont, George E. Sokolsky and American East Asian Relations* (New York, 1978); Robert J. C. Butow, *Tojo and the Coming of the War* (Princeton, N.J., 1961), and *The John Doe Associates: Backdoor Diplomacy for Peace* (Stanford, Calif., 1974); Herbert Feis, *The Road to Pearl Harbor: The Coming of the War between the United States and Japan* (Princeton, N.J., 1950); Jonathan Utley, *Going to War with Japan, 1937–1941* (Knoxville, Tenn., 1985); Robert Dallek, *Franklin D. Roosevelt and American Foreign Policy, 1932–1945* (New York, 1979); Waldo H. Heinrichs, *American Ambassador: Joseph C. Grew and the Development of the United States Diplomatic Tradition* (New York, 1966), and *Threshold of War: Franklin D. Roosevelt and American Entry into World War II* (New York, 1988); Frederick Wakeman, Jr., *Policing Shanghai, 1927–37* (Berkeley, Calif., 1995), and *The Shanghai Badlands: Wartime Terrorism and Urban Crime, 1937–1941* (New York, 1996); Michael Schaller, *The U.S. Crusade in China, 1938–1945* (New York, 1975).

FOUR

The Chinese–American Alliance

The startling attack on the American fleet at Pearl Harbor on December 7, 1941, followed by the Japanese sweep over the Philippines and most of Southeast Asia, shattered all hope that aid to China would deter Japan from fighting the United States. When Germany entered the war against the United States a few days later, the American people and their allies faced the Axis powers along two global fronts. Stunned by Japan's opening-round victory, many Americans found comfort in their link to a "battle tested" Chinese army. An editorial in the *The New York Times* on December 9 declared:

> We are partners in a larger unity. . . . We have as our ally China, with its inexhaustible manpower—China, from whose patient and untiring and infinitely resourceful people there will now return to us tenfold payment upon such aid as we have given.

The "Battle Cry of China," a U.S. Army training film produced later in the war by Hollywood director Frank Capra, expressed similar faith in the U.S. alliance with China:

> The oldest and the youngest of the world's great nations, together with the British commonwealth, fight side by side in the struggle that is as old as China herself. The struggle of freedom against slavery, civilization against barbarism, good against evil.

When news reached battle-weary Chungking that Japan and the United States were at war, KMT officials celebrated what they considered their salvation. Novelist Han Su-yin, then married to one of Chiang Kai-shek's officers, recalled the reaction to news that America had entered the war.

> Almost immediately there were noises in the street . . . people surging out of their houses to buy the newspapers, crowding together . . . the military council was jubilant. Chiang was so happy he sang an old opera aria and played "Ave Maria" all day. The Kuomintang government officials went around congratulating each other as if a great victory had been won. From their standpoint, it was a great victory. . . . At last, at last, America was at war with Japan. Now China's strategic importance would grow even more. American money and equipment would flow in; half a billion dollars, one billion dollars. . . . Now America would have to support Chiang, and that meant U.S. dollars into the pockets of the officials, into the pockets of the army commanders, and guns to General Hu Tsung-nan for the coming war against Yenan.

Japan's attack on the United States not only brought the United States fully into China's corner, but also changed the political equation in Asia. Japanese forces quickly overran the Dutch, British, French, and American colonies of mainland and island Southeast Asia. Although most Asians were not eager to exchange, say, British for Japanese imperialism, they were nevertheless astounded by the ease with which Japan defeated their old colonial masters. The humiliating rout of European and American forces in Southeast Asia foretold the demise of colonialism in the postwar years.

In China, despite American aid and advice, Chiang proved unable or unwilling to fight the Japanese effectively, diminishing his stature and grasp on power. In contrast, the Chinese Communists emerged from the cauldron of war as national heroes in the struggle against Japan. Communist success in carrying forward the banner of nationalism in the war against Japan created both the momentum and a sort of political cover that the party used to advance a social revolution in the civil war against the Kuomintang.

Until his death in April 1945, President Roosevelt struggled both to win the war and assure the peace by harnessing the nationalist forces unleashed by Japan's rampage through Asia. Roosevelt expected Japan's defeat, but worried about what the postwar order would look like. What would replace the Dutch, French, and British colonial governments? With Japan eliminated as a major power, what would restrain Soviet expansion in Asia? And how would China, with a fourth of the world's population, influence events in East Asia? Would postwar China be pro-American, antiforeign, or pro-Soviet? U.S. policymakers grappled with the challenge of steering these forces of change in the most friendly, least dangerous direction.

Ideally, postwar China and Asia would be governed by moderate nationalists sympathetic to American political and economic values. Gradual reform and liberal capitalism, Roosevelt believed, not revolutionary social struggle, held the key to progress. A stable, united, pro-American China could be the linchpin of Asian security—replacing Japan, restraining the Soviet Union, and acting as an "elder brother" to the people emerging from colonial control. Even if China played only a limited role in defeating Japan, it could exercise critical influence in shaping this postwar order. As Roosevelt explained his vision to skeptical British leaders, China, with its vast population, would be "very useful twenty-five years hence, even though China cannot contribute much military or naval support for the moment." At the very least, China continued to tie down millions of Japanese troops merely by staying in the war. This alone justified generous aid.

China also comprised a key element in Roosevelt's postwar diplomacy. He hoped the wartime allies, the so-called Four Policemen, including the United States, Great Britain, the Soviet Union, and China, would forge a postwar partnership for peace. Wartime trust and cooperation could assure that inevitable strains and rivalries after the war would be contained and mitigated by revitalized world trade and collective security pacts. China could become an Asian policeman and an American proxy, as Roosevelt hoped, or a "faggot vote" for the United States as British prime minister Churchill complained.

In discussing wartime China, we must recognize that the bulk of the president's attention, as well as most U.S. troops and supplies, were committed to the war in Europe. The naval war in the mid-Pacific and the army's assault on South Pacific islands took second place. China placed a distant third in strategic priority. Yet for a variety of practical and romantic reasons, Roosevelt insisted on including China in the ranks of the wartime Grand Alliance. A circle of like-minded enthusiasts convinced the president that he could join American power to the Kuomintang and create an effective wartime and postwar ally. A strong, united, and pro-American China would replace the influence of Japan and the European empires and counter the spread of revolutionary doctrines among the masses of Asia. Also, as Roosevelt's close aide Harry Hopkins remarked, "in any serious conflict of policy with Russia," Chiang's government "would line up on our side."

Although Chinese Nationalist leaders had divergent wartime priorities, their vision of postwar Asia resembled Roosevelt's. Chiang and his inner

Uncle Sam feeding a Chinese child, by Ed. Hunter. This poster was one of many similar depictions circulated in the United States by United China Relief, Inc., during World War II. (B.A. Garside Collection, Hoover Institution Archives)

circle hoped that by cleaving closely to the United States, China could recover its "lost territories" (Manchuria, Taiwan, Hong Kong, Outer Mongolia). They worried about Soviet expansion and aid to the CCP. In fact, the Nationalists favored lenient treatment of Japan after the war to encourage its cooperation against Moscow and Yenan.

Before any of these plans could be realized, however, the war against Japan had to be won, and this meant breathing new life into the Kuomintang. Before that, little could be expected from this "fourth policeman." Unfortunately, Roosevelt never quite realized that like the German tie to Austria in World War I, the United States had allied itself to a corpse. After 1941, despite massive infusions of American money (a half-billion dollars in 1942 alone) and arms, the Kuomintang's hold on power and popular support steadily diminished. At the same time, the power and appeal of the Communists grew far stronger. Without intending to do so, the United States would become a crutch sustaining Chiang.

Warning signals reached Washington even before the smoke cleared from the burning ships at Pearl Harbor. General John Magruder, a U.S. military observer in China, warned his superiors that Chiang intended to hoard whatever aid America gave him, "largely with the idea of postwar military action." Chinese military strategists, he wrote, lived in a "world of make believe," and Chiang considered his troops and equipment "static assets to be conserved for assistance in fighting against . . . fellow countrymen for economic and political supremacy." U.S. ambassador to China, Clarence Gauss, a brooding man jaded by long years in the foreign service, believed Chiang "suffered from a touch of unreality derived from a somewhat grandiose or ivory tower conception of his and China's role."

Roosevelt hated hearing these negative reports. Like most people, he preferred reality to confirm his expectations. When it failed to do so, he sought out messengers carrying more compatible messages. Once again, Lauchlin Currie—who played a key role in expanding aid to China before Pearl Harbor—provided the assurances Roosevelt wanted. After a fact-finding mission to China in 1942, Currie told the president:

> We have a unique opportunity to exert a profound influence on the development of China and hence Asia. It appears to me to be profoundly in our national interest to give full support to the Generalissimo both military and diplomatic. I do not think we need to lay down any conditions nor tie any strings to this support . . . we can rely on him so far as lies within his power to go in the direction of our wishes in prosecuting a vigorous war policy and in creating a modern, democratic and powerful state.

Here was ample justification for assisting Chiang without requiring or expecting much, for the moment.

Not only Roosevelt, but much of the American public bought into this romantic view of China. Mme. Chiang toured the United States from November 1942 through the following May. In February 1943, amidst a prolonged stay in the White House (where she snapped at the staff, demanded silk bed sheets, and drove Franklin and Eleanor Roosevelt to distraction), she delivered a dramatic speech to Congress. What politician could remain unmoved by her uplifting assurance that China and the United States fought together "for a better world, not just for ourselves alone, but for all mankind." Mme. Chiang's underlying theme, that the war against Japan and aid to China should take priority over the defeat of Germany, infuriated FDR and his aides. During a cross-country speaking tour, the "First Lady of China" told large audiences that China was America's foremost fighting ally and deserved more assistance, not closer scrutiny. *Time* and *Life* magazines were especially generous in their coverage of Mme Chiang. To a great extent, the American people, like their president, became captives of their optimism and their ignorance.

The celebration of the Chinese alliance prompted Congress to partially redress a running sore. Since the 1880s, under a variety of laws, nearly all Chinese had been barred from immigrating to the United States. In 1943, acknowledging China as an ally, Congress amended the exclusion provisions to permit 105 Chinese to immigrate annually. Steps were also begun to amend the "unequal treaties" imposed on China during the nineteenth century.

THE REAL WAR IN CHINA

Only by disregarding the inspired news stories from the White House and *Time* magazine could Americans discover the tragic dimensions of wartime China. Many American journalists and diplomats in China observed and tried to report the despair, corruption, and defeatism of Nationalist China. Wartime censorship, however, blocked most critical news from appearing in print. Theodore White, a *Time* reporter in China who was both well informed and a protégé of Henry Luce, wrote incisively about real events. Few of his reports appeared during the war, although White published many of his wartime pieces in a postwar collection, *Thunder Out of China* (1946). His description of the famine in Henan province during 1942–43 revealed a China unknown to most Americans.

> The peasants as we saw them were dying. They were dying on the roads, in the mountains, by the railway stations, in their mud huts, in the fields. And as they died, the government continued to wring from them the last possible ounce of tax. . . . The government in county after county was demanding of the peasant . . . more grain than he had raised. No excuses were allowed; peasants who were eating elm bark and dried leaves had to haul their last sack of seed grain to the tax collector's office. Peasants who were so weak they could barely walk had to collect fodder for the army's horses. . . . One of the most macabre touches of all this was the flurry of land speculation. Merchants, small government officials, army officers, and rich land owners who still had food were engaged in purchasing the peasants' ancestral areas at criminally low figures. . . . We knew there was a fury, as cold and relentless as death itself, in the bosom of the peasants of Henan, that their loyalty had been hollowed to nothingness by the extortion of their government.

This horror, occurring in many regions of China during the war, belied Mme. Chiang's words about building better worlds, and the heroic portrayals of *Time* magazine, which described Generalissimo Chiang as a "Christian and scholar first," a soldier only be necessity. It seemed to observers like White, as well as to several American diplomats, that Chiang and the Kuomintang had abandoned all principle except for anticommunism and the drive to remain in power. The regime's growing dependency on a combination of landlord support and American aid severed its connection to the mass of poor Chinese.

AMERICAN MILITARY STRATEGY AND THE KMT

When Chiang requested that Roosevelt send a military advisor to Chungking, T. V. Soong—the Generalissimo's brother-in-law and sometime foreign minister—had suggested that "the officer need not be an expert on the Far East." In fact, Chinese Nationalist leaders hoped Washington would send a pliant "yes man" who merely endorsed aid requests. Ironically, the officer selected to coordinate U.S. military affairs was General Joseph W. Stilwell, who knew more about China than practically anyone else in the army. "Vinegar Joe," as his men affectionately called the blunt-speaking officer, was a tough, no-nonsense soldier who had spent years in China as a young officer and military attaché. During the 1920s and 1930s, he had learned Chinese and traveled widely in the countryside, often on foot. A close friend of Army Chief of Staff General George C. Marshall, Stilwell seemed an inspired choice to command the American effort in China. At the peak, barely 100,000 U.S. technical and support troops served in China, but as theater commander, Stilwell was expected to advise Chiang and to reorganize his large but unwieldy army into an effective fighting force.

Almost three years later, in the fall of 1944, a despondent Stilwell described how political intrigue had undercut all his reform efforts. "American aid," Stilwell complained, "had to take into consideration the domestic side of every move we have undertaken . . . so that the Gimo's (Generalissimo Chiang) own command will get the most benefit from it." All serious military effort had been sacrificed to achieve Roosevelt's goal of "preserving China's precarious unity" under Chiang's leadership. As he saw it, "the cure of China's trouble is the elimination of Chiang Kai-shek."

Stilwell's harsh view gelled soon after he arrived in China in March 1942. Although his actual authority was unclear, he immediately attempted to assume command of Chinese troops fighting to keep open the Burma Road, which carried military supplies from India to China. Stilwell assumed command of front-line troops, but discovered that Chiang continually undercut his orders. When Burma fell, Stilwell was caught behind Japanese lines, but led his troops out of the Burmese jungle on foot, telling journalists when they reached India, "we took a hell of a beating."

Chiang's conflicts with Stilwell lasted until Vinegar Joe left China. The reason was clear: the Generalissimo opposed committing his troops and equipment to fighting the Japanese in Burma or elsewhere. If American planes could fly supplies into China over the Himalaya Mountains, a route known as the "Hump," why should Chiang squander his forces on a fight to keep open a land route? Although air transport was costly and dangerous—at least for the Americans—and could not carry nearly as much equipment as the Burma Road, it did not require that Chiang sacrifice very much.

The defeat in Burma convinced Stilwell that only a reformed Chinese army, committed to opening a Burma supply route, could play a role in defeating Japan. Chiang, he believed, stood in the way of this reform. During the next two and one-half years, Stilwell struggled to create and command what he called a "new army." While the "wasteful and inefficient system of juggling" of Chinese armies and commanders might be valuable for keeping Chiang in power, Stilwell remarked, "it emasculated the effectiveness of Chinese troops." But even Stilwell failed to realize how his reform plan threatened the jerry-built structure of Nationalist power.

As of 1942, the Chinese army, if it could be called that, consisted nominally of four million men organized into 316 divisions. Chiang directly controlled only about thirty divisions. The rest were commanded by a dozen

Generalissimo Chiang Kai-shek and General Joseph W. Stilwell share an uncharacteristic lighter moment in Chungking, 1942. (National Archives)

or so generals, some allied to the Generalissimo and others bitter rivals. One of the most powerful army groups, of 400,000 troops under General Hu Tsung-nan, was not even deployed against Japan. Instead, it blockaded Yenan, seat of Chiang's nominal Communist allies.

The quality of many KMT troops can be gauged by a report prepared by American army officials during the war. It described the formation of a typical unit.

> Conscription comes to the Chinese peasant like famine or flood, only more regularly—every year twice—and claims more victims. Famine, flood, and drought compare with conscription like chicken pox with plague. The virus is spread over the Chinese countryside. . . . There is first the press gang. For example, you are working in a field looking after your rice [when suddenly] a number of men tie your hands behind your back and take you with them . . . Hoe and plow rust in the field, the wife runs to the magistrate to cry and beg for her husband, the children starve.

This report described prison officials making money by selling convicts into service. Roped together, peasants and convicts were marched hundreds of miles to training camps. Some fled along the way. Those caught were beaten and forced on. Disease felled many conscripts, which also profited officers.

> If somebody dies, his body is left behind. His name on the list is carried along. As long as his death is not reported, he continues to be a source of income, increased by the fact he has ceased to consume. His rice and his pay become a long-lasting token of memory in the pocket of his commanding officers. His family will have to forget him.

The account also compared Chinese army hospitals to Nazi death camps.

Stilwell, who respected individual Chinese soldiers, found these conditions appalling and hoped to create a more effective and humane force. To begin, he called for reducing the overall size of the Nationalist armies and handpicking thirty divisions for special training. Stilwell would select a Chinese officer to command the new divisions and to lead them jointly in the struggle to reopen a land route through Burma. Stilwell would use the supplies brought in by truck to create a lean, efficient national army.

Although a keen observer of Chinese affairs, Stilwell never fully realized how his plan threatened to upset the Nationalist grip on power. In his diary, the general wrote "why doesn't the little dummy [Chiang] realize that his only hope is the thirty division plan and creation of a separate, efficient, and well-equipped and well-trained force?" But in his way, Chiang understood quite well the implications of Stilwell's reform plan. Giving an American general the power to select, promote, or sack Chinese officers, as well as to give or withhold aid, would cut the heart out of Chiang's authority. If the Generalissimo lost the power to reward his subalterns, Stilwell, rather than himself, would command their obedience. Rather than acquiesce to his own obsolescence, Chiang did all he could to delay military reform and rid himself of Stilwell.

The American commander of what was called the China–Burma–India (CBI) Theater grew livid at Chiang's refusal to initiate either a Burma campaign or army reform. "The stupid little ass fails to grab the opportunity of his life," Stilwell complained. The "Chinese government" he concluded, was a "structure based on fear and favor in the hands of an ignorant and stubborn man." Denigrating Chiang as the "peanut," Stilwell believed that "only outside influence can do anything for China—either enemy action will smash her or some regenerative ideas must be formed and put into effect at once." By the end of 1942, Stilwell concluded that he himself embodied that regenerative idea, and he began to challenge Chiang for control. Stilwell hoped to force Chiang's compliance by getting Roosevelt to order the Generalissimo to give him control of distributing Lend-Lease aid and China's armies—or face the cut-off of U.S. support. The president refused to act until September 1944, and then he withdrew his support for Stilwell almost as soon as he offered it.

Meanwhile, Chiang resisted reform pressure but continued accumulating money and equipment. He guessed that Roosevelt's intention to utilize China as an American protégé in postwar Asia would blunt Stilwell's demands. Chiang gambled that the president would back down before undercutting the Nationalist regime he hoped to build up as one of the future "Four Policemen."

CHINESE MANIPULATION OF AMERICAN POLICY

Even as he resisted Stilwell, Chiang recognized that he could not appear totally negative. To assure the continued flow of current and future aid, he had to offer a constructive alternative to the military strategy demanded by Stilwell. Adopting an old Chinese adage of "playing the barbarians off against each other," the Generalissimo identified American military commanders who advocated policies that did not threaten his hold over the KMT, but still presented China as a useful ally against Japan. The antidotes to Stilwell came in the persons of Navy Commander Milton Miles and Army Air Forces General Claire Chennault.

Miles, a naval officer searching for a role in landlocked wartime China, hit on the idea during 1942 of creating a "secret," commando-style unit in which American and Chinese personnel engaged in anti-Japanese operations. In Washington, navy admirals hoped wartime cooperation would yield bases in postwar China. Miles's Naval Group China eventually allied with General Dai Li, one of Chiang's most reactionary henchmen.

Their "Sino–American Cooperative Organization," or SACO, funneled military aid to the Kuomintang with little oversight by Stilwell. Although only a small number of navy personnel served in SACO, it spent much of its energy helping Dai Li fight Communists and undercutting Stilwell and American diplomats critical of Chiang by leaking sensitive information to the Chinese.

Chiang found a far more influential American in Claire Chennault, former head of the American Volunteer Group (Flying Tigers) and now commander of a small air task force in China. Like Miles, Chennault felt a deep bond with Chiang and deeply resented Stilwell's emphasis on a ground war in China. Air power, he argued, held the key to low-cost victory. The flier knew that only by winning adherents to the air power cause could he rise from his marginal role in the China theater. Chiang championed Chennault's arguments for an air campaign because it served several needs. If the limited air freight capacity of the Hump route was filled with supplies of fuel, ammunition, and spare parts for Chennault's planes, Stilwell would lack the equipment needed to begin a ground offensive. More importantly, a powerful American air force operating in China posed no threat to the KMT power structure, especially if commanded by an acolyte such as Chennault. Finally, permitting Chennault's warplanes to spearhead attacks against the Japanese would cost Chiang nothing while fostering the illusion that China pulled its weight in the war. In return, Chiang hoped, the American people would lavish more aid on China.

Chennault tried hard to vault over Stilwell and capture Roosevelt's support. Distrustful of the War Department (which considered him a publicity hound), the airman communicated directly with the president through several selected intermediaries. Among the most important was an aide to Chennault named Joseph Alsop, who happened to be a distant cousin of the Roosevelts. Alsop and Chinese foreign minister T. V. Soong deluged the White House with advice over how to fight the war. Calling Stilwell's policy a "national disgrace," they claimed that if Chennault received even a handful of bombing planes he could cripple Japanese forces in China and bring Japan to its knees. Chennault boasted that that he could "not only bring about the downfall of Japan" but also "make the Chinese lasting friends of the United States." He promised to "create such good will that China will be a great and friendly trade market for generations."

Stilwell despised Chennault as a toady and flawed strategist. An air campaign would not only dissipate resources for the ground war and army reform, but made no sense. As soon as air attacks on Japanese forces and shipping had an impact, Stilwell predicted, Japanese troops would attack and overrun China's unprotected air bases. Certainly, the Chinese army in its current state could not protect the bases.

The president and most of his aides resented Stilwell's warnings, along with his descriptions of the incompetence and veniality of Chiang. Chennault, on the other hand, soothingly told presidential aide Harry Hopkins that if Roosevelt supported an air war, "there was no doubt of success." Chennault's supporters chanted their mantra of air war and claimed it would not only kill Japanese, but would also magically improve the political atmosphere in Chungking.

All during 1943 and the first half of 1944, Stilwell tried in vain to get Chiang and the reluctant British (who held India) to begin a military drive to open a supply route through Burma. But without Roosevelt's firm backing, nothing happened. In May 1943, the president attempted to resolve the conflict of strategies by inviting both Stilwell and Chennault to present their cases directly to him in Washington. The questions posed by Roosevelt were centered more on politics than military strategy. What did Stilwell think of Chiang, asked the president. "He's a vacillating, tricky undependable old scoundrel who never keeps his word." Chennault disagreed. "Sir, I think the Generalissimo is one of the two or three greatest military and political leaders in the world today."

Roosevelt ignored the detailed analysis Stilwell presented in favor of the feel-good promises offered by Chennault. An air campaign promised easy, cheap, and quick success. Stilwell's approach involved protracted, difficult combat, requiring complex negotiations with the British and Chinese. Not surprisingly, the president came down on Chennault's side and decided to allocate the bulk of the precious Hump cargo flown into China for an air campaign. Roosevelt came close to recalling Stilwell from China, but relented when Army Chief of Staff Marshall and Secretary of War Stimson expressed their confidence in him.

THE RISE AND FALL OF AIR WARFARE IN CHINA

Roosevelt's decision to indulge Chiang by shifting support to an air war strategy reflected his hope that he had made a wise investment in future cooperation. As he told General Marshall in 1943, Chiang should not be threatened into reform. It would be counterproductive to bully a man who had created in China "what it took us a couple of centuries to attain." The president called the Generalissimo the "undisputed leader of 400,000,000 people," who could not be dictated to like "the Sultan of Morocco."

Marshall then understood why the president had accepted Chennault's absurd claims. It was not that anyone with a grain of military sense believed that air power alone could defeat Japan, but that Chiang wanted Chennault. As Marshall put it:

> Since the Chinese wanted what Chennault wanted, and Roosevelt wanted to give the Chinese what they wanted, all these things fit together very neatly and required no further presidential effort or analysis.

At another level, of course, the president's decision demonstrated the extent to which he was divorced from the reality of the situation. In contrast to Roosevelt's sophisticated understanding of European rivalries, he and most of those around him had only the dimmest comprehension of Chinese conditions. They failed to realize that Chiang's military policy overlay a much deeper political crisis in China and that these problems could not be resolved by placating Chiang. Furthermore, their glib faith in China's immediate postwar importance led them to postpone the day of reckoning with Chiang, unintentionally encouraging his most destructive tendencies.

While Chennault celebrated the go-ahead to begin an air campaign, Stilwell brooded over being cut adrift by Washington. His diary entries during 1943 reveal tremendous resentment toward Roosevelt, Chennault, and Chiang. "Back again on the manure pile after that wonderful trip home," he wrote, back "to find Chiang the same as ever—a grasping, bigoted, ungrateful little rattlesnake."

For the next year, through the spring of 1944, Stilwell bided his time, doing what little he could to reorganize thirty Chinese divisions with the meager resources left him. Chiang continued to interfere with all reform efforts and came perilously close to open warfare against the Chinese Communists. The Generalissimo complained frequently to Washington about Stilwell's arrogance, while the general did what he could to channel American supplies to Chiang's KMT rivals. He even dabbled in a few plots to overthrow the Kuomintang leader.

Meanwhile, Chennault built up his Fourteenth Air Force and prepared to launch attacks on Japanese positions at the end of 1943. The results of the attacks proved devastating, but not exactly in the way Chennault promised. As soon as the air attacks began to hurt the Japanese, they launched massive counterattacks and quickly overran Chennault's undefended air bases. The Chinese armies supposedly protecting them dissolved into a rabble. The Japanese offensive, code named *Ichigo*, succeeded in overrunning large parts of China that had resisted conquest since 1937. By the spring and summer of 1944, it appeared the Japanese might subdue the entire country. These events proved Stilwell correct in his estimation of the military and political bankruptcy of the Chennault-Chiang strategy. In the

From left to right, Chiang Kai-shek, Franklin Delano Roosevelt, Winston Churchill, and Mme. Chiang, at Cairo Conference, 1943. (National Archives)

process, however, it appeared that a member of the Grand Alliance was about to fall to Japan.

The disaster overtaking China finally impressed itself on President Roosevelt. It not only confirmed Stilwell's prediction, but compelled the president to reexamine his faith in Chiang. In fact, as early as November 1943, when Roosevelt met Chiang face to face during a meeting at Cairo, the president began to reassess his ally. Chiang harangued FDR for hours, demanding a billion dollars in new economic aid and more weapons. At the same time, the Chinese leader refused to commit himself to military reform or an offensive against Japan. Roosevelt came away from Cairo disgusted by the British priority of recapturing lost colonies and the Chinese determination to do as little as possible.

In marked contrast, when the president went on from Cairo to Teheran to meet with Josef Stalin, the Soviet leader promised to enter the war against Japan soon after Hitler's defeat. Promised Russian assistance, along with recognition that China was unlikely to do much against Japan, forced Roosevelt to rescind his blanket endorsement of Chiang. At Cairo, the president even quipped to Stilwell that if Chiang were deposed in a coup, the United States would gladly support whomever was "next in line."

When Treasury Secretary Henry Morgenthau, Jr. discovered massive fraud by high KMT officials, the president blocked new economic aid. Morgenthau claimed he would not give Chiang's clique "another nickel" and the crooks could "go jump in the Yangtze." Roosevelt's disillusionment with Chiang increased after April 1944 when Stilwell took charge of the few divisions of Chinese troops under American control and began a campaign to retake Burma. When Chiang interfered with the flow of supplies and replacements to these units, Roosevelt threatened to cut off aid. How, Americans asked, could Chiang block sending Stilwell reinforcements when the KMT kept a half-million troops blockading the Chinese Communists?

ROOSEVELT AND CHIANG: ULTIMATUM AND RETREAT

By June 1944, about the time the Allies began the liberation of Western Europe, Roosevelt decided to compel Chiang to fight Japan actively. It became clear to him that unless the Chinese government and military were revitalized, they would be unable either to help win the war or secure the peace. Since Chiang argued that he had to use many of his troops to guard the Communists rather than fight the Japanese, the president insisted on an effort to improve the United Front. This would free KMT units to fight Japan and would allow the United States to tap the growing military strength of the Communist armies in north China. Wartime unity, Roosevelt hoped, would prevent the renewal of civil war after Japan's defeat. With this in mind, the president dispatched Vice President Henry A. Wallace to China in June 1944, with instructions to press Chiang to negotiate a settlement with the Communists. Washington, he implied, would help mediate their disputes.

Roosevelt also insisted that an American military and diplomatic observer team be allowed passage through the KMT blockade to the Communist capital, Yenan. This was designed to put some fear into Chiang by letting him know that the United States could "back more than one horse" in China. It would also provide the U.S. government with first-hand knowledge about the rapidly growing Communist movement. In his report to Roosevelt, Wallace revealed growing frustration.

> Chiang, at best, is a short-term investment. It is not believed that he has the intelligence or political strength to run postwar China. The leaders of postwar China will be brought forward by evolution or revolution and it now seems more like the latter.

As the military situation in China deteriorated, Stilwell seized the moment to ask Roosevelt again to compel Chiang to turn over to him command of all Chinese armies. The American general wanted complete freedom to direct China's war effort and even to aid and utilize Communist units. On July 4, 1944, the president approved a telegram to Chiang warning him that "the future of all Asia is at stake." Air power had failed and now Stilwell must be given "command of all Chinese and American forces . . . including the Communist forces."

Rather than rebuff this demand outright and risk the loss of American aid, Chiang responded in his usual way, giving vague assurances of compliance, stalling, and playing off American rivalries. Stilwell, he informed the White House, would soon be given the power of command. But first the president should send a personal emissary to China to smooth relations.

Army Chief of Staff Marshall wanted to move quickly and also to make certain that any emissary sent by Roosevelt would take Stilwell's side. For somewhat murky reasons, both Marshall and Secretary of War Stimson proposed sending Patrick J. Hurley, a Republican oil company lawyer and former secretary of war in the Hoover administration. During a previous mission to China, Hurley had gotten on well with Stilwell. Also, Marshall and Stimson, like Roosevelt, may have thought it good politics to send a Republican as intermediary. In any case, no one in Washington expected Hurley to play more than a supporting role in the unfolding Chinese drama.

On September 6, 1944, after a brief stop in Moscow where he received a Soviet pledge to support Chiang's government rather than the Chinese Communists, Hurley arrived in Chungking. There he found Stilwell anxiously waiting to take command of KMT troops and making plans to "get arms to the Communists who will fight" Japan. On September 19, Stilwell personally delivered a presidential ultimatum to Chiang, informing the Generalissimo that unless he immediately transferred command power, all U.S. aid would stop. This, he believed, would bring down the KMT government.

Stilwell gloried in delivering this ultimatum. He wrote in his diary:

> Mark this day in red on the calendar of life. At long last, at very long last FDR has finally spoken plain words, and plenty of them, with a firecracker in every sentence. "Get Busy or Else." A hot firecracker. I handed this bundle of paprika to the Peanut and then sank back with a sigh. The harpoon hit the little bugger right in the solar plexus, and went right through him. It was a clean hit, but beyond turning green and losing the power of speech, he did not bat an eye. He just said to me, "I understand." And sat in silence jiggling one foot.

Stilwell's victory proved temporary. Just as the American commander prepared to assume command of Chinese troops, Hurley secretly took it upon himself to cooperate with Chiang to get rid of Stilwell. Hurley worked openly and behind the scenes to sustain Chiang's rule. He worried that a KMT collapse would open China to domination by Mao's Communists or the Soviet Union. Thus, a man almost completely ignorant of China conspired to remove Stilwell and crush the Chinese Communists.

Hurley's motives and betrayal of Stilwell have long puzzled historians. Some have speculated that personal ambition or extreme anti-communism motivated his behavior. After returning to the United States at the end of 1945, Hurley became a strident anti-Communist, accusing the Truman administration of coddling Reds and abetting treason. But Hurley's motives were partly rooted in his unstable personality. In 1982, a conference brought together several American journalists, diplomats, and military officers who had served in wartime China. Many had known Hurley and witnessed his erratic behavior. Several recalled encounters in which he ranted incoherently about personal demons, seemed to forget he was in China, and confused them with relatives and old friends. *Time* journalist Anna Lee Jacoby was astounded when Hurley insisted she was his wife. But neither she nor other correspondents were able to convince their editors to publish accounts of this behavior. Decades later, these "old China Hands" still trembled with rage when they recalled these incidents. Somehow, Hurley displayed more rational behavior when conferring with officials.

On September 24, 1944, Hurley joined Chiang and T. V. Soong in sending a message to Roosevelt. They insisted that the only real problem in China was Stilwell. Because of his impudence and caustic personality, they said, he must be removed. Once this happened, the Generalissimo would gladly do everything Roosevelt asked of him.

As the president wavered, Hurley peppered the White House with additional warnings. On October 10, he asserted that "there is no other Chinese known to me who possesses as many of the elements of leadership as Chiang Kai-shek. Chiang and Stilwell are fundamentally incompatible." Hurley claimed that only jealousy and revenge inspired Stilwell's demand to control Chinese troops. Foolishly, he sought to "subjugate a man who has led a nation in revolution and who had led an ill-fed, poorly equipped, practically unorganized army against an overwhelming foe for seven years." Playing his ultimate card, Hurley told Roosevelt that if he "sustained Stilwell in this controversy you will lose Chiang Kai-shek and possibly you will lose China with him."

Events forced Roosevelt to choose between two extreme positions—sustaining Stilwell even at the cost of a break with Chiang, or replacing Stilwell with a deferential commander and accepting the fact that China would play only a small role in defeating Japan. To make matters worse, Roosevelt faced an unprecedented fourth-term election in just a few weeks time, running on his record as a leader of a successful coalition. Hurley tried to alleviate the president's discomfort by framing the issue as a mere personality clash, not as a question of Chiang's competence or China's importance as an ally. The entire problem was merely Stilwell's arrogance. It was a comparatively easy solution to choose between a quarrelsome general and the "indispensable" leader of China.

Roosevelt made the expedient decision, issuing orders on October 18, 1944 that Stilwell be recalled to the United States. The president selected General Albert Wedemeyer, a man Stilwell despised as the "world's most pompous prick," as his replacement. U.S. aid would continue, but Chiang would not have to give military command to Wedemeyer. Finally, Roosevelt promoted Hurley from special emissary to ambassador, replacing Clarence Gauss who shared Stilwell's opinions. The Generalissimo appeared to have snatched victory from the jaws of defeat.

Because of his pungent and accurate descriptions of Chiang's shortcomings, as well as the sacrifices he made on China's behalf, it is tempting to see Stilwell as a potential "savior" of China. He certainly recognized the faults of the Kuomintang, understood the Chinese Communist commitment to resist Japan, and appreciated the desperate need for reform in China. Stilwell knew first hand the depth of China's poverty and the misery into which millions of its peasants were born and died. Unlike Chennault or Miles, he did not see China as a stage on which to find his glory. He wanted to fight Japan, help China, win the war, and go home.

If Stilwell had succeeded in gaining command of large numbers of Nationalist troops, and had also been permitted to utilize Communists forces, he probably could have mounted a major offensive against Japanese forces in China. However, by the end of 1944, the war in the Pacific was passing China by. The navy's massive central Pacific offensive had pushed Japanese forces back toward their inner ring of islands. Armies under General Douglas MacArthur had already begun the reconquest of the Philippine islands. Soon, long-range B-29 bombers, operating from the Pacific islands seized by the navy and marines, would begin pummeling Japanese cities. China, in other words, had already moved to the margins of the Pacific War and was merely a secondary consideration in the strategy to defeat Japan.

It is possible, of course, that one or more of the Nationalist generals tapped by Stilwell to lead the reorganized Chinese army he envisioned could have replaced Chiang Kai-shek and revitalized the Kuomintang. The

American commander certainly hoped this might occur. Whether or not such a new leader would have reached a compromise with the Chinese Communists after 1945 or, unlike Chiang, beaten them in a civil war, is speculative. China, ultimately, had to find its own solutions. In the aftermath of Stilwell's recall, it seemed increasingly likely that the path to be followed led directly to civil war.

SELECTED ADDITIONAL READINGS

Joseph W. Stilwell, *The Stilwell Papers* (New York, 1948); Theodore White and Annalee Jacoby, *Thunder Out of China* (New York, 1946); Theodore White, *In Search of History* (New York, 1978); Han Su-yin, *Birdless Summer* (New York, 1968), and *Destination Chungking* (Boston, 1942); Gordon Seagrave, *The Soong Dynasty* (New York, 1985); T. Christopher Jespersen, *American Images of China, 1931–39* (Stanford, Calif., 1996); Graham Peck, *Two Kinds of Time* (Boston, 1967); John W. Dower, *A War without Mercy: Race and Power in the Pacific War* (New York, 1968); John W. Garver, *Chinese–Soviet Relations, 1937–1945, The Diplomacy of Chinese Nationalism* (New York, 1988); Christopher Thorne, *Allies of a Kind: The United States, Great Britain, and the War against Japan, 1941–1945* (New York, 1978); Herbert Feis, *The China Tangle* (Princeton, N.J., 1953); Barbara Tuchman, *Stilwell and the American Experience in China, 1911–1945* (New York, 1971); Robert Dallek, *Franklin D. Roosevelt and American Foreign Policy, 1932–1945* (New York, 1979); Lloyd Eastman, *Seeds of Destruction: Nationalist China in War and Revolution, 1937–1949* (Stanford, Calif., 1984); Xiaoyuan Liu, *A Partnership for Disorder: China, the United States, and Their Policies for the Postwar Disposition of the Japanese Empire* (New York, 1996); Ronald Spector, *Eagle against the Sun: The American War with Japan* (New York, 1985); Michael Schaller, *The U.S. Crusade in China, 1938–1945* (New York, 1979).

FIVE

Americans Encounter the Chinese Revolution, 1942–1945

Tensions between the United States and the Kuomintang regime formed only part of a larger Chinese drama. Throughout the vast Chinese interior, the Communists and Nationalists continued their rivalry, with civil war simmering just below the surface. Centered in their remote northwestern capital of Yenan, where they lived in caves carved into the sand hills, the Communists spent the war years resisting Japan and building a mass peasant army. When they joined the United Front in 1937, Mao's Communists controlled a few thousand square miles of territory, a population of about one million people, and an army of 80,000. Compared to Chiang's Nationalists, they appeared a negligible force. When Japan surrendered eight years later, the Communists fielded a million troops, controlled one-fourth of China, and governed 100 million people. Four years later, after Chiang and his defeated army fled to a small offshore island, all China was theirs.

Several factors account for this reversal of fortune. In the 1950s, many Americans believed their own failures explained the massive upheaval in China. Republican politicians accused the Democratic Truman administration and the State Department of "losing China" through treason or incompetence. These charges resonated in the atmosphere of the cold war, but had only a glancing relation to reality. More than anything, the different ways in which the Kuomintang and the Chinese Communist party responded to the challenge of the Japanese invasion explained why Mao, not Chiang, led China by 1949.

After the first year of the Sino–Japanese war, the Japanese occupied the most valuable part of China, roughly the eastern third of the country on a line from Beijing to Canton. When the Nationalists withdrew to Chungking, they left the fate and loyalty of hundreds of millions of Chinese up for grabs. Chiang followed a simple strategy that made some sense: he would trade space for time and wait for the United States to enter the war. Both before and after that occurred, the Nationalists hoarded much of the American aid they received for eventual use against the Communists. Chiang failed, however, to account for the fact that Communist organizers entered the vacuum created by the Nationalist retreat. Moving through the countryside, behind Japanese lines, they organized political support and recruited soldiers for an army that eventually swept away the KMT.

The flaw in Chiang's plan was not a mere oversight. Challenging the Japanese effectively required appealing to and empowering peasants. A peasant-guerrilla army threatened not only the Japanese, but also the landlord class that formed a pillar of KMT support. Chiang faced a dilemma. To win the peasants, he risked losing his base of support among landlords. If he lost the landlords, how would he organize campaigns against the Communists? Chiang became a hostage to his backers. His best—possibly only—way out lay with the United States. If America fought Japan and provided needed military assistance, he could amass the strength he needed for a showdown with the Communists without alienating his wealthy supporters or being forced to placate the peasantry.

The circumstances that paralyzed the KMT energized the Communists. As the Nationalists deserted countless villages in occupied or semi-occupied China, Communist organizers arrived to rally the peasants against the Japanese. During most of the war years, the CCP stressed its patriotic mission against the Japanese invader. A report by U.S. military intelligence chronicled Communist methods at the village level.

> Its retinue of propagandists, social and economic workers, school teachers . . . immediately started organizing and training the peasant masses for resistance through guerrilla warfare. Their central idea in all these efforts was that the social and economic level of the peasants had to be improved in order to maintain morale and to instill among the people a will to resist Japan and support their own armies.

Rather than promote radical land redistribution or impose rigid Marxist schemes that would divide the community, the Communists at this stage undertook moderate reforms, such as reducing rents and intervening on behalf of peasants in debt to notorious landlords or money lenders.

The details of the CCP program were often less important to peasants than the mere fact that they were being treated as valuable human beings. Journalist Theodore White, who witnessed these events, described what he believed to be the secret of the Communists' success.

> If you take a peasant who has been swindled, beaten and kicked about for all his walking days and whose father has transmitted to him an emotion of bitterness reaching back for generations—if you take such a peasant, treat him like a man, ask his opinion, let him vote for a local government, let him organize his own police . . . decide on his own taxes and vote himself a reduction in rent and interest—if you do all that the peasant becomes a man who has something to fight for, and he will fight to preserve it against any enemy, Japanese or Chinese.

The Communists, White reported, helped the peasant gather his harvest, would "teach him to read and write and fight off the Japanese who raped his wife and tortured his mother." Because of this, the peasant developed "loyalty to the army and the government and to the party that controls them. Gradually the peasant votes for that party, thinks the way that party wants him to think, and in many ways becomes an active participant."

In village after village, Communist activists sponsored local defense groups, agricultural cooperatives, schools, and political indoctrination. Peasants felt that the Communists were in the forefront of the struggle against Japan and for restructuring society. The Communist party gave voice to peasant demands for social and economic justice against landlords. As a result, many villagers joined the Red forces either as regular soldiers or members of a part-time militia.

The Japanese responded to guerrilla activities by waging a terror campaign. They unleashed the "Three-All Policy" of "Burn all, Kill all, Loot All" against villages or regions that harbored Communists. In the long run, Japanese brutality served as the Communists' most efficient recruiting tool, driving nearly a million new soldiers to fight under the CCP banner. The Communists asserted that for China to be free and powerful, it must throw off the shackles of foreign domination and internal oppression. They harnessed powerful revolutionary and nationalist impulses that formed a wave that eventually carried them to power.

AMERICANS AND THE CHINESE COMMUNISTS, 1942–1944

Given the attention lavished on the Kuomintang by both President Roosevelt and the media, Americans were slow to take notice of the Communist's rise in importance. When the United States joined China in the war against Japan, there had been little contact between American diplomats and the CCP, even though the United Front made the Communists an implicit ally. In the late 1930s, a handful of American journalists and adventurers, such as Edgar Snow, Peggy Snow, Owen Lattimore, T. A. Bisson, Agnes Smedley, Phillip Jaffe, and Evans Carlson, had sneaked through the KMT blockade into Communist territory. All praised the high morale, social reform, and commitment to fighting Japan that they observed. However, most of these Americans were committed leftists, a fact that diminished their credibility.

As noted earlier, official American views of the Chinese Communist movement since the 1920s alternated between uncertainty and hostility. Most U.S. experts on communism were baffled by the appeal of a Marxist–Leninist party to Asian peasants. Some diplomats considered the Reds "agrarian reformers" or folk bandits who labeled themselves revolutionaries. They were uncertain whether or how closely the CCP was tied to Moscow.

Following the Pearl Harbor attack, many more American diplomats, soldiers, and journalists entered China. They included a group of Chinese-speaking Foreign Service officers, several of whom had grown up as "missionary kids" in China. These diplomats, members of Stilwell's staff, and the journalists expressed growing interest in the Communist movement, especially as they witnessed the deterioration of Nationalist rule.

The American presence created danger and opportunity for the CCP. Mao, like most Chinese, rejoiced when the United States joined the war against Japan, but worried that Chiang might turn U.S.-supplied weapons against the CCP. The Communists hoped that by participating in the American war effort they could restrain Chiang, receive badly needed aid, and win a measure of recognition. This effort was led by the CCP's chief representative in Chungking, Zhou Enlai. From Lauchlin Currie in 1940 through Henry Kissinger in the 1970s, nearly every American who encountered Zhou came away charmed. Permitted by the United Front agreement to reside in Chungking, Zhou entertained and cajoled journalists, diplomats, and military officers in his tiny apartment. He invited Americans he met to visit Yenan as private citizens or government representatives, to contrast life there to the squalor of Chungking.

During 1942 and 1943, American diplomats in Chungking urged their superiors to give them approval for official visits to the Communist region. John S. Service, a member of the embassy staff and an adviser to Stilwell, feared that not only the Communists but Chinese "liberals" deeply resented the American policy of exclusive aid to the KMT, and these groups might turn "toward friendship with Russia." The embassy staff agreed that Washington had much to learn about the CCP. Service speculated:

> What is the form of their local government? How "Communistic" is it? Does it show any Democratic character or possibilities? Has it won the support of the people? How does it compare with the conditions in Kuomintang China? What is the military and economic strength of the Communists and what is their probable value to the Allied Cause?

As frustration with Chiang increased, Service, like fellow diplomats John P. Davies and Raymond Ludden, worried that the alliance with the KMT might drag the United States into a Chinese civil war. If America continued to side with Chiang, the Communists would almost certainly move closer to the Soviet Union. These Foreign Service officers predicted that radical nationalism would sweep postwar Asia. If the United States hoped to influence the direction of this movement, Davies wrote his superiors, American policy must "move with the historical stream rather than fighting it." Whether one liked it or not, these diplomats asserted, the Communists would play a major role in China's future. It seemed the greatest folly to support Chiang exclusively and risk conflict with the Communists while knowing practically nothing about them.

For complementary reasons, General Stilwell and members of the Office of Strategic Services (OSS) hoped to cooperate with Yenan. Stilwell, for example, favored arming and enlisting Communist troops in his planned ground offensive. Based on what he had heard about Yenan and seen in Chungking, he thought it important to enlist Communist troops. He faulted the KMT for "corruption, neglect, chaos, trading with the enemy" and a "callous disregard for all the rights of men." The Communists, in contrast, "reduced taxes, rents and interest" and "practiced what they preached."

Roosevelt, however, refused to distance himself from Chiang by authorizing contact with the CCP. As discussed earlier, the president changed course in the summer of 1944, as a result of the collapse of KMT armies in the face of the Japanese *Ichigo* offensive. This effort to knock China out of the war followed Chennault's air attacks. Chiang's refusal to send vital supplies to key Chinese generals resisting the Japanese because he questioned their personal loyalty, appalled Stilwell. It also convinced Roosevelt to explore the option of dealing with the Communists, either as a junior partner in coalition with Chiang or separately. If nothing else, putting out feelers in Yenan might frighten Chiang into cooperation.

Pushed by Washington, Chiang reluctantly gave way in the summer of 1944 and allowed two groups of Americans into the Communist zone. A delegation of journalists went first. After three years in squalid Chungking, these Americans found Yenan a remarkable improvement, even a "wonderland city." In dozens of articles sent home, they described the populace under Communist rule as "better fed, huskier, and more energetic than in other parts of China." Peasants considered the local government an asset, not an oppressor. Brooks Atkinson, of *The New York Times*, believed the soldiers of the Communist Eighth Route Army were "among the best clothed and best fed this writer has seen anywhere in China." Another journalist wrote that any American general would be "proud to command these tough, well-fed, hardened troops." Kuomintang censors removed much of the praise from the news copy sent back to the United States. Chiang so resented these favorable reports that he blocked additional visits.

The first official American representatives reached Yenan in July 1944. The so-called Dixie Mission (a code name selected because of the location in "rebel" territory) consisted of about two dozen military personnel, weather specialists, translators, and Foreign Service officers. The group outnumbered the handful of Soviet personnel in Yenan. For the first time, the U.S. government could gather direct information about the CCP while the Communists could gauge American intentions.

The Dixie Mission quickly took on a life of its own. Most of the American personnel shared the enthusiasm voiced by John Service. "We have come into a different country and are meeting a different people," he wrote in his first dispatch. The Communists were equally excited by their contacts. Between July and November 1944, they treated the American visitors as honored guests. Top CCP leaders mixed closely with the junior diplomats and military officers. Mao questioned Service in detail about the American policy and attitude toward his movement. The party leaders declared that the United States had nothing to fear from the CCP. "Even the most conservative American businessman can finding nothing in our program to object to." Yet, Mao admitted, the Communists were extremely vulnerable to American policy.

> America does not need to fear we will not cooperate. We must cooperate and we must have American help. This is why it is important to us Communists to know what you Americans are thinking and planning. We cannot risk crossing you, cannot risk conflict with you.

Dixie Mission member John S. Service in Yenan, 1944. (Left to right) Zhou Enlai, Zhu De, Service, Mao Zedong, Yeh Jianying. (National Archives)

The force of Mao's personality and the material strength of the CCP convinced Service that if current trends continued, within a few years the Communists would become the "dominant force in China."

During the final months of 1944, Communist leaders addressed their own tenuous position in relation to the KMT, United States, and the Soviet Union. With limited resources, they were fighting the Japanese, continuing an armed truce with the KMT, developing strategies for agrarian reform, conducting a series of shake ups within the party to suppress both liberal and Soviet influences, and trying to sort out a new relationship with Washington. For at least the short run, they admitted, good relations with the United States were vital to forestall attacks by the KMT. They had little prospect of aid from Stalin. None of the Americans who spoke with Mao doubted either his commitment to communism or his nationalist determination to restore China as a great power. Mao implied, and the Americans who talked with him inferred, that he envisioned a Communist China that could be a stabilizing force in Asia and a possible counterweight to Soviet influence. While not denying their goal of transforming China, the CCP leaders told Americans that a Communist China need not threaten postwar U.S. interests. In the interim, Mao pledged to cooperate with both Washington and the KMT by forming a coalition government that would avert civil war.

At the practical level, OSS officers in Yenan began to offer Communist troops basic instruction in the use of donated American weapons. They hoped to train sabotage squads for deployment against the Japanese. These small, individual acts of cooperation convinced Mao that U.S. policy was flexible and that Washington had begun to shift away from exclusive support for Chiang. The Communists understood that the growing command crisis between Stilwell and Chiang revolved, in part, around the general's desire to distribute American weapons to the Communists who, as he put it, "will fight."

Stilwell, of course, never got to implement this plan. In October 1944, Chiang and Patrick J. Hurley convinced the president to fire Stilwell and continue exclusive aid to the Nationalist regime. From this point on, Hurley, with Roosevelt's tacit consent, pressed the Communists to accept a subordinate role in a coalition dominated by Chiang. American diplomats who questioned this approach were removed from China. In February 1945, when Roosevelt met Stalin at the Yalta conference, the president pressed for a Soviet pledge to steer clear of the CCP and deal only with Chiang.

On November 7, 1944, soon after Stilwell's recall, Hurley, now U.S. ambassador to China, paid an unannounced visit to Yenan. As he stepped off the plane and was greeted by the American commander of the Dixie Mission, a clearly shocked Zhou Enlai learned that an emissary of the president had just arrived. "Keep him here until I can find Chairman Mao," Zhou yelled, as he dashed off. Hurley, who privately called Mao "Moose Dung" and Zhou "Joe N. Lie," stunned his Chinese hosts by bellowing a Choctaw Indian war cry as he deplaned. It proved the first of many bizarre outbursts. Soon, the Communists referred to Hurley as "the clown."

In the initial Hurley–Mao discussions, the American proposed that the Communists join a coalition under Chiang. To alleviate Communist doubts, Hurley offered to guarantee a coalition based on equality. Washington, he promised, would recognize the equality of the two partners. and would distribute aid to both. Mao and Hurley even signed a "Five Point Agreement" to this effect. In mid-November, Hurley accompanied Zhou to Chungking to finalize the arrangement. Once there, however, the deal collapsed. In

The mercurial and immaculately tailored Patrick Hurley escorting Mao Zedong to peace talks in Chungking, 1945. (National Archives)

Chiang's presence, Hurley informed Zhou that the Communists must dissolve their armed forces as the price for admission into a coalition. Given the twenty-year record of KMT–CCP hostility, unilateral disarmament by the Communists was akin to mass suicide. Negotiations ended on November 21, when an embittered Zhou returned to Yenan. The Communists deeply resented Hurley's role, believing he had used bait-and-switch tactics to get them to meet with Chiang.

Hurley, in contrast, blamed the impasse not on his own or Chiang's positions, but on sabotage by American diplomats and military personnel who sympathized with the Communists. He hoped to force Zhou and Mao back into negotiations by throwing these American sympathizers out of China and showing the CCP that they had no allies to rely upon.

Aware of Hurley's plan, Mao and Zhou made a secret effort to meet directly with President Roosevelt. On January 9, 1945, they asked members of the Dixie Mission to forward a secret message to Washington. Mao and Zhou offered to fly to Washington and explain to Roosevelt the muddle Hurley had made. They still believed that U.S. policy could be altered and that cooperation between the CCP and America was possible.

Unfortunately, Hurley again blocked this path. The ambassador found out about the secret offer, probably from a Naval Group China radio operator on the Dixie team who passed the text along to Hurley, General Albert Wedemeyer—Stilwell's successor—and Chiang. The ambassador promptly warned Roosevelt not to meet with the Communists. He accused them and their American sympathizers of causing all China's problems. China, Hurley insisted, could be saved only by forcing Mao to submit to Chiang.

Roosevelt, weighed down by a thousand problems related to coalition warfare, preparing for the end of the war in Europe, and desperate to preserve cooperation with the Soviets, spent little time examining this latest China flap. Without much hesitation, he spurned Mao's request for a meeting and authorized Hurley to purge those American officials in China the ambassador considered "disloyal." This meant anyone who questioned Hurley's judgments or Chiang's virtue, or who advocated forcing the CCP into a KMT-led coalition. At one point, he even threatened to shoot an embassy staffer who wrote a report critical of Chiang. Those who opposed the new line were sent home or, as some put it, "Hurleyed out of China."

THE PRESIDENT'S NEW ASIA POLICY: YALTA

By February 1945, the president realized that his dream of fostering a "powerful, united and pro-American China" was turning into a nightmare. Not only would China be useless in the war against Japan, but it seemed likely to become a postwar disaster. At best, China might survive with a weak KMT government or a fractious coalition. At worst, it could erupt in civil war and go Communist. Civil war in China would likely draw the Soviets into the region. To prevent this, Roosevelt decided to make a deal with Soviet dictator Josef Stalin. (By then Stalin, like Chiang, had added Generalissimo to his impressive string of titles.)

Since the 1920s, Stalin had exhibited an ambivalent attitude toward most foreign Communists, including those in China. Beneath the facade of support for foreign revolutionary movements, Stalin remained suspicious of nominal allies. He questioned the loyalty of most foreign Communists and worried about those who, like Mao, created a power base independent of the Soviets. The prospect of a powerful but independent Communist China along the Soviet border made Stalin uneasy. During the 1920s and late 1930s, most Soviet assistance to China went to the KMT. Although Mao paid homage to Stalin and the Soviet Union, before World War II, Stalin had several times promoted policies that nearly led to the destruction of the Chinese Communist movement. From Stalin's perspective, Soviet interests in China might best be served by either a weak KMT or CCP regime, or by a coalition. As events over the next year showed, Stalin's main interest in northeast Asia was acquiring and keeping an economic and strategic buffer zone in Manchuria. He would deal with any Chinese government that provided what he wanted. A strong China, ruled by either party, or a U.S. military presence in China, were the least attractive alternatives.

In February 1945, Roosevelt, Stalin, and British Prime Minister Winston Churchill conferred at Yalta, a city in the Soviet Crimea. There, the "big three" discussed the final stages of the war against Hitler and tried to arrange the future of liberated Europe. Stalin insisted on Soviet domination of Poland and much of Eastern Europe—most of which was already falling under control of the Red Army. Roosevelt argued for granting the region a measure of autonomy.

In spite of tensions over European policies, Roosevelt and Stalin found common ground on Asian issues. To the relief of American military planners, the Soviet leader pledged to join the war against Japan by invading Manchuria three months after Germany's defeat. This would speed victory and save American lives. Nevertheless, Roosevelt worried that in the process of fighting Japan's armies, Soviet forces might assist the CCP. Stalin reassured the president that he would support Chiang's regime exclusively. In return, however, he demanded that the Soviet Union be given control over two major ports and two railroads in Manchuria and continue its de facto rule in Outer Mongolia. Roosevelt considered this a reasonable price to pay for military cooperation and political moderation.

The so-called Yalta Far Eastern Agreement, concluded on February 11, 1945, remained secret until the following summer, although details leaked out earlier. Both Chinese factions found it a bitter pill to swallow. The Nationalist regime was expected to concede ports, a naval base, and rail lines to Moscow, diminishing its sovereignty in Manchuria and abandoning all claims to Outer Mongolia. The Communists were equally uneasy with these concessions and appalled to see Stalin's willingness to sign a treaty of friendship and alliance with Chiang, cutting them adrift.

Roosevelt's actions at Yalta showed that he had little faith in either the Chinese Communists or the Nationalists. Instead, he hoped to stabilize East Asia through Soviet–American agreement. The president probably hoped that his deal with Stalin would push the Chinese Communists into entering a coalition, since they would have no foreign sponsors. But Chiang's rigidity and Mao's independent streak made this problematic.

By the spring of 1945, Mao had little faith in the United States playing a balancing role in China. In March, John Service briefly rejoined the fast diminishing ranks of the Dixie Mission. Mao pleaded with him to get Washington to change course and stop supporting Chiang. Hurley's hostility would ensure that "all that America has been working for will be lost." Mao stressed that "there is no such thing as America not intervening in China! You are here as China's greatest ally. The fact of your presence is tremendous."

Service and his colleagues tried desperately to alert Washington to Hurley's mischief. On February 28, while the ambassador was home for consultations, virtually the entire embassy staff sent a joint telegram to the State Department warning that Hurley's actions would drag the United States into a Chinese civil war. The diplomats stressed the "advantage of having the Communists helped by the United States rather than seeking Russian aid or intervention, direct or indirect." Solomon Adler, a Treasury Department representative in China and a friend of Service, spoke even more bluntly in a message to Washington. America's future in Asia, he lamented, "should not be left in the hands of a bungler like Hurley."

Once more, however, Hurley and General Wedemeyer shaped the president's response. In discussions with Roosevelt, they disputed every point of the embassy critique. They dismissed the CCP as a weak, unpopular group disrupting China's unity. Chiang, they assured Roosevelt, could easily "put down the communist rebellion" if he received full U.S. backing. Troubled and disillusioned by this conflicting advice, and only weeks away from a fatal stroke, the president accepted the advice given by Hurley and Wedemeyer. On April 2, 1945, Hurley emerged from a meeting with Roosevelt and told a group of reporters that the Chinese Communists were the main source of disorder in China. By implication, even the president had now abandoned an even-handed policy.

AMERICAN-COMMUNIST HOSTILITY, JUNE TO AUGUST 1945

In the wake of the April 2 announcement, Chinese Communist authorities publicly denounced Hurley and other American "reactionaries" who plotted civil war. When Mao addressed the Congress of the CCP that month, he warned that the Americans and Kuomintang were planning to attack the

CCP as soon as Japan surrendered. Mao's suspicions increased in June, when word came from Washington that John Service had been arrested for passing classified documents critical of Chiang and Hurley to the leftist *Amerasia* magazine. The arrest of the American diplomat most trusted by the CCP seemed proof that the new president, Harry Truman, and his administration had decided to oppose the Communists. (Charges against Service were later dropped, but the complex case left a stain on his reputation and ended his influence. Five years later, he was dismissed from the State Department as a security risk.) Yenan's reaction to Service's arrest appeared in a radio broadcast beamed to the United States. If the American imperialists did not "withdraw their hands . . . then the Chinese people will teach them a lesson they deserve."

Denunciations of U.S. policy grew in intensity as the war in the Pacific drew to a close. Roosevelt's death in mid-April added to the problem. Even though he had failed to support them, Roosevelt remained a symbol of the anti-Fascist alliance to Chinese Communists. They harbored some hope that he might not fully back Chiang. Harry S. Truman, the new president, was largely unknown in China, but soon gained attention for firing several liberal advisers and for his verbal sparring with the Soviet Union.

By the time Germany surrendered in May, Truman fell under the sway of several of Roosevelt's more conservative foreign policy aides, including Navy Secretary James Forrestal and Ambassador to the Soviet Union Averell Harriman. They condemned Soviet domination of Eastern Europe as Stalin's effort to export communism. They viewed Soviet interest in Manchuria and the growth of Chinese communism as a prelude to Soviet expansion in Asia. By their calculus, Mao was Stalin's puppet. Influential spokesmen on foreign affairs, such as John Foster Dulles—a future secretary of state—argued vehemently on behalf of more aid to Chiang. The essence of U.S. policy in Asia, he told an audience early in 1945, must be a "determination that the 400,000,000 people of China shall not become harnessed to the predatory design of an alien power." Chiang chose to "rely on the ultimate support of the Christian democracies, notably the United States." Deserting him would be a sin.

Truman's approach to China reflected the ideas of advisers such as Harriman and Forrestal. They identified China as one of several flash points where Stalin was likely to challenge U.S. interests. If Washington wavered in support of Chiang, Harriman warned, "we should have to face ultimately the fact that two or three hundred millions of people would march when the Kremlin ordered." The same Chinese masses Americans had hoped to mobilize against Japan were now a potential "red horde."

By July 1945, the Grand Alliance persisted in name only. Although the United States still fought Japan and hoped for Soviet assistance in the final stages of the war, the Truman administration considered Moscow an emerging threat to Western Europe and Asia. The president, like his advisers, was torn between the desire to defeat Japan quickly with few American casualties and the fear that Soviet entry into the Pacific war would give Stalin a foothold in China and northeast Asia.

The Potsdam Conference, held in the suburbs of conquered Berlin in mid-July 1945, revealed these fissures. Soviet and American delegates, led by Truman and Stalin, accused the other of bad faith. Americans denounced creation of Soviet "puppet regimes" in Poland and Eastern Europe, while Stalin accused the United States of breaking promises to give the Soviet Union reparations from Germany and even of plotting to rebuild a Germany hostile to Moscow. Were it not for the American desire for Soviet help in defeating Japan, the conference might have ended in total disarray.

In the midst of angry discussions at Potsdam, Truman received word that American scientists in New Mexico had secretly tested an atomic bomb. The new weapon held out hope of defeating Japan without a costly invasion and with minimal Soviet help. If Soviet forces were kept out of Manchuria and Mongolia by a quick Japanese surrender, Stalin would have less opportunity to help Mao or seek occupation zones in Korea or Japan. As Truman's new Secretary of State James F. Byrnes put it, the atomic bomb might get Japan "to surrender before Russia goes into the war and this will save China. If Russia goes into the war . . . Stalin will take over and China will suffer." A reassured Truman told a group of naval officers on his way home from Potsdam that with the new weapon, "we did not need the Russians or any other nation." Most historians now agree that Truman's primary motive in using the atomic bomb against Japan was to minimize casualties and end the war quickly. Objectively, Japan was beaten, but U.S. leaders guess correctly that the militarists in charge were not ready to surrender. Still, it is equally clear that Truman and his advisers hoped the atomic bomb would speed Japan's defeat before Soviet forces moved into China or the Japanese home islands.

Information from Soviet sources suggests that Truman had an exaggerated notion of Stalin's appetite. The Soviet leader clearly hoped to control parts of Manchuria, much as the Czars had before 1904. A naval base or two in northeast China and control of North Korea would strengthen the Soviet presence in northeast Asia and could be a useful counterweight to a revived Japan. But Stalin had made no commitment to the Chinese Communists and was quite willing to cooperate with Chiang's regime if it acceded to the Yalta accords.

On August 14, 1945, after the United States dropped two atomic bombs on Japan and Soviet forces had joined the war, and only hours before Japan surrendered, Chinese Nationalist and Soviet negotiators in Moscow signed a Sino–Soviet treaty that implemented the Yalta accords. Chiang accepted a Soviet-dominated Outer Mongolia and a Soviet controlling interest in the Manchurian ports of Dalian and Port Arthur, as well as in the province's two main railroad lines. In return, Stalin pledged his government's "moral, material, and military support to China and solely to the Chinese Nationalist Government" led by Chiang. American observers in Yenan described Communist leaders as stunned by the terms of this deal. Not only had Stalin infringed Chinese sovereignty, but he seemed eager to cooperate with the KMT regime at the expense of the Communists.

THE JAPANESE SURRENDER AND ITS AFTERMATH, AUGUST TO NOVEMBER 1945

Japan's surrender on August 14 brought peace to the United States, but not to most of Asia. Tokyo had failed to create a "co-prosperity sphere," but its military victories and wartime occupations had fatally undermined Dutch, French, and British colonialism. Within a few years, India, the Philippines, and Indonesia were independent, and the French in Indochina were losing a war to Communist-led guerrillas. Japan's occupation of China had weakened the KMT and given a tremendous boost to the Communist movement. Japan's defeat set the stage for resumption of China's civil war.

On August 14, the day Japan agreed to surrender and the Soviets signed a treaty with Chiang's representative, Stalin sent Mao a message urging him to resume peace talks in Chungking. Soviet motives were clear: peace talks would reduce tensions with the United States and allow time to consolidate gains in Manchuria. Confronted with pressure from the Soviet, American, and Chinese governments, Mao consented to negotiations, but also committed Communist forces to the task of seizing territory and extending their influence in Manchuria.

Both Chinese factions rushed to seize the territory and weapons held by the three million or so Japanese and puppet troops in Manchuria and north China. Whichever side acquired these resources would gain an invaluable advantage, a fact Washington recognized. On August 15, 1945 upon announcing Japan's surrender, President Truman issued "General Order # 1." Among other things, this instructed all Japanese-controlled forces in China to surrender their positions and arms only to Chiang's representatives, not to Communist forces in the field. They were ordered to hold and defend their positions—against the Communists—until properly relieved. By this act, Truman committed the United States even more directly to the KMT. Yenan denounced American action as a betrayal of wartime cooperation and declared that Communist commanders would move to disarm the Japanese wherever possible.

Because KMT forces were unreliable and located mostly in the interior, the United States quickly redeployed almost 60,000 Marines from the Pacific to secure rail lines, ports, and airfields in north China. At the same time, American ships and aircraft began transporting several hundred thousand KMT soldiers from the south and west to north China. During the autumn of 1945, American and KMT units cooperated closely with nominally defeated but still armed Japanese forces to bar the Communists from seizing cities and lines of communication. One disgruntled Marine described this situation to his senator:

> We were told when en route [to north China] that we were to assist in the disarming of Japanese troops in this area. Before we arrived, the Chinese had the situation well in hand, and have since gone so far as to re-arm some Japanese units for added protection against Chinese Communists. Recently, we have been told that the reason for our prolonged visit is to hold the area in lieu of the arrival of General Chiang Kai-shek's Nationalist forces. In other words, we are here to protect General Chiang's interests against possible Communist uprisings. Everything we do here points directly or indirectly toward keeping the Chinese Communists subdued.

In addition to dispatching Marines and transporting KMT troops, U.S. Lend-Lease assistance to China actually increased in the six months following the Japanese surrender.

Initially, Soviet occupation forces in Manchuria provided little assistance to newly arrived CCP troops. By the end of October, however, the nearby presence of U.S. Marines, the American air and sea lift of several hundred thousand KMT troops to Manchuria, and the general deterioration in U.S.—Soviet relations angered Stalin. Soviet commanders in Manchuria began cooperating with CCP troops by turning over to them stockpiles of captured Japanese weapons and by blocking landings by KMT armies.

In late November, Hurley's resignation and the appointment of General George C. Marshall as mediator in China prompted another Soviet reversal. From then until shortly before the withdrawal of Soviet troops from Manchuria in April 1946, Soviet commanders kept their distance from the CCP and adopted a more cooperative attitude toward both the KMT and the United States.

In light of substantial American aid to Chiang and very modest Soviet assistance to Mao, the Communist leader faced a difficult choice. An immediate civil war favored the Nationalists. Since Communist strength was growing, it made sense to postpone fighting until the party could muster greater power. This, along with Stalin's prodding, convinced Mao in late August to accept U.S. calls for renewed negotiations on forming a coalition government and averting civil war.

Peace talks resumed in Chungking in September 1945, but they soon deadlocked. Chiang, backed up by Hurley and the Truman administration, again demanded that the CCP surrender its armed forces and its territory as a precondition for joining a coalition. Both the Nationalists and the Americans believed that Mao would relent in the face of their superior military power. However, this optimism soon faded, as fighting spread throughout north China during the autumn months of 1945. Although KMT armies held urban areas, they were often surrounded and isolated by Communist forces. Decisionmakers in Washington realized that assisting Chiang would require far greater and more direct U.S. intervention than had been planned. If the Truman administration intended to "save" the Nationalist regime, it would have to commit substantial American military forces to the task.

Ambassador Hurley recommended just this sort of open-ended commitment, but his over-confidence and erratic behavior had eroded his credibility. From China, General Wedemeyer wrote that Chiang had little hope of unifying China without direct American intervention. Despite their wariness of the Chinese Communists, the president and most of his advisers recognized that the CCP could hold its own against Chiang's armies. The only way to defeat them would be to dispatch a large expeditionary force to China—something Chiang hoped for but most Americans recoiled at. Truman and his advisers believed the United States faced more critical challenges in Europe than in Asia. Millions of American soldiers and sailors were clamoring for demobilization, the huge wartime army was fading away, and the public had no interest in sending combat forces to China just months after Japan's surrender. China was important, but not so overwhelmingly important as to justify committing American lives to keeping it out of Communist control.

The political situation grew more uncertain on November 27, 1945, when Ambassador Hurley, then visiting Washington, called a news conference at which he resigned. Fearful of being blamed for the chaos in China, Hurley condemned the "Hydra-headed direction" of China policy promoted by State Department officers who "sided with the Communist armed party . . . against American policy." Although these charges were nonsense, they provided fuel for political fires, including brief Senate hearings in December. Later, when a search began for a scapegoat to explain

Mao's 1949 victory, Republican critics of Truman revived Hurley's charges of treason and took aim at Chiang's critics in the State Department.

The same day that Hurley resigned, President Truman asked retired Army Chief of Staff General George C. Marshall to go to China as his personal representative. The selection of the immensely respected Marshall, Truman guessed correctly, would mute Hurley's accusations. Truman also hoped that the architect of victory in World War II could salvage American interests or at least prevent China from becoming a flashpoint with the Soviet Union in the emerging cold war.

SELECTED ADDITIONAL READING

Michael Schaller, *The U.S. Crusade in China, 1938–1945* (New York, 1979); Joseph Esherick, ed., *Lost Chance in China: The World War II Dispatches of John S. Service* (New York, 1974); John S. Service, *The Amerasia Papers: Some Problems in the History of U.S.–China Relations* (Berkeley, Calif., 1971); Harvey Klehr and Ronald Radosh, *The Amerasia Spy Case: Prelude to McCarthyism* (Chapel Hill, N.C., 1996); John Patton Davies, *Dragon by the Tail* (New York, 1972); Janice MacKinnon and Stephen MacKinnon, *Agnes Smedley: The Life and Times of an American Radical* (Berkeley, Calif., 1988); Stephen MacKinnon and Oris Friesen, *China Reporting: An Oral History of American Journalism in the 1930s and 1940s* (Berkeley, Calif., 1987); Tracy B. Strong and Helene Keyssar, *Right in Her Soul: The Life and Times of Anna Louise Strong* (New York, 1983); Kenneth Shewmaker, *Americans and Chinese Communists: A Persuading Encounter* (Ithaca, N.Y., 1971); Carol Carter, *Mission to Yenan: American Liaison with the Chinese Communists, 1944–1947* (Lexington, Ky., 1997); Mark Galicchio, *The Cold War Begins: American East Asia Policy and the Fall of the Japanese Empire* (New York, 1988); Odd Arne Westad, *Cold War and Revolution: Soviet-American Rivalry and the Origins of the Chinese Civil War, 1944–46* (New York, 1993), and *Brothers in Arms: The Rise and Fall of the Sino–Soviet Alliance, 1945–1963* (Washington, D.C., 1999); Xiaoyuan Liu, *A Partnership for Disorder: China, the United States, and Their Policies for the Postwar Disposition of the Japanese Empire* (New York, 1996).

SIX

"Who Lost China?"

The United States and the Chinese Revolution, from the Marshall Mission to the Creation of the People's Republic

In December 1945, President Harry S. Truman sent one more American mediator to try to avert disaster in China. Although neither the president nor his emissary, General George C. Marshall, held out much hope for a "united, democratic, pro-American China," they desperately wanted to avoid a worst case scenario: a civil war between the KMT and CCP that dragged in stranded Japanese armies, Soviet troops in Manchuria, and U.S. Marines in north China. Meanwhile, the American public demanded the rapid demobilization of the wartime army, including the Marines in north China. This attitude, which Henry Luce attributed to American gullibility and Communist propaganda, prompted him to place Chiang's portrait an unprecedented sixth time on the cover of *Time* in the fall of 1945, and to publish an editorial on the subject in *Life* magazine. In a postwar world, he wrote, "the safest thing for us to do is rededicate our wartime alliance with China and its government." Luce dismissed those who criticized Chiang's regime as unpopular reactionaries. "Man for man," he countered, Chiang's advisers were "probably as able and as liberal as Truman's cabinet."

At the time of Marshall's appointment, the Truman administration pursued several contradictory goals in China. U.S. policymakers wanted to remove quickly two million Japanese troops from north China and replace them with KMT forces. They hoped to speed Soviet evacuation of

Manchuria, but also to block Communist movement into areas evacuated by the Japanese and Russians. U.S. officials were anxious to keep the Marines in north China out of combat and, finally, sought to encourage KMT–CCP peace talks. In practice, since U.S. policy centered on helping the Nationalists, more attention was paid to utilizing the Japanese against the Communists than in repatriating them to Japan. This, along with continued American military aid to the KMT, did nothing to boost CCP confidence in Washington's impartiality.

The Joint Chiefs of Staff had informed Truman that the Marines were needed in north China both to hold back the Reds and to repatriate the Japanese. If civil war erupted with the Japanese still present, both the KMT and CCP would try to enlist them. This would probably provoke wider Soviet intervention. The Joint Chiefs doubted that Kuomintang armies alone could hold north China or Manchuria against the Chinese Communists once Japanese, American, and Soviet forces departed. Thus, whether or not the Marines and Japanese left quickly or lingered, the result was likely to be civil war.

Since the Truman administration did not intend to send more Americans to garrison north China, Marshall had few alternatives. He decided that the best way to prevent civil war was to extricate the Soviets, Americans, and Japanese quickly, while pressing the CCP and KMT to create a coalition government. There were, in fact, moderate elements in both Chinese camps who favored this arrangement, at least on a temporary basis. To encourage compromise, Marshall needed the authority to threaten or reward the Chinese rivals.

On December 9, 1945, Truman and Secretary of State James F. Byrnes told Marshall that if the CCP proved cooperative but the KMT balked at compromise, he should deal directly with the Communists. If the CCP proved obdurate, Marshall could give full support to Chiang and move additional KMT armies north. Just two days later, however, the administration reversed itself. Truman decided that no matter what happened, the United States would provide "at least indirect support of Chiang Kai-shek's activities against dissident forces in China." If the Communists refused to make "reasonable concessions," Marshall was instructed to assist the KMT in moving more troops north. But even if Chiang blocked a compromise, the United States would not abandon him because America could not accept a "divided China" or the "resumption of Russian power in Manchuria." As Marshall admitted, no matter what Chiang did, Washington "would have to swallow its pride and much of its policy" and continue to support the Kuomintang.

U.S. mediator General George C. Marshall with Mao Zedong in Yenan, 1946. Marshall had kept the Grand Alliance together during World War II, but could not arrange a coalition government in China. (National Archives)

Marshall's instructions, along with the extreme animosity between the KMT and CCP, probably doomed prospects for a lasting, peaceful coalition. But a temporary armistice stretching out for a few years was not impossible to imagine. Stalin continued his interest in working with the KMT. In December 1945, for example, he discussed Chinese events with Jiang Jingguo, Generalissimo Chiang's son, during a visit to Moscow. Stalin told Jiang that he would remain neutral in China's political struggle if the Nationalist government maintained its neutrality in the larger U.S.–Soviet struggle. The Soviet leader praised Marshall's effort and confirmed his own intention of withdrawing Soviet forces from Manchuria in early 1946.

For their part, the Chinese Communists also greeted Marshall's appointment as a favorable "change in American policy" and sent Zhou Enlai back to Chungking to participate in a "political consultative conference." But when Communist delegates went to meet Marshall's incoming flight in Chungking, a squad of KMT police "started to chase the Communist representatives off the field" and beat them until a group of American diplomats intervened.

As 1946 began, Mao admitted to his inner circle his disappointment with the lack of Soviet support. The CCP had relied on the classic Chinese tactic of "using barbarians to deal with barbarians," meaning countering U.S. power and aid to the KMT with Soviet backing for the Communists. However, Stalin's tacit cooperation with the Nationalists and Americans, and the refusal of Soviet commanders to help Red forces take control of cities and railroads in Manchuria, left him no option but to concentrate on rural areas and make a short-term deal with Chiang.

Although he had little room to maneuver, Marshall tried to be even-handed. The CCP insisted that they must share real power in a coalition and maintain a separate army. Chiang, concerned that the Reds were playing for time and convinced that he enjoyed full support from Washington and tacit backing from Moscow, demanded immediate dissolution of Communist armed forces, with the CCP taking the role of a very junior coalition partner. Peace talks in Chungking soon deadlocked on these issues, and disputes arose over control of Manchuria. Soviet–KMT relations also deteriorated early in 1946, when Chiang balked at Stalin's proposals to create joint trading companies along the Soviet–Chinese border. Even though U.S. ships and planes continued to transport KMT armies north, Marshall managed to get both sides to accept a temporary cease fire in January and February 1946.

The Manchurian truce lasted until April 1946. Then, as Soviet troops withdrew from the region, they again coordinated their movements with Communist forces. This provoked a scramble between KMT and CCP armies for control of cities and other strategic territory. One side or the other called for or broke numerous cease fires as their battlefield fortunes fluctuated over the following months.

As the fighting escalated, U.S. civilian relief supplies continued to be distributed almost exclusively in KMT zones. In June, American and Nationalist negotiators reached agreement to turn over $1 billion worth of Lend-Lease equipment already in China to Chiang's forces. Mao denounced these actions as proof of American bias. He told party leaders that it had become vital to resist the KMT, even if it involved an all-out civil war. Mao declared that "American reactionaries" were engaged in a global effort to seize what he called the "intermediate zone" of semi-colonial and colonial countries as a prelude to attacking the Soviet Union. Chiang seemed to prove Mao correct. On July 1, he ordered a nationwide offensive against the Communists.

Facing the collapse of his mediation mission, Marshall pressed Truman for authority to cut off military aid to the KMT. The American envoy argued that Chiang would almost certainly *lose* a military showdown, and the best way to stem a Communist victory was to force Chiang to offer the Reds a meaningful compromise. The president reluctantly agreed and on July 29, 1946, Marshall imposed an embargo on the transfer of American arms to China that lasted about one year. Surprised by this forceful action, Chiang agreed to establish three party truce teams (comprised of CCP, KMT, and U.S. members) to prevent fighting in north China. This slowed, but did not stop, the spread of civil war. Marshall took the opportunity to withdraw most of the U.S. Marines and two million Japanese troops in north China, although a few thousand Japanese stayed and fought the Communists alongside the KMT until 1949.

Ironically, from 1946 through early 1948, Stalin pressed Mao to compromise with the Nationalists because he feared that the Communists would either lose an all-out struggle or would provoke U.S. intervention. The Soviet leader publicly condemned American aid to the KMT, but privately suggested that Moscow and Washington adopt a "common policy" to stabilize China. Presumably, he had in mind some kind of imposed truce.

Chinese public opinion during 1946–47 placed most of the blame for Chiang's hard line on U.S. support. Criticism of American policy boiled over in December 1946, when several young Marines raped a Beijing college student named Sheng Chong. The notorious attack and subsequent court martial in which U.S. authorities dealt lightly with the offenders, provoked anti-American demonstrations throughout China. Outraged students viewed the incident as a metaphor for foreign assault and demanded not only harsh punishment for the attackers, but the withdrawal of all U.S. forces and the cessation of military aid to the KMT.

The student demonstrations coincided with the collapse of peace talks and the cease fire at the end of December 1946. Both KMT and CCP forces launched attacks when local conditions seemed favorable. Chiang remained hopeful that despite the arms embargo, the United States would back him when full-scale civil war broke out. In January 1947, Truman called Marshall home to become secretary of state. As the envoy departed, he condemned both Chinese factions for betraying peace. Peace in China had eluded him, but Marshall had facilitated the removal of Japanese, Soviet, and American troops and prevented the civil war from becoming an international conflict.

The end of the Marshall Mission coincided with a broader review of American foreign policy. The Truman administration all but acknowledged that it had no solution to China's crisis. It also recognized that China's fate was not central to American security. Influenced by the ideas of George Kennan, the head of Policy Planning in the State Department, Truman, Marshall, and others decided that in the emerging cold war with the Soviet Union, certain areas mattered more than others. Western Europe, the western zone of Germany, and Japan, for example, had major military-industrial potential, despite their temporary poverty. If the United States concentrated on rebuilding these areas and binding them to America, it would enjoy a vast advantage over the Soviet Union. Conversely if these areas passed under Soviet control, the world power balance could tilt against the United States.

Kennan argued that the key to cold war victory was rebuilding Western Europe and Japan and harnessing their industry to the United States. The overwhelming economic power and the political stability it created would "contain," as Kennan put it, Soviet influence far more effectively than fighting the Soviets for influence over large, but essentially weak, areas of the world. China was simply too weak and too poor to justify a major commitment of American resources. In Asia, Japan, with a tenth of China's population and territory but far more industrial potential, held the key to regional control. As Navy Secretary James Forrestal remarked, to "have a run for our side in the competition with the Soviet Union," the time had come to "put Germany, Japan and the other affiliates of the Axis back to work." By the spring of 1947, Under-Secretary of State Dean Acheson, in a speech anticipating the soon to be announced Marshall Plan, declared America's intention to rebuild the "two great workshops of Europe and Asia," Germany and Japan.

CIVIL WAR TO LIBERATION

Almost three years elapsed between Marshall's departure from China and creation of the People's Republic in October 1949. As civil war flared in 1947, KMT forces scored some deceptively easy gains, what *Time* magazine called "brilliant victories," over the poorly armed Communists. But during 1948, the tide of battle turned. Chiang and his American backers blamed the previous year's arms embargo for these reversals. But a senior American military observer countered that the KMT troops suffered from "the world's worst leadership." Ill-equipped but highly motivated Communist forces routed them from positions they could have "defended with broomsticks" if they had the will. A French military observer remarked that, as much as anything, KMT corruption destroyed civilian morale, and this totally undermined the quality of the Nationalist troops. A soldier in Chiang's armies was:

> Generally considered to be the scum of humanity. Except in several elite divisions, such a conception could not be changed and morale remained low despite promised reforms. The soldier of Chiang Kai-shek knew not why he

> fought. Against the Japanese he could fight for his country and his people; but in this civil war a peasant soldier from Kwangtung province had no idea why he should be fighting in Shansi or Manchuria. Poorly fed, poorly paid, poorly clothed, poorly cared for, poorly armed, often short of ammunition—even at decisive moments—unsustained by any faith in a cause, the Nationalist soldier was easy prey for the clever and impassioned propaganda of the Communists.

Kuomintang officials not only squandered their military advantages, they alienated almost all segments of civil society. As they reoccupied territory from the Japanese, KMT civil and military officers indulged in an orgy of personal aggrandizement. They seized for personal use vast amounts of property and land held by the Japanese, made deals with wealthy Chinese who had collaborated with the Japanese, ignored the suffering of the poor in liberated areas, and attacked real and alleged Communists instead of addressing the desperate need to reconstruct the country. In rural areas, KMT officials spent much of their energy helping landlords and rent collectors reassert authority, further alienating the peasants.

In contrast to KMT blundering, the Communists adopted flexible approaches to governing areas over which they gained control. During the civil war, the CCP promoted two agendas: the fight against the Kuomintang and the transformation of village life. As they had done behind Japanese lines in wartime, Communist organizers infiltrated villages and stoked the fury of the poorest peasants against large landlords, of debtors against usurers, of the exploited against the exploiter. By pushing land and social reform, the Communists created a mass base of support and a steady supply of military recruits. During 1948, in massive battles in Manchuria and the north China plain, the KMT lost a million troops through death and desertion, while the Communists seized the offensive.

Once the tide of battle turned in the Communists' favor, Stalin provided some assistance to the CCP, especially in Manchuria. There, during 1948, Soviet technical experts helped repair and run damaged railroad lines and trained Communist troops. Of course, stabilizing Manchuria was of special interest to Stalin since he possessed and planned to retain special Soviet privileges there. Even after Stalin approved this limited aid, he still counseled Mao to exercise restraint. For example, in January 1949, the Soviet leader urged Mao to halt his advancing armies at the Yangtze River, effectively cutting China in half. Mao ignored the advice, attacked across the Yangtze, and assured the CCP a victory.

Only when a CCP triumph appeared inevitable did Stalin approve high-level contacts with the Chinese Communists. In February 1949, he sent

Anastas Mikoyan, a top aide, to confer with Mao. The meeting soothed Mao's anger at Stalin's past advice, and Mikoyan promised that once the CCP established a national government, the Soviet Union would quickly recognize and assist the new regime.

As the civil war raged on, China became a domestic as well as foreign policy issue in American politics. In 1948, a group of mostly Republican members of the House and Senate criticized Truman's effort to promote a coalition government in China and accused him of doing too little to help Chiang beat the Communists. At the same time, Republicans and the Luce publishing empire repeated the charges made by Ambassador Hurley when he resigned in 1945, blaming treasonous State Department China specialists for the Communists' success.

The Truman administration was forced to take on the defensive in part because it had succeeded so well in selling the "Containment doctrine" to the public. In 1947–1948, Truman had overseen the Greek–Turkish aid bill (Truman doctrine), the multi-billion-dollar European Recovery Program (Marshall Plan), the Berlin Airlift, the creation of the C.I.A. and a unified Defense Department, and had implemented an internal security program. All were designed to bolster Europe and Japan against communism and to improve domestic security. Chiang's supporters in and out of Congress questioned why so much less had been done to block Communist encroachment in China. The answer, of course, was that few foreign policy experts thought China mattered as much as Europe or Japan or that communism there could be stopped at a reasonable cost. But the Truman administration failed to answer this question directly, leaving critics free to snipe with impunity.

The make-believe world of many of Chiang's American allies was depicted in a May 1947 *Time* story discussing Ch'en Li-fu, one of Chiang's most notoriously reactionary advisers. *Time* portrayed Ch'en as a modern Confucius, wise and modest, struggling to build a democratic China. Even though former *Time* journalist Theodore White published a best-selling, damning critique of Chiang, *Thunder Out of China*, in 1946, the 400,000 readers who purchased his book were a fraction of the several million weekly subscribers to Luce's *Time* and *Life*.

Cynical members of Congress discovered that China was a "hot button issue" that they could use against the Democratic administration. Since few Americans knew very much about real political conditions there, almost anyone could, and did, claim to be a "China expert." The Republican party, desperate for a winning issue with which to attack the Democrats, found China an ideal weapon. It was hard to score points against Truman by criticizing the Berlin airlift or Marshall Plan, but condemning the "sell out of China" proved strong medicine.

Many of Chiang's ardent advocates in Congress were demagogues who cared little about China one way or the other, but found it a useful issue. Senators William F. Knowland (dubbed the "senator from Formosa"—the Portuguese word for Taiwan), Styles Bridges, Owen Brewster, Kenneth Wherry, and Pat McCarran, fell into this category. Others, such as Senator H. Alexander Smith and Congressman Walter Judd (a former medical missionary in China), believed in Chiang's cause. Richard Nixon, then an ambitious young representative from California, had a foot in both camps.

Some members of this so-called congressional China bloc were remarkably obtuse. Senator Wherry, for example, was fond of saying that "with God's help we [in the United States] will lift up Shanghai, up and up, ever up, until it is just like Kansas City." Senator Pat McCarran of Nevada was eager to give Chiang a special loan of several hundred million silver dollars. The State Department objected, saying that if China needed anything, it was food and medical relief. But McCarran's real interest lay in finding an outlet for surplus silver produced in his state. When talk of assistance turned away from silver, he quickly lost interest.

In 1949, Congressman John F. Kennedy of Massachusetts, like McCarran one of the few Democrats focused on China, delivered a bitter attack on Truman's handling of the civil war. He accused the president and his entourage of deserting China, "whose freedom we once fought to preserve. What our young men had saved, our diplomats and president have frittered away."

Chiang's most influential American friend, Henry Luce, turned *Life* and *Time* into virtual Kuomintang party publications. Between 1931 and 1949, Chiang appeared on eight *Time* covers, more than any other mortal. In October 1947, after General Albert Wedemeyer returned from a fact-finding trip to China where Secretary of State Marshall had sent him largely to placate Republican critics, *Life* denounced the administration for ignoring Wedemeyer's plea to increase aid. The magazine carried a sensationalist article by former ambassador to Russia and full-time gadfly, William Bullitt. A liberal turned arch-conservative, Bullitt insisted that China must be "kept out of the hands of Stalin." This could be done "at a cost to ourselves which would be small compared to the magnitude of our vital interests in the independence of China."

Bullitt claimed that Roosevelt had begun the sell-out of China at Yalta, and Truman perpetuated the outrage. To reverse it would require spending one billion dollars in China and sending the Occupation commander in

Japan, General Douglas MacArthur, to supervise the distribution of equipment and "prevent subjugation of China by the Soviet Union." If China fell into Stalin's hands, Bullitt warned, "all Asia, including Japan, sooner or later, will fall into his hands. The manpower and resources of Asia will be mobilized against us. The independence of the U.S. will not live a generation longer than the independence of China."

Time played up the military danger of Stalin turning China against the United States much like Roosevelt had tried to use it against Japan. On March 29, 1948, the magazine published vivid maps depicting a blade jutting out of a Communist China and slicing through Southeast Asia and Japan. Soviet aircraft operating from China, *Time* warned, could easily occupy Alaska and threaten the rest of North America.

In July 1949, *Life* ran a story focused on the effort by retired General Claire Chennault to revive his wartime Flying Tigers airforce as a weapon to save Chiang. "Last Call for China," proposed upgrading Chennault's Civil Air Transport company by the addition of warplanes that would help Chiang hold a free zone in south and west China. This "fighting American," as *Life* described him, could save "a third of the Good Earth and 150,000,000 people" from Red domination. In October, *Reader's Digest* reprinted Chennault's plan under the title "Hold Em! Harass Em! Hamstring Em!" Unknown to the public, the CIA did secretly acquire control of Chennault's air transport company, but used it as a cover for supplying anti-Communist forces in Asia, not as a combat unit.

In spite of these hysterical and partisan demands to intervene in China, the Truman administration resisted a major involvement in the civil war. Truman personally loathed Chiang's inner circle, remarking that the Generalissimo and his wife, the Kungs, the Soongs, etc., "were all thieves, every last one of them." Senator Arthur Vandenberg, a leading Republican foreign policy spokesman, privately admitted in 1948 that despite his sympathy for China, "there are limits to our resources and boundaries to our miracles." In China, he sighed, "we are facing the conundrum of the ages." Democratic Senate leader Tom Connally spoke more bluntly: "Any more aid to Chiang would be money down a rat hole." By 1948, nearly all Americans who knew much about China—academics, business leaders, missionaries, journalists—favored minimizing aid to the Nationalists. Most had lost confidence in Chiang and many believed that even a Communist regime might be better than a prolonged civil war.

According to a Gallup Survey of April 1948, 55 percent of the American public approved giving some form of aid (military, economic, or humanitarian) to the Chinese government. A third of the public were opposed to giving any more aid, while 13 percent voiced no opinion. A year later, in the summer of 1949, less than a tenth of Americans favored extending more aid to China, and only one in five retained a favorable view of Chiang.

In spite of mixed public sentiment and nearly unanimous "expert" opinion opposing aid to Chiang, the Truman administration agreed to a small assistance package in 1948. (This in addition to postwar Lend-Lease and "surplus" military aid valued at over $2 billion.) Concerned that Republicans would delay funding the Marshall Plan for Western Europe and Japan unless something was done for Chiang, Truman agreed to allocate $125 million for a China Aid Act. The funds could be used "at the discretion of the Chinese government." But before most of the money reached China, the Communists were in control. In 1949, some of the unexpended funds, along with new appropriations, were redirected for use "in the general area of China," meaning Southeast Asia.

President Truman's decision to sit out the final stage of China's civil war reflected the judgment of most of his foreign policy advisers. Secretary of State Dean Acheson, who succeeded George Marshall early in 1949, director of policy planning, George F. Kennan and W. Walton Butterworth, head of the State Department's Bureau of Far Eastern Affairs, all counseled restraint. American interests in Asia, in general, and China, specifically, they insisted, did not depend solely on the survival of Chiang and the KMT. None of these advisers was sympathetic to the Soviet Union or the Chinese Communists. But they doubted that anything short of massive military intervention could slow the Red tide in China. Moreover, they harbored some hope that once the CCP took power, it might follow a semi-independent path. If Washington increased its aid to the doomed KMT, it might only succeed in driving Mao more tightly into Stalin's embrace.

But even Asia experts opposed to intervention in China's civil war were determined to contain communism elsewhere in Asia. The State Department actively promoted the so-called Reverse Course in Japan, a program to shift occupation policy away from liberal reform to promote rapid economic recovery. American planners transferred many of their earlier designs for China to Japan. As its economy recovered and it was groomed for restoration of sovereignty, Japan was poised to become the "anchor" of containment in East Asia.

The clearest statement of American intentions in Asia appeared in a policy approved by the president at the end of December 1949, known by its acronym, NSC 48/2. In it, Secretary of State Acheson guided an interagency task force to devise a policy premised on "blocking further communist expansion in Asia." Doing this required building up Japan and giving "particular attention . . . to the problem of French Indochina." In 1949, the Truman administration committed to more actively assisting the French effort to defeat Communist insurgents in its colony of Indochina (Vietnam). In fact, the first direct military aid sent to Vietnam early in 1950 came partly from unexpended funds originally allocated by Congress to China.

George Kennan, widely praised as the "father of containment," typified this new thinking about Asia. In his view, China, even if it became a Soviet satellite, would for many years remain a "vast poorhouse," encumbering, not enhancing, Soviet power. "Nationalistic elements" among Mao's followers, he predicted, would eventually split from the Soviet bloc. The worst thing Washington could do was adopt policies that pushed Mao and Stalin closer together. When the KMT government and army fled to the island of Taiwan (sometimes called Formosa) in the summer of 1949 (about three million mainlanders eventually fled across the 150-mile-wide Taiwan Strait, joining ten million Taiwanese), Acheson, Kennan, and others convinced Truman to retain nominal relations with the KMT, but to leave the door open to possible ties with the emerging Communist regime. In a series of decisions during 1949, the president agreed to permit limited trade between the United States, its allies, and Communist-held areas of China. He rebuffed proposals to provide substantial military aid to anti-Communist guerrillas on the mainland or to defend Taiwan from a Communist invasion.

Administration policies reflected realities on the ground. By mid-1949, the Communists controlled most of China, Nationalist troops were defecting to the Reds en masse, and Chiang had decamped for Taiwan, leaving a caretaker government in south China. Officially, the Truman administration hesitated to do anything that might "deliver the knock-out blow to the Nationalist government." Some officials insisted it was better to keep the "facts from the American people and thereby not be accused later of playing into the hands of the Communists." Privately, however, Acheson told members of Congress that Chiang had been doomed by his own mistakes, not Soviet subversion or American inaction.

In August 1949, the administration decided to take its case to the public by releasing a massive "China White Paper," an official review of relations with China over the past decade. Acheson and Truman hoped the document would clear the air by showing the tawdry record of KMT corruption and incompetence. In a bid to placate Republicans and counter any claim that the administration was "soft on communism" or had "stabbed Chiang in the back," Secretary of State Acheson appended a "cover letter" to the White Paper that contradicted many of the report's conclusions. For example, the letter condemned Mao and his followers as brutal thugs who had "foresworn their Chinese heritage and have publicly announced their subservience to a foreign power, Russia." This, of course, was precisely what Henry Luce and Chiang's congressional allies charged.

As the certainty of a Communist victory became clear at the end of 1948, Mao Zedong began speaking and writing more critically of the United States. He accused the American government and its diplomats in China of organizing an "imperialist conspiracy" to mobilize non-Communist opposition within China. During the final year of the civil war and even after the creation of the new Communist government, CCP officials believed that the continued presence of U.S. diplomats, businessmen, and missionaries in Chinese cities encouraged counterrevolutionaries. At the end of 1948, Communist authorities in Shengyang (Mukden), a city in Manchuria, put the staff of the U.S. consulate under house arrest for several months, charging them with espionage. But a few months later, in May 1949, several of Mao's closest aides approached Ambassador John Leighton Stewart who had remained in Nanjing after the Communist takeover. They invited Stewart, a former educator in Beijing, to return there for a visit and confer with CCP leaders. Stewart wanted to accept the offer, but President Truman ordered that "under no circumstances" should the ambassador travel to Beijing. The president feared a Republican backlash and cited the detention of the consulate staff in Shengyang as reasons to spurn the offer. Stewart soon left China, but a handful of American diplomats, businessmen, missionaries, and educators stayed on.

Communist motives for approaching Stewart are uncertain. Perhaps, as some argue, the CCP merely wanted to deflect any last-minute American military intervention. Although Mao certainly expected the new China to be close to the Soviet Union, he probably did not want to sever all links to the United States or its allies, many of whom could provide vital trade and technological assistance. Whatever the explanation, the lack of a positive response from Washington reinforced the anti-American sentiment already ascendant among the CCP leadership.

In June, Mao broke off contacts with American diplomats and declared that henceforth, in the struggle against the forces of imperialism, China would "lean to the side" of socialism and the Soviet Union. Some time in the future, after reforms had taken place, China would be ready to reopen diplomatic and trade contacts with the West; but he intended to "clean house before entertaining guests." He followed up on this by sending his second in command, Liu Shaoqi to Moscow. Mao had hoped to go himself, but Stalin declined to meet the revolutionary leader before the establishment of a new Chinese government.

Liu remained in the Soviet Union for most of July and August 1949. In discussions with Stalin, Liu pledged Chinese Communist loyalty to Soviet policies. Stalin, in turn, promised future economic and military assistance to China and urged Mao to delay establishing diplomatic relations with the Americans and British. He warned against an early assault on Taiwan, fearing it might provoke U.S. military action. Although Liu made clear CCP interest in revising the "unequal" 1945 Sino–Soviet treaty, Stalin gave no sign that he intended to give up Soviet privileges in Manchuria and Mongolia.

On October 1, 1949, Mao finally stood atop Tiananmen to proclaim creation of the People's Republic of China (PRC). This set the stage for his long delayed journey to Moscow and his acceptance by Stalin. Mao spent nearly two months in the Soviet Union, from December 1949 to February 1950, much of it shadow-boxing with the Kremlin leadership. Stalin offered the PRC a loan valued at $300 million, trade credits, and technological assistance. He also provided a security pledge, promising to assist China if it were attacked by Japan or a country allied to Japan, i.e., the United States. But the Sino–Soviet Friendship Treaty, signed on February 14, denied Mao something equally important: the restoration of full Chinese sovereignty in border areas. Stalin insisted on retaining, for at least a while, the extensive Soviet port and rail privileges in Manchuria, as well as control over Outer Mongolia, extracted from Chiang in 1945. Mao's disappointment showed in the official photograph of the treaty ceremony, where he and a grim faced Stalin appeared as if no one had reminded them to smile.

Events in Moscow nearly overshadowed a budding Sino–American rivalry in French Indochina. Mao viewed U.S. involvement with Indochina, South Korea, Taiwan, and Japan as an effort to contain and intimidate China. He planned to counter this "encirclement" through Chinese aid and involvement in Indochina, Korea, and Taiwan and, in Japan's case, through cooperation with the Soviet Union. Early in February, China recognized the Democratic Republic of Vietnam, led by veteran Communist Ho Chi Minh, who fought against France and its Vietnamese client, Emperor Bao Dai. Mao even considered sending troops to fight alongside Ho's Viet Minh guerrillas, but bowed to Soviet advice to send only military aid.

Before China recognized Ho's regime, U.S. officials had ridiculed the French effort to cloak their colonial war in nationalist garments by working through Bao Dai. But the Truman administration held its nose, recognized Bao Dai's puppet regime, and in the spring of 1950, allocated military aid to him and his French masters. The war in Vietnam quickly took on the trappings of a proxy fight between the United States and the PRC.

While Mao and Stalin negotiated in Moscow, Chinese–American relations deteriorated further. The U.S. consulate in Beijing had continued to operate as a contact point between the two governments following the departure of Ambassador Stewart from Nanjing. In January 1950, the Chinese government announced it would seize the consular property of foreign governments that had not yet recognized the PRC. Mao may have done this to impress Stalin with his revolutionary fervor or, alternatively, to pressure the Truman administration into breaking ties with Taiwan and recognizing the PRC. (It was often hard to know where Stalin stood on this question, since a year before he had urged the CCP to shun contact with foreign powers, but now he spoke in favor of PRC diplomatic and trade ties with the West and Japan. Mao may have felt it a safer bet to show Stalin his anti-Western face.) When the State Department refused to act under pressure, China seized the consulate, and the diplomats left for home. This ended official contact between Washington and Beijing.

Acheson had previously told Congress that before the United States took any dramatic, new initiatives in China, it should "wait for the dust to settle." He implied that once Mao's regime began governing, and after the expected collapse of the Nationalists on Taiwan, the PRC might act more moderately and seek a diplomatic accommodation with the United States. In January 1950, both Acheson and Truman issued what they hoped was their epitaph on China's civil war. The United States would cease military aid to Taiwan and not shield the island from an anticipated Chinese invasion, at least while Chiang remained in power. As the clock ran down on Taiwan, most China experts in America voiced quiet hope that after the civil war finally ended, Washington and Beijing could resume a dialogue leading to a live-and–let-live diplomatic relationship. Events in both countries soon confounded this possibility.

SELECTED ADDITIONAL READINGS

Suzanne Pepper, *Civil War in China: The Political Struggle, 1945–49* (Berkeley, Calif., 1978); James Reardon-Anderson, *Yenan and the Great Powers* (New York, 1980); Steven I. Levine, *The Anvil of Victory: The Communist Revolution in Manchuria, 1945–48* (New York, 1987); John Melby, *The Mandate of Heaven: Record of a Civil War in China, 1945–1949* (Toronto, 1968); Nancy B. Tucker, *Patterns in the Dust:*

Chinese–American Relations and the Recognition Controversy, 1949–50 (New York, 1983), and, *China Confidential: American Diplomats and Sino–American Relations, 1945–1996* (New York, 2001); E. J. Kahn, *The China Hands: America's Foreign Service Officers and What Befell Them* (New York, 1976); Gary May, *China Scapegoat: The Diplomatic Ordeal of John Carter Vincent* (Washington, D.C., 1983); Robert P. Newman, *Owen Lattimore and the Loss of China* (Berkeley, Calif., 1992); Robert M. Blum, *Drawing the Line: The Origin of American Containment Policy in East Asia* (New York, 1982); William W. Stueck, *The Road to Confrontation: American Policy Toward China and Korea, 1947–1950* (Chapel Hill, N.C., 1981); Dorothy Borg and Waldo Heinrichs, eds., *Uncertain Years: Chinese–American Relations 1947–50* (New York, 1980); John L. Gaddis, *Strategies of Containment* (New York, 1982); Gary R. Hess, *The United States Emergence as a Southeast Asian Power, 1940–1950* (New York, 1987); Michael Schaller, *The American Occupation of Japan: The Origins of the Cold War in Asia* (New York, 1985); Chen Jian, *China's Road to the Korean War* (New York, 1996), and, *Mao's China and the Cold War* (Chapel Hill, N.C., 2001); Michael Hunt, *The Genesis of Chinese Communist Foreign Policy* (New York, 1998); Odd Arne Westad, ed., *Brothers in Arms: The Rise and Fall of the Sino–Soviet Alliance, 1945–1963* (Washington, D.C., 1999); Harvey Klehr and Ronald Radosh, *The Amerasia Spy Case: Prelude to McCarthyism* (Chapel Hill, N.C., 1996); Harvey Klehr and John Earl Haynes, *Venona: Decoding Soviet Espionage in America* (New Haven, Conn., 2000); Allen Weinstein and Alexander Vassiliev, *The Haunted Wood: Soviet Espionage in America—The Stalin Era* (New York, 1999).

SEVEN

Red Scare and Yellow Peril

The Korean War

In spite of their dim opinion of the new Chinese Communist regime, President Truman and Secretary of State Acheson hoped to avoid direct conflict with the PRC. While waiting, in Acheson's phrase, for the "dust to settle" in China, the United States would build strength along the arc or "great crescent" that stretched from Japan through Okinawa, the Philippines, and Southeast Asia. American strategists considered this a viable "defense perimeter" from which they could deter or contain Chinese expansion and wait for Mao's revolutionary fervor to mellow. Whether either the United States or People's Republic could, in the near term, reach a peaceful accommodation remained uncertain. Unfortunately, political developments in both countries frustrated compromise.

Anti-American sentiment ran deep among rank and file Communists in China, and Mao often mobilized the masses by stoking this anger. Many American politicians found it equally useful to foment fear that, because of the "loss of China," the United States was losing the cold war. Just one year after Mao stood on Tiananmen to proclaim creation of the PRC, Chinese and American soldiers clashed on the Korean peninsula. Dean Rusk, assistant secretary of state (later secretary under presidents Kennedy and Johnson), declared that the "peace and security of China" had been "sacrificed to the ambitions of a communist conspiracy." China had been "driven by foreign masters into an adventure of foreign aggression." Rusk insisted that Red China (as American officials called the PRC until 1971) was a "colonial Russian government . . . not the government of China. It is not Chinese." The slaughter in Korea lasted three years, but Chinese–American hostility continued for two decades.

As 1950 began, the United States had achieved several of its most important cold war security goals. Marshall Plan aid had promoted economic recovery in Western Europe and Japan. The appeal of communism in both regions had diminished significantly. U.S. resolve had frustrated the Soviet blockade of Berlin and created a strong Federal Republic of Germany in the heart of Europe. By most relevant measures, "containment" had blunted the Soviet threat to Western Europe and Japan, and the United States held an improving hand in the cold war. The public, however, remained skeptical. Ordinary Americans agonized over the Soviet testing of an atomic bomb in August 1949, followed by the Chinese Communist victory that October, and Mao's signing a friendship treaty with Stalin in February 1950.

All three events were significant, but none altered the basic global power balance, already in America's favor. For example, for most of the decade, the Soviets lacked atomic weapons capable of reaching the United States, and the Chinese Communist victory of October 1949 had long been anticipated; further the Sino–Soviet treaty proved both a source of strength and weakness for the Communist allies. Nevertheless, many Americans feared that China, backed by a nuclear-armed Soviet Union, stood poised to dominate Asia.

RED SCARE AT HOME

The Truman administration's efforts to present Asian developments in a calm and measured fashion became more difficult after February 1950. As Congress and the public lost faith in "official" explanations, China policy became political fodder for wildly irresponsible demagogues, both in government and the press. Placing blame for "who lost China" became a means to an end—gaining political power by stoking fears of treason committed by career diplomats and Democrats.

Public accusations of disloyalty and treason erupted first in November 1945, when Ambassador Patrick Hurley resigned, accusing State Department China experts of aiding the CCP. The controversy subsided after a brief Senate inquiry and Truman's dispatch of George Marshall as emissary to China. The issue resurfaced early in 1950, following creation of the new Communist government in Beijing and its alliance with the Soviet

Union. By then, a series of spy charges and trials had also stoked popular fears.

In January 1950, after being accused in testimony before Congress of being a Communist and spy, former State Department official Alger Hiss was convicted by a federal jury of lying about past Communist affiliations. (The statute of limitations had prevented the government from charging him with espionage.) In February, British police arrested Klaus Fuchs, an émigré German scientist, who confessed to being part of a spy ring that had passed atomic secrets to Moscow while he worked at the American nuclear laboratory at Los Alamos, New Mexico during World War II. Fuchs provided evidence that led to the arrest in June of an American couple, Julius and Ethel Rosenberg, as "atomic spies." Reacting to these events, Senator Homer Capehart, an Indiana Republican, rose to ask: "How much more are we going to have to take? Fuchs and Acheson and Hiss and hydrogen bombs threatening outside and New Dealism eating away at the vitals of the nation. In the name of Heaven, is this the best America can do?"

Capehart's Republican colleague from Wisconsin, Senator Joe McCarthy, answered his call. On February 9, 1950, McCarthy delivered a speech in Wheeling, West Virginia, that pointed to a massive conspiracy. America faced defeat in Asia, he asserted, because Dean Acheson, a "pompous diplomat in striped pants and a phony British accent" had turned over policymaking to a subversive clique. "I have in my hand," McCarthy claimed, "a list of two hundred and five [names] known to the Secretary of State as being members of the Communist Party and who nevertheless are still working and shaping policy of the State Department." McCarthy's targets were "individuals who are loyal to the ideal and designs of Communism rather than those of the free, God-fearing half of the world. . . . I refer to the Far Eastern Division of the State Department and the Voice of America."

In fact, McCarthy utterly failed to connect State Department China experts to espionage. His charges were mostly recycled rumors from earlier inquiries or groundless accusations. When he named diplomats who had criticized Chiang Kai-shek, he could not link them to espionage. When he identified persons whom the FBI had linked to espionage, he was unable to show their role in making China policy. As one contemporary journalist remarked, McCarthy "couldn't find a communist in Red Square. He didn't know Karl Marx from Groucho." Nevertheless, the recklessness and volume of McCarthy's accusations, as well as the encouragement he received from more respectable Republicans, spread terror through the Foreign Service. His two favorite targets were Foreign Service officer John S.

Senator Joseph McCarthy, who had blamed American diplomats for "losing China" to the Reds, shares a joke with one of his chief targets, John S. Service. (National Archives)

Service and Professor Owen Lattimore of Johns Hopkins University. Service, who worked in China during World War II, and Lattimore, who briefly served as an adviser to Chiang, had both criticized the KMT and predicted its defeat. In McCarthy's mind, this made them agents of a "communist conspiracy." McCarthy branded the bookish Lattimore, an expert on Mongol culture and editor of the journal *Pacific Affairs,* "the number one Soviet agent" in America.

At one Senate hearing in 1950, McCarthy questioned Service about what he saw as the curious fact that three China specialists (Service, Davies, and Vincent) all shared a first name. Was it "mere chance" McCarthy asked skeptically that "three Johns lost China"? Service retorted that actually "four Johns lost China." Who was the fourth, McCarthy demanded. "John K. Shek," Service answered, to the delight of the audience. The diplomat won the verbal exchange, but soon lost his job.

Although McCarthy opened the attack on "China experts," other politicians joined in. Senator Pat McCarran, a conservative Democrat from Nevada, played nearly as destructive a role as his better known colleague. As chair of the Senate Internal Security Subcommittee (SISS) beginning in 1951, McCarran spent several years hounding diplomats, journalists, and scholars who had been affiliated with groups such as the Institute for Pacific Relations, a non-governmental, international organiation concerned with Asian affairs. By the time his crusade against "interlocking subversion" ended in the late 1950s, one official described the Far Eastern Division of the State Department as a "disaster area" filled with "human wreckage."

In a series of security investigations begun under Truman and continued by the Eisenhower administration after 1953, several of the most talented China specialists in the State Department were dismissed or pressured to resign. John S. Service, John P. Davies, John Carter Vincent, and O. Edmund Clubb, for example, were all judged security risks or insufficiently loyal to serve the government. Owen Lattimore was exonerated only after two trials in which he was accused of lying about harboring pro-Communist sentiment. His career in ruins, he took a job teaching in England.

In both administrative hearings and legal cases, the charges against the so called China Hands focused on their criticism of the KMT and predictions of CCP victory. For example, Foreign Service personnel stationed with the Dixie Mission in Yenan were accused of "consorting with Communists." This, of course, had been their assignment! Some lesser-known China experts were permitted to remain in the State Department provided they steered clear of Asian affairs. Promising junior officers learned quickly to avoid specializing in this minefield area. By 1954, when McCarthy's power began to wane, and for many years afterward, few diplomats with expert training or experience in China remained in the Far Eastern Division of the State Department. The U.S. government was ostracizing Americans who had contact with the Chinese Communists just as the Chinese government launched a campaign to punish their own citizens whom they considered tainted by past friendship with Americans.

During the spring of 1950, perhaps prodded by Senator McCarthy's escalating charges of treason, the Truman administration inched back toward support of the Kuomintang. In January, Acheson and the president had all but written off Chiang and the KMT remnant on Taiwan. By April, small amounts of U.S. assistance were again sent to the island. Some American officials even toyed with schemes to depose Chiang in favor of a more moderate leader whom Washington would defend against a Communist invasion. Truman also countered Chinese aid to Ho Chi Minh by approving direct military aid to French forces fighting Communist insurgents in Indochina. From his headquarters in Tokyo, General Douglas MacArthur, bored by occupation duties, called for extending his authority over Taiwan—which he described as an "unsinkable aircraft carrier"—as part of a strategy to defend Japan and Southeast Asia from Chinese assault. Some members of the administration, including Dean Rusk and John Foster Dulles in the State Department, as well as the Joint Chiefs of Staff, agreed with the idea of defending Taiwan. Meanwhile, in April, a special interagency task force issued an alarming report, NSC-68. Describing the Soviet a-bomb and Chinese Communist victory as major threats, NSC-68 called for sharp increases in military spending to meet a global challenge.

Despite rising tension between Washington and Beijing over Taiwan, President Truman hesitated to authorize the huge weapons outlays called for in NSC-68. Only a crisis, it seemed, would persuade Congress and the public to support intervention on Taiwan or major increases in military spending. One Truman aide recalled: "We were sweating over" what to do "in June 1950 and then, thank God, Korea came along."

THE KOREAN WAR

North Korea's invasion of the South on June 25, 1950, unlike the far larger Chinese civil war, pulled American combat forces into northeast Asia. Within a week, President Truman had committed the United States to defending South Korea, protecting Taiwan, and increasing aid to the Philippines and the French in Indochina. These decisions reinforced Mao's belief that the United States intended to surround, undermine, and perhaps overthrow the PRC. Because of this fear, as well as his belief in Communist solidarity, Mao sent a "volunteer" army to defend North Korea. Before the end of 1950, Chinese and American troops were locked in a brutal war that lasted until July 1953.

At the end of World War II, Korea—a Japanese colony for almost half a century—had been split at the 38th parallel into Soviet and U.S. occupation zones. Designed as a temporary expedient, the division hardened as the cold war set in. Ignoring Korean hope for unification, each occupying power gradually established a client regime in its half of Korea. In the north, a former anti-Japanese guerrilla leader and Communist, Kim Il Sung, ruled with Soviet support. American authorities created a southern regime under Syngman Rhee, a conservative nationalist who had lived for many years in the United States. By 1949, both the Soviets and Americans had withdrawn most of their own troops, leaving two rival regimes—the northern Democratic People's Republic of Korea and the southern Republic of Korea—each claiming the right to rule the entire peninsula. The governments of both Koreas relied on domestic repression and aid from their foreign patrons to maintain control. In the three years leading up to the 1950 clash, tens of thousands of Koreans died in internal fighting and cross-border skirmishes.

Both Moscow and Washington had misgivings about the ambitions of their respective clients. Syngman Rhee's frequent calls to march north led Washington to equip his forces mostly with defensive weapons. Kim had better luck getting military aid from his patrons. In late 1949 and early 1950, China released to North Korea a large number of Korean soldiers who had fought alongside the CCP in China's civil war. During the same period, Kim pressed Stalin to authorize an invasion of the south. He assured both the Soviet leader, and later Mao, that North Korean troops would finish the job before America could intervene. Such intervention seemed unlikely because in both public and private, U.S. policymakers had excluded Korea (and Taiwan) from a defense perimeter that ran from Japan through Okinawa and the Philippines. American military planners considered Korea a strategic backwater and in case of a major war did not anticipate defending it.

From the perspective of Stalin and Mao, Communist unification of Korea appeared a low-risk, modest-gain operation. A victory by Kim would eliminate ongoing threats of a South Korean invasion of the north and would counterbalance American plans to rebuild Japan economically and as a base for U.S. forces in Asia. Mao went along with but did not initiate plans for a North Korean attack broached to him by Stalin and Kim early in 1950. The Chinese leader's main interest remained liberating Taiwan. In late January 1950, Stalin gave the North Korean leader tentative approval to invade the south, and during the spring, Mao gave the plan his blessing.

Kim Il Sung's prediction that his Soviet-equipped forces could quickly overrun South Korea's defenses proved correct. His assumption that the United States either would not react at all or would do so too late to make a difference proved disastrously wrong. The Truman administration interpreted the attack as "part of a global challenge directed from Moscow [rather than Beijing] at American collective security systems." The relationship between Stalin and Kim, one presidential aide quipped, was the same as that between "Walt Disney and Donald Duck." Truman and Secretary of State Acheson were especially concerned that if they abandoned South Korea, American "credibility" would suffer and more important allies, including the Japanese and West Germans, would lose faith in Washington's security guarantee. This concern outweighed Korea's marginal importance.

Within days of the North Korean attack, Truman ordered U.S. air, sea, and land forces to defend the south. He sent the Seventh Fleet to protect Taiwan from invasion and substantially increased military aid to fight Communist insurgencies in the Philippines and Indochina. These actions were designed to show Moscow and Beijing, as well as America's friends, that Washington would resist Communist expansion. The president declared that the "attack on Korea makes it plain beyond all doubt that communism had passed beyond the use of subversion to conquer independent nations and will now use armed invasion and war."

Even though Truman was prepared to act unilaterally, the United States managed to win UN support for a call on member states to dispatch troops to help South Korea restore the prewar boundary. For some time, the Soviet delegate to the UN had boycotted Security Council sessions to protest America's refusal to seat the new Chinese government in place of the rump Nationalist regime on Taiwan. This ill-timed absence allowed the UN resolution to pass.

Mao assisted the North Korean offensive in several ways, including allowing Kim to move troops from China's Shandong peninsula across the water to South Korea. Like Stalin and Kim, Mao was stunned by the rapid U.S. decision to defend South Korea. On June 28, Zhou Enlai declared that U.S. intervention in Taiwan and Korea constituted "aggression against the territory of China" and marked a "further act of intervention by American imperialism in Asia." Truman's decision to shield Taiwan from invasion was seen, correctly, as the first step in the resumption of U.S. support for the Kuomintang. Protection soon led to military assistance, then to cooperation in KMT raids on China, and finally to a formal security treaty. The Communist plan to invade Taiwan by the end of 1950 was first delayed and then postponed indefinitely.

For the PRC, however, the greatest security threat came from the large American combat force that arrived in South Korea, commanded by General Douglas MacArthur. Even if U.S. troops confined themselves to operations south of the 38th parallel, Mao worried that their proximity would destabilize Manchuria and embolden "reactionary" elements still active in

China. Thus, even before U.S. troops crossed into North Korea and pushed toward China's border in October–November, Mao felt threatened, but he was uncertain how to respond.

Until mid-September, U.S. and South Korean (ROK) forces could barely hold a small perimeter near the southern port of Pusan. But Chinese strategists guessed that MacArthur would send in a large invasion force that would overwhelm the North Koreans. At that point, they guessed, Washington would expand the war and attempt to crush North Korea. In anticipation, during the summer Mao ordered creation of a special "Northeast Border Defense Army" of over 300,000 men and made tentative plans for Chinese troops to move into North Korea in August or early September. However, supply problems, as well as Kim Il Sung's reluctance to invite a Chinese army into Korea before absolutely necessary, delayed deployment until after the American breakthrough in the south. Meanwhile, Beijing initiated a mass anti-U.S. propaganda campaign among Chinese civilians, stressing the need to "Beat American Arrogance" by defending North Korea. The "Resist America, Aid Korea" movement also provided a patriotic context for Communist efforts to seize control of all U.S. cultural, religious, and business organizations that remained in China. American-educated Chinese were stigmatized as potential traitors at the same time that U.S. diplomats who had been in Yenan were fired as security risks.

As Chinese analysts predicted, General MacArthur carried out a bold amphibious invasion at the South Korean port of Inchon in mid-September. Although Chinese and North Korean intelligence may have had advance knowledge of the assault, North Korean forces were too weak to respond. Within two weeks of the landing, U.S. troops had retaken most of South Korea, including the capital of Seoul, and had achieved the goal set by the UN of restoring the 38th parallel as the boundary between the two Koreas.

Success proved intoxicating to both General MacArthur and President Truman. They and their advisers worried that victory had come almost too easily. Failed North Korean aggression had cost the Soviets and Chinese so little, American leaders believed, that Kim's defeat would not deter future threats. To teach Stalin and Mao a lesson, the Truman administration decided to destroy the North Korea regime and unify the country under southern rule. Although America's allies were lukewarm to this idea, the United States pushed a vague resolution through the UN sanctioning this goal.

Domestic politics also prompted this decision. Large-scale rearmament, as called for by NSC-68, had barely begun by September. Ending the war too quickly, high officials worried, would undermine the arms build up.

Also, MacArthur, who hoped to be elected president in 1952, and Truman, who wanted to keep his job, recognized the political appeal of rolling back communism in Korea and achieving a cold war victory. For MacArthur, a big win would cement his heroic image, while Truman hoped that unifying Korea would put to rest charges that his administration was "soft" on communism. In late September, Truman ordered U.S./UN forces to cross into North Korea and destroy its army as it fled toward the Yalu River border with China. MacArthur was free to move north unless he encountered major Chinese or Soviet resistance—by which time disengagement would be impossible. American planners appeared barely to notice that Manchuria, China's industrial heartland, lay on the other side of the Yalu.

Although official U.S. policy specified halting troops at the Yalu River and confining the war to Korea, MacArthur sent home mixed and often quite provocative signals. In the two and a half months before the September 15 Inchon landing, he continually pushed for greater authority, often taking controversial stands without Washington's approval or even knowledge. For example, at the end of July, MacArthur flew to Taiwan where he embraced Chiang and spoke of their "coordinated" effort to resist Communist aggression. He followed this by transferring jet fighter aircraft to Taiwan and issuing calls for Washington to assist KMT troops in forays against south China. Officially, Truman had decided only to shield Taiwan from invasion, not to assist Chiang's attacks on China. But MacArthur's actions reentangled the United States in the Chinese civil war. The general told several visitors to his headquarters in Tokyo that although it was U.S. policy to avoid war with China, he "got down on my knees and prayed nightly" that the Chinese would intervene in Korea or Taiwan, as this would free him to "deliver such a crushing defeat" against communism that it would prove "one of the decisive battles of the world." At other times, he described Taiwan as the key to future efforts to roll back Communist rule in China. After September 27, when the Joint Chiefs of Staff (JCS) authorized him to cross the 38th parallel and destroy North Korean forces, the general told a colleague he felt ready to "take on the Chinese or even the Russians." Such statements, often purposely leaked, stoked Mao's fear of a growing American threat.

On October 2, Mao told Stalin he was reluctant to send Chinese troops into Korea because a major war meant "our entire plan for peaceful reconstruction will be completely ruined and many people in the country will be dissatisfied." Stalin warned Mao that China faced an even greater threat if it did nothing to stop the American advance. It required additional meetings a week later between Stalin and a Chinese delegation headed by Zhou Enlai and Lin Biao to convince the Chinese to reverse their decision. On

October 13, Mao informed the Soviet government that China would send troops to Korea, and he began doing so on October 19.

After Zhou Enlai and other PRC representatives warned that China would not stand "idly by" if American troops entered North Korea, intelligence reports suggested large-scale Chinese troop movements toward the border region. A nervous Truman even flew to Wake Island in the Pacific on October 15 to confer with MacArthur. The general glibly dismissed Zhou's warnings as a bluff and assured the president that if the Chinese intervened in Korea, they would be "slaughtered." Truman pinned a medal on MacArthur's chest and returned to Washington.

Chinese leaders initially hoped to stop the Americans in the southern end of North Korea. But problems in transportation and supply delayed the confrontation until the end of October, by which time American forces were midway through North Korea. When Truman and the JCS issued some half-hearted appeals to MacArthur to slow his advance and avoid a clash with the Chinese, the general leaked stories to the press accusing weak-willed Democrats of undermining his imminent victory. A supreme egotist, he often complained that rivals in Washington would "rather see America lose a war than MacArthur win a battle."

Chinese troops struck at and defeated several small American and South Korean units in late October, but they soon broke off contact. MacArthur dismissed these attacks as insignificant, and he pushed forward. Chinese strategists had carried out the hit-and-run attacks with the twofold purpose of either giving the Americans a chance to withdraw or, if they refused, luring them deeper into a trap. Insisting that no more than 30,000 to 60,000 Chinese were in Korea (the actual number was at least 300,000), the general ordered an "end the war" push toward the Yalu River at the end of November and predicted that American boys would be "home by Christmas." Privately, he worried that resistance might continue even after his forces reached the Yalu, leaving him no choice but to "begin bombing key points in Manchuria."

China's *People's Daily* explained what happened on November 25, 1950: 300,000 People's Volunteers launched a counterattack against advancing Americans. The Volunteers would "check them with force and compel them to stop" because there was "no alternative." Soviet planes and pilots provided air cover along the Yalu River, and Stalin provided substantial military equipment—on credit—to Chinese troops. During the next few weeks, the Chinese badly mauled U.S. Army and Marine units, which suffered over 11,000 casualties fighting their way to safety on the coast or to the south. It was, a stunned MacArthur admitted, "an entirely new war."

Only five years before, American and Chinese forces had been allies against Japan. Now, as newspaper headlines trumpeted, "Red Chinese Hordes" were slaughtering GIs and Marines. By January 1951, the Chinese had pushed the Americans south of the 38th parallel and, possibly, might drive them entirely out of Korea. MacArthur and much of the American press described Chinese intervention as both unexpected and irrational. As one newsreel put it:

> Americans were being routed by Chinese Red Army Legions, treacherously forced into this war by the unscrupulous leaders of international communism. The G.I.s battle the new elements with everything they have, but the latest Communist perfidy in Korea makes the picture grim.

During the first half of 1951, the "new war" in Korea presented Washington with a terrible dilemma. Most of Truman's military and civilian advisers feared getting "sewed up" in Korea against the "second team" (China), while the greater danger remained the Soviet threat to Europe and Japan. They also feared that expanding the war against China might provoke Soviet intervention. MacArthur dismissed both notions. China, he insisted, was the central threat to American global security. He and a growing number of Republican supporters in Congress called on Truman to widen the war by authorizing air and naval attacks on China and by accepting Chiang's offer to send Nationalist troops into Korea and south China. Those demanding a wider war minimized the risk of Soviet intervention. When MacArthur failed to sway Truman, he began a campaign via the press and congressional Republicans charging that weak-willed Democrats risked complete defeat in Korea by forbidding him to expand the war. By accusing his superiors of tying his hands, MacArthur hoped to shift the blame for his humiliation by the Chinese onto the president.

Not surprisingly, Truman, Secretary of State Acheson, and even the JCS had other ideas. By early 1951, top decisionmakers in Washington had pretty much abandoned their idea of unifying Korea by force. While not saying so publicly, they were ready to accept their original war aim of restoring the 38th parallel. MacArthur, of course, claimed that even this was impossible because the Chinese threatened to overrun South Korea. Mao had, in fact, succumbed to the same euphoria that afflicted Truman and MacArthur in September 1950. The Communist leader ignored advice from his field commander, Peng Dehuai, that China halt its offensive at the 38th parallel. Instead, Mao ordered his armies to unify Korea under a Red banner. As Peng feared, extended and inadequate supplies lines, bad weather, U.S. control of the air, and more effective leadership by a new American field commander, General Matthew Ridgway, halted the Chinese offensive just south of the 38th parallel. Despite MacArthur's dire warnings, by March, there was little likelihood of a Communist sweep south.

This rough balance of power created the possibility of compromise. In December 1950 and January 1951, several UN members called for a cease-fire in place, followed by political negotiations on Korea's future and China's seat in the UN. Beijing rejected this, arguing that it would give the United States time to regroup without guaranteeing Korean unification, the liberation of Taiwan, or Chinese UN representation. In return for agreeing to a cease-fire, China demanded the immediate withdrawal of U.S. troops from Korea and Taiwan, as well as a UN seat. Mao, in particular, hoped to boost his revolutionary stature by unifying Korea and also felt pressure from the North Koreans to achieve unity.

At times during 1950–51, some American officials, such as George Kennan, suggested making a deal with China. In exchange for a cease-fire (which, they hoped, would promote tension between Mao and Stalin), the United States would recognize the PRC, abandon Taiwan, and evacuate South Korea. Truman, who feared a political backlash at home, refused to link the issues. When China spurned as biased and inadequate the UN armistice proposal, Washington convinced the UN General Assembly to pass a resolution condemning China as the aggressor in Korea. This made future UN mediation difficult.

In March 1951, Truman and Acheson shifted course, a bit, and decided to offer China a plan that called first for a cease-fire in place and later for political discussions of outstanding problems. This left open the possibility of compromise on Taiwan and UN membership. The prospect of a peace without victory horrified MacArthur. Fearful that he would be blamed for the stalemate, the general sabotaged the peace plan by broadcasting a garbled version to Beijing on March 24, accompanied by a threat that unless Chinese military commanders in Korea surrendered to him personally, he would attack China's "coastal and interior bases." He had, in fact, devised a series of contingency plans to bombard Chinese cities with conventional and atomic weapons and to unleash Chiang's troops against China. MacArthur's threat buried Truman's peace initiative and convinced the president that the "Big General in the Far East must be recalled."

MacArthur, who probably preferred the martyrdom of being fired to presiding over a stalemate, made Truman's decision to dismiss him easier. In early April 1951, GOP Representative Joseph Martin, the House minority leader, released a letter from MacArthur sent in response to a message from the congressman. The general voiced support for Martin's call to arm KMT troops for an invasion of China and agreed with the assertion that unless Truman planned to "win" the war, he bore responsibility for the "murder" of thousands of Americans. There was, MacArthur crowed, "no substitute for victory." On April 11, with the backing of the JCS, Truman sacked MacArthur and appointed Matthew Ridgway occupation commander in Japan and theater commander in Korea.

MacArthur privately groused that his firing was part of a plan to sell out Taiwan, Korea, and even Japan to "Red China." Many conservative newspapers in America, such as the *Chicago Tribune* and the New York *Journal American*, denounced Truman as "unfit to be president" and under the influence of Communist agents. Senator Richard Nixon remarked that with MacArthur's firing, the "happiest group in America are the communists." Senator Joe McCarthy demanded that the "son-of-a-bitch ought to be impeached." The Gallup Poll found that two-thirds of Americans opposed the general's recall and only one-third supported the president.

MacArthur returned to a series of gala parades and delivered a stirring speech to both houses of Congress. He angrily condemned "those who would appease Red China," and he rejected a compromise peace in Korea. There was, he repeated, "no substitute for victory." Although he closed his speech with the line of an old army ballad that lamented "old soldiers never die, they just fade away," MacArthur had no intention of going quietly. He testified for a week before a special Senate committee, only to discover that the JCS strongly supported Truman's strategy over his own. JCS chairman General Omar Bradley fired off the best line, declaring that MacArthur would get the United States into the "wrong war, at the wrong place, at the wrong time, and with the wrong enemy." General Dwight D. Eisenhower, MacArthur's deputy during the 1930s and now NATO commander in Europe, privately compared MacArthur to Senator Joe McCarthy: both were "opportunists, seeking to ride the crest of a wave." In May, MacArthur launched a speaking tour to denounce Truman's policies, but when the crowds grew smaller, he canceled future appearances.

Developments in Korea explain why MacArthur faded away. During April and May, General Ridgway rallied American troops. Without attacking Manchuria, using Nationalist forces, or dropping atomic bombs, U.S./UN forces beat back a Chinese offensive. Shaken by these heavy losses, Mao and other CCP leaders convinced themselves that they had humiliated American imperialism and could now accept an armistice based on the restoration of the 38th parallel. Mao agreed to postpone the issues of UN representation for China and a pullout of U.S. forces from South

Korea and Taiwan. With Stalin's approval, U.S.–PRC armistice talks began in Kaesong, Korea on July 10, 1951.

To the surprise of all participants, the talking—and fighting—dragged on until July 1953. Within a few months, both sides tacitly agreed to restore the north-south boundary close to the 38th parallel. The major stumbling block turned out to be prisoner repatriation. International law specified (and the United States had always agreed) that all prisoners of war (POWs) should, at the conclusion of fighting, be returned to their country of origin, regardless of personal preference. However, when Truman learned that only 70,000 (later raised to 83,000) of about 116,000 Chinese/North Korean POWs wanted to go home, he refused to compel their return. The president considered this both a human rights issue and an effective psychological and propaganda weapon. He also guessed how, in an election year, Republicans would savor the sight of a Democratic president forcing POWs back to Communist lines.

America's claim to occupy the moral high ground was clouded by the fact that Communist prisoners were often brutally intimidated by U.S., South Korean, and Chinese Nationalist prison camp guards. Thus, in January 1952, when American negotiators explained their position, the Chinese considered it a cynical ploy to embarrass China and keep the war going. Beijing tried to recapture the moral heights by charging that American planes had used biological weapons against North Korea and Manchuria. (The United States had not done so, although when Chinese officials first made the charges they thought they were valid.) Later, when U.S. negotiators spoke of prisoner rights, the Chinese retorted with (false) confessions of biological warfare wrung from captured Americans. The result was an eighteen-month impasse during which both sides bolstered their forces, which periodically struck at the other.

The logjam broke in March 1953, following the death of Stalin. The Soviet dictator had seemed comfortable continuing a war that tied Americans down in Korea and forced greater Chinese dependence on the Soviet Union—all at little risk to the U.S.S.R. Accordingly, he had not encouraged a settlement. Stalin's death brought to power a group of Soviet leaders eager to improve relations with the United States. Mao, too, recognized that the Korean stalemate paid diminishing returns. China and North Korea had suffered nearly a million battlefield casualties, including the death of Mao's son. The war had retarded economic growth, blocked trade with Japan and Europe, and put China in debt to the Soviet Union. When Zhou Enlai attended Stalin's funeral, he and the new Soviet leadership agreed to make compromises designed to end the fighting.

The American public was equally disillusioned with a stalemated war that had cost them almost 150,000 casualties, including nearly 50,000 deaths. The new president, Dwight D. Eisenhower, had been elected in November 1952, in part because of his promise to end the war promptly. Eisenhower and his secretary of state, John Foster Dulles, adopted a two-track plan. They issued veiled threats to expand the war beyond Korea, possibly with atomic weapons used against China, unless the peace talks made rapid progress. The administration also announced that the Seventh Fleet would no longer "shield" the Chinese mainland from attacks by Chiang's forces. They had, as journalists put it, "unleashed" the Nationalists in order to pressure China. But even as they made these threats, Eisenhower and Dulles hinted to the Chinese that once a Korean settlement was achieved they were prepared to deal flexibly with several outstanding issues between the United States and PRC.

In late March, China accepted a U.S. suggestion for an interim exchange of sick and wounded POWs. Three days later, Zhou proposed a broader exchange in which prisoners who opposed repatriation would be transferred to a neutral state "so as to ensure a just solution to the question of their repatriation." This would permit both sides to save face. After serious armistice talks resumed at the end of April 1953, a commission of neutrals was created to screen POWs in Korea. All major issues were settled by mid-June, when Syngman Rhee attempted to derail a settlement. On June 18, he suddenly released 18,000 POWs whose fate had yet to be resolved. The Chinese responded by launching a fierce attack on South Korean forces. Eisenhower, furious at Rhee's ploy, nearly ordered his overthrow. Finally, on July 27, all participants signed an armistice that left Korea divided, in a technical state of war, and still full of foreign troops.

The dreadful loss of life was only one consequence of the Korean War. By 1953, the U.S. government had implemented the concept of NSC-68, expanding military spending nearly fourfold, from $13 billion annually before the war to over $50 billion in 1953. Most of the funds were expended on a military build-up in Western Europe and Japan. Defense spending came down a bit after the Korean armistice, but remained at a historically high level for the rest of the decade.

Policies adopted by Washington from 1950–53 embittered Chinese–American relations in several ways. The U.S. public overwhelmingly considered China a brutal aggressor, responsible for the deaths thousands of young Americans. Demagogues such as Sen. Joe McCarthy stoked this anger to a fever pitch. The battles with China revitalized support for the disgraced Kuomintang on Taiwan and made it politically difficult, if not impossible, for any politician to discuss diplomatic recognition of the PRC. By 1953, the CIA was actively assisting Nationalist guerrilla raids on the China coast and helping to support a KMT army fighting on the China–Burma border. The Defense, State, Treasury, and Commerce Departments, as well as U.S. intelligence services, were committed to isolating China in every way possible. This isolation forced the PRC even closer to the Soviet Union.

During the Korean War, Washington not only stopped its own small trade with China, but also organized an embargo among its allies. Congress, for example, passed the Battle Act, which threatened penalties against any country that sold any of a wide variety of products to China. After the 1953 armistice, the United States continued its own total trade embargo and worked to restrict China's trade with other non-Communist nations. Washington operated through the China Committee (CHINCOM) of the Paris-based Coordinating Committee For Export to Communist Areas (COCOM). This U.S.-dominated group set guidelines for which manufactured products the European allies and Japan could sell to China and worked to restrict China's access to credit. Pressured by the United States, CHINCOM imposed far stricter trade barriers on China than were applied to the Soviet Union or its Eastern European satellites. Before ending the occupation of Japan in April 1952, the United States insisted that Tokyo agree to even more stringent limits on exports to China. Washington did this out of an exaggerated fear that trade with China would seduce Japan to become either "neutral" or even pro-Communist.

Despite the unpopular restriction on trade with China, Japan received exceptional benefits from the Korean War. Still economically vulnerable when the fighting began, a flood of American war orders—called "divine aid" by business leaders—spurred industrial production. For example, the Toyota corporation, nearly bankrupt in June 1950, found salvation in a contract from the U.S. Army to build military trucks for use in Korea. The company not only earned badly needed dollars, it also gained access to new technology, which it applied to building automobiles. Between 1950 and 1954, Japan earned nearly $4 billion in U.S. military procurements, more money than it had received in postwar reconstruction aid. As Ambassador Robert Murphy remarked, these orders turned Japan into "one big supply depot without which the Korean War could not have been fought." Most economists believe Japan's economic surge in the 1950s through the 1980s had its roots in the Korean War.

The war also prompted Washington to sign a long-delayed peace and security treaty with Japan. Drafted solely by the United States and signed at a ceremony in San Francisco in September 1951 (from which China was excluded), the treaties linked Japan closely to the United States. Although the United States terminated its formal occupation, the security pact allowed a large number of American troops to remain in bases on Japan and Okinawa, with virtually no restrictions on their activities. These Japanese air, sea, and ground bases, along with others in the Philippines, formed the spearhead of U.S. military power in East Asia for the next quarter century. In addition to the military pact, the Truman administration required that the Japanese government recognize only the Nationalist regime on Taiwan and strictly limit economic contacts with the PRC. Even though most Japanese deeply resented the large U.S. military presence and the restrictions on contact with China, they had to accept the terms in order to end the occupation and be assured of access to the American market.

Among the most dramatic unintended consequences of the conflict in Korea was the rapid increase of both Chinese and American involvement in the French colonial war in Indochina. The Truman and Eisenhower administrations were certain that the PRC would use a Communist Vietnam to dominate Southeast Asia and choke Japan economically. Mao was equally convinced that the United States planned to develop Vietnam as an anti-Communist base from which to threaten China.

John Foster Dulles, a Republican foreign policy expert (and future secretary of state) hired by the Truman administration to negotiate the peace treaty with Japan (signed in September 1951 and effective in April 1952), articulated this view. Speaking to French officials in Paris in May 1952, he described the wars in Korea and Indochina as a single struggle to contain China. Unfortunately, some Americans misinterpreted the French war as "an effort by a colonial power to maintain its rule." In fact, Dulles declared, French Indochina—or Vietnam—was the "key to Southeast Asia upon the resources of which Japan is largely dependent." If communism triumphed in Vietnam and the rest of Southeast Asia, Dulles warned upon becoming secretary of state in January 1953, "from there on out" the economically desperate "Japs would be thinking on how to get to the other side." The loss of Japan, like the loss of Germany, could alter the global balance of power and had to be prevented.

At the time of the Korean armistice, the United States already paid nearly three-fourths of the cost of the French Indochina war. When the French quit fighting in 1954, Washington had provided over $2 billion in aid. During the next twenty years, presidents Truman, Eisenhower, Kennedy, Johnson, and Nixon built on this Korean War-era commitment to hold the line in Southeast Asia against communism and China.

SELECTED ADDITIONAL READING

William W. Stueck, *The Road to Confrontation: American Policy Toward China and Korea, 1947–1950* (Chapel Hill, N.C., 1981), and, *The Korean War: An International History* (Princeton, N.J., 1997); James I. Matray, *The Reluctant Crusade: American Foreign Policy in Korea, 1941–50* (Honolulu, 1985); Bruce Cumings, *The Origins of the Korean War, 1947–1950* (2 vols.; Princeton, N.J., 1981–90); Chen Jian, *China's Road to the Korean War* (New York, 1996), and, *Mao's China and the Cold War* (Chapel Hill, N.C., 2001); Robert Accinelli, *Crisis and Commitment: United States Policy toward Taiwan, 1950–1955* (Chapel Hill, N.C., 1996); Rosemary Foot, *The Wrong War: American Conflict and the Dimensions of the Korean Conflict, 1950–53* (Ithaca, N.Y., 1985) and, *A Substitute for Victory: The Politics of Peacemaking and the Korean Armistice Talks* (Ithaca, N.Y., 1990), and *The Practice of Power: U.S. Relations with China since 1949* (New York, 1997); Sirgei N. Goncharov, John Lewis, and Xue Li Tai, *Uncertain Partners: Stalin, Mao and the Korean War* (Stanford, Calif., 1993); Allen S. Whiting, *China Crosses the Yalu* (New York, 1960); Michael Schaller, *Altered States: The U.S. and Japan since the Occupation* (New York, 1997), and, *Douglas MacArthur: The Far Eastern General* (New York, 1989); Qiang Zhai, *The Dragon, the Lion, and the Eagle: Chinese–British American Relations, 1949–58* (Kent, Ohio, 1994), and, *China and the Vietnam Wars, 1950–1975* (Chapel Hill, N.C., 2000); Shu Guang Zhang, *Deterrence and Strategic Culture: Chinese–American Conflicts, 1949–1958* (Ithaca, N.Y., 1992); Thomas Christensen, *Useful Adversaries: Grand Strategy, Domestic Mobilization, and Sino American Conflict, 1947–1958* (Princeton, N.J., 1996); Odd Arne Westad, ed., *Brothers in Arms: The Rise and Fall of the Sino–Soviet Alliance, 1945–1963* (Washington, D.C., 1999); O. Edmund Clubb, *The Witness and I* (New York, 1974); Daniel M. Oshinski, *A Conspiracy So Immense: The World of Joe McCarthy* (New York, 1985); Robert P. Newman, *Owen Lattimore and The Loss of China* (Berkeley, Calif., 1992).

EIGHT

From Old Frontiers to New Frontiers

Chinese–American Conflict during the Eisenhower, Kennedy, and Johnson Administrations, 1953–1969

The Korean stalemate discredited President Truman and hobbled a Democratic party already staggering under the charge that it had lost China and coddled Communists. During the 1952 presidential campaign, Republicans coined the slogan K–1, C–2, signifying Democratic responsibility for "Korea, Communism, and Corruption." Democrats, Senator Joe McCarthy added, had perpetrated "Twenty Years of Treason." Republican presidential candidate, Dwight D. Eisenhower, who promised to "go to Korea" and end the war, along with running-mate Senator Richard M. Nixon, rode a tide of voter discontent into the White House. During the next decade and a half, Eisenhower, as well as his two Democratic successors, John F. Kennedy and Lyndon B. Johnson, made a fetish of their hostility to China. In public, at least, it appeared that Sino–American relations lurched from crisis to crisis, with almost no improvement over time.

Between 1953 and 1969, presidents Eisenhower, Kennedy, and Johnson pursued four interrelated goals in Asia. These included containing and isolating China, protecting Taiwan, maintaining Japanese prosperity, and keeping communism out of Southeast Asia. To achieve these ends, all three presidents supported the Nationalist regime on Taiwan, expanded military involvement in Vietnam, opened U.S. markets to Japan, and provided security guarantees to most non-Communist nations in East and Southeast Asia.

By the time of the Korean armistice, the United States had resumed large-scale military aid to the KMT and often assisted Nationalist raids against the mainland. In the language of the era, Washington "unleashed" Chiang Kai-shek. When Truman first sent the Seventh Fleet into the Taiwan Strait in June 1950, it was ordered to stop attacks by China or by Nationalists against the PRC. In his inaugural speech, Eisenhower announced that the navy would no longer "shield" the People's Republic from attacks by Taiwan. Despite this public bravado, right after the new president announced this policy change, he slowed delivery of weapons to Taiwan until Chiang "made a commitment" to "play ball" and not act "recklessly."

In addition to military assistance, throughout the 1950s and early 1960s, the United States provided generous development aid to Taiwan. Although Chiang had previously ignored most outside advice, on Taiwan he proved more flexible. This was not merely a case of learning from past errors. Native Taiwanese landlords, rather than mainland Chinese who had come over in 1949, owned much of the island's farmland. With the United States providing money, Chiang purchased and redistributed land to Taiwanese farmers. This weakened the power of the local landlord class, which disliked Chiang and the KMT, while boosting the Generalissimo's support among landless peasants who had resented the influx of mainlanders. American agricultural, economic, civil service, health, and other advisers flocked to the island. By the early 1960s, despite continued political repression, Taiwan boasted the second highest standard of living in East Asia, trailing only Japan.

The United States maintained a much higher level of involvement in Asia during the 1950s and 1960s than it had before World War II. The effort to contain China, build up Japan, protect Taiwan, and stabilize South Vietnam transformed a backwater of U.S. foreign policy into a focal point. At the same time, American policies in the region often antagonized U.S. allies in Europe, who considered Washington's diplomacy too moralistic, rigid, and reflexively anti-Communist.

EISENHOWER AND CHINA

The Eisenhower administration placed the final bricks in the American-designed wall around China. These consisted of strict trade controls, new or expanded security pacts with Japan, Korea, Thailand, the Philippines, and Taiwan, and creation of a non-Communist state in southern Vietnam. Even though the president and some of his aides occasionally voiced private misgivings about their own hard line, their public rhetoric on China remained unbending.

Eisenhower's secretary of state, John Foster Dulles, brought a particularly strident moralism to discussions of foreign policy. An accomplished international lawyer and lay activist in the Presbyterian Church, Dulles, in a double pun attributed to British Prime Minister Winston Churchill, was described as the "only bull who carried around his own China shop." Partly to insulate himself from the attacks by Chiang's American allies that undermined his predecessor, Dean Acheson, Dulles voiced an unstinting critique of China. He appointed Scott McCleod, an aide to Senator Joe McCarthy, to smoke out State Department personnel of dubious loyalty. To appease Taiwan's supporters in Congress and the media, the so-called China Lobby, Dulles fired one of the few senior "China hands" left in the department, John Carter Vincent. Ironically, after sacking Vincent, Dulles asked the stunned diplomat if he would be willing to consult anonymously from time to time on China policy! Vincent declined.

In his public rhetoric, Dulles often described the People's Republic of China as a godless, illegal regime that did "not conform to the practices of civilized nations." By the "test of conception, birth, nature and obedience," he argued, the "Mao Tse-tung (Mao Zedong) regime is a creature of Moscow's Politburo." According to an aide, he hoped to "reactivate the civil war in China" (although without U.S. participation) and see Mao's regime swept away. In 1957, Dulles declared, "we owe it to ourselves, our allies, and the Chinese people to do all that we can to contribute to that passing."

Although Dulles despised the PRC and felt politically compelled to verbally support Chiang's claim to reconquer the Chinese mainland, he was not entirely naïve. For example, he dismissed the views of the China Lobby and Henry Luce that Chiang was a paragon of democratic virtue. In the words of one Dulles biographer, he considered Chiang an "arrogant, manipulative schemer more interested in self-aggrandizement than in the welfare and security of the Chinese people." Chiang, he sensed, would happily drag the United States into war with China. Dulles privately remarked that the Nationalist leader had a "vested interest in World War III."

Both Dulles and Eisenhower hoped to contain and eventually get rid of the Chinese Communist regime without becoming completely enmeshed with Chiang or fighting a major war. Like their predecessors, at various times they considered deposing Chiang in favor of a more moderate Taiwan leader, turning the island into a UN trusteeship, or even recognizing two separate Chinese governments. Ultimately, the president and secretary of state favored a "wedge" strategy to drive the PRC and Soviet Union apart. Rather than try to subdue China by "subsidizing a vast military operation," the administration implemented a combined program of "economic embargo, political isolation, and subversion" to force China out of the Soviet orbit.

The so-called wedge strategy could be "hard" or "soft." Officials such as Dulles, Assistant Secretary of State for the Far East Walter Robertson, Treasury Secretary George Humphrey, and Admiral Arthur Radford, Chairman of the Joint Chiefs of Staff (JCS), condemned Mao and his followers as fanatics who would never respond to positive inducements. They believed a tight embargo on China's trade with non-Communist nations would force Beijing's complete reliance on Moscow. They reasoned that as the Soviet economy could not meet China's needs, the People's Republic would be forced to its knees—and its senses—and return to the Western fold.

Within his administration, President Dwight D. Eisenhower was the most articulate advocate for a "soft wedge" policy. He considered it "hopeless to imagine we could break China away from the Soviets and communism short of some great cataclysm." Trade flexibility, not rigidity, he insisted, could encourage change in China and be "a weapon on our side." He also worried that a strict embargo would create economic strains between the United States, Great Britain, and especially, Japan, which looked to China as a major export market. If all trade "between the free world and Soviet bloc" was severed, he asked, how much would it cost the United States to subsidize "countries that depend on trade, such as Japan?" A total embargo on China "simply slammed the door in Japan's face" and would probably cause more problems than it solved, Eisenhower declared.

At the end of 1953, the president told his cabinet that the only "sensible course of action" in regard to trade with China was to "apply the criterion of the net gain. What do we get out of this policy in terms of what we put in?" He added, only half joking, that he would send jet fighter aircraft to Mao instead of Chiang "if it could be shown to our net advantage." Speaking to legislative leaders in June 1954, Eisenhower chided key groups in Congress who seemed set on "no trade with Red China," opposed sending U.S. troops to Vietnam, and insisted on "no further liberalization of trade with Japan." Unless the United States allowed some trade with China, defended Vietnam, and accepted more Japanese exports, the president warned, "we would lose Japan" and the Pacific "would become a communist lake." The problem, Eisenhower told aides, came from "demagogues" like Senator Joe McCarthy and the China Lobby, who incited the public to fear and oppose any dealing with China.

For much of his presidency, Eisenhower seemed the chief, if not the only, high-level advocate of a flexible China policy. At least within the private confines of the White House, he dismissed Chiang's pretensions of retaking the mainland, advocated greater European and Japanese trade with the PRC, dismissed the China Lobby as a collection of ignorant partisans, and recognized incipient tension between Beijing and Moscow. Unfortunately, Eisenhower seldom articulated these thoughts in public. Instead, he allowed more extreme notions voiced by Dulles and Vice-president Nixon to frame the debate. This lapse of leadership confused both the American public and Chinese government.

The result of these divisions in American ranks was a policy that sometimes combined the worst of both worlds. The United States imposed rigid, but not absolute, limits on British and Japanese industrial exports to China. Eisenhower publicly justified the restrictions, but privately ridiculed them. At times, he virtually encouraged London and Tokyo to defy U.S. restrictions. The trade barriers infuriated the British, French, and Japanese, (not to mention the Chinese), but allowed just enough trade to keep American allies in line. Often, China simply bought forbidden goods via the Soviet Union or Eastern Europe, which were permitted to import a wider category of products. Under mounting pressure from London and Tokyo, in late 1957, the American government finally abandoned the so-called China Differential. Until 1971, the United States continued its own nearly total embargo on trade with China, but after 1957, it permitted its allies to sell China the same products they were authorized to sell to the Soviet Union. Ironically, just as the United States relaxed export controls in 1958, Mao Zedong launched a radical program called the Great Leap Forward, which isolated China further.

Stalin's death in 1953, followed by the Korean armistice, temporarily improved relations between the Communist allies. Nikita Khrushchev, who eventually succeeded Stalin, accommodated Chinese needs more willingly than his stingy and suspicious predecessor. Khrushchev pleased Mao by visiting Beijing in 1954 and offering to return the Manchurian naval base at Lushun (Port Arthur) taken by Stalin in 1945. He followed this with loans, military aid, and technical assistance vital to Chinese development. These actions undercut American hope of driving a wedge between Moscow and Beijing.

Mao had mixed feelings about Khrushchev's attack on Stalin's memory, begun in 1956. As Mao acknowledged, had he always followed Stalin's advice, the CCP would not have triumphed and "I would have been dead." Nevertheless, Mao resented Khrushchev's failure to consult him in advance about this policy change and faulted the Soviet leader for unleashing anti-Communist protests in Eastern Europe. He even blamed growing criticism of the CCP among Chinese during 1957 on forces unleashed by Moscow.

From the end of the Korean War until 1958, the PRC relied on Soviet development aid and pursued modest trade with non-Communist nations. After 1958, Mao proposed to speed China's economic development by rejecting both Soviet and capitalist models. He ordered creation of large agricultural communes and backyard industry, spurning Soviet advice and foreign trade. Mao's defiance of economic logic resulted in widespread famine, which demographers estimate killed twenty to thirty million people and led to economic stagnation during the late 1950s and early 1960s.

In the aftermath of the Korean War, the United States and China nearly came to blows on three occasions: in Vietnam in 1954, and in the Taiwan Straits in 1954 and again in 1958. In each incident, Beijing and Washington approached what John Foster Dulles called "the brink," but pulled back before direct fighting began. To some degree, the painful lessons both sides learned in Korea modified their behavior. During most of the 1950s and 1960s, Mao denounced the United States as an imperialist enemy of China and a "paper tiger" doomed to destruction. At the same time that the PRC supported calls for revolution in poor countries, it stressed that oppressed peoples must accomplish their own liberation and that it was willing to accept "peaceful co-existence" with the United States. China would resort to arms only in self-defense or to defend territory along its borders.

Chinese and American interests collided in Vietnam in the spring of 1954. Despite the U.S. grant of more than $2 billion in military aid to French forces fighting the Communist Viet Minh guerrillas, the insurgents had worn down the French. U.S. military planners had encouraged the French to lure the Viet Minh into a pitched battle at Dien Bien Phu, a valley in northern Vietnam. But instead of decimating the insurgents, the French garrison was surrounded by the Viet Minh, assisted by Chinese advisers and supplies. Given the French public's growing disillusion with the war, the loss of Dien Bien Phu looked likely to end armed resistance and clear the path for Communist control of all Vietnam.

Months before, Dulles had warned that the Soviets and Chinese had hatched a plan to seize Japan, not through direct assault but "through what they are doing in Indochina. If they could get this peninsula of Indochina, Siam, Burma, Malaya, they would have what was called the rice bowl of Asia." The JCS similarly worried that a Viet Minh victory would result in Communist control of all Southeast Asia. Japan, the "keystone of U.S. policy in the Far East," would then be forced by "economic and political pressure" to reach an "accommodation with the Communist bloc." Standing with one foot in Southeast Asia and the other in Japan, China would "ultimately control the entire Western and Southwestern Pacific region and would threaten South Asia and the Middle East." The administration considered direct intervention in Vietnam if Chinese combat troops joined the struggle.

Early in 1954, when he dispatched additional military advisers to Vietnam, Eisenhower declared "My God . . . we must not lose Asia." In a speech about the danger of Japan being toppled by a "row of falling dominoes," and in a private appeal to British Prime Minister Churchill for joint intervention, Eisenhower warned that the loss of Vietnam and Southeast Asia would allow the Soviets and Chinese to "combine the manpower and natural resources of Asia with the industrial potential of Japan." This would alter the global balance of power.

Despite his advisers' calls for American air strikes, or even use of tactical nuclear weapons against the Viet Minh, Eisenhower stepped back from the brink. Congressional leaders made clear their opposition to direct military involvement in Southeast Asia. Most of America's allies spurned Dulles's call for "United Action" to save all Vietnam. The British, who had abandoned India without a fight, were not eager to defend the French empire. Even the French were lukewarm about U.S. intervention. Paris wanted help in saving its troops at Dien Bien Phu, but rejected Washington's price: that it continue to fight under American command. On May 7, Viet Minh guerrillas overran the French base and effectively ended colonial rule in Indochina.

At the same time as Dien Bien Phu fell, an international conference had convened in Geneva, Switzerland, to discuss several Asian issues, including Vietnam. The Soviet Union, France, Great Britain, and China formally participated. The United States sent an observer team, briefly led by Dulles. Americans feared that in his determination to end the war in Indochina, French Prime Minister Pierre Mendes-France would cut a deal that turned over all Vietnam to Ho Chi Minh. This, Eisenhower and Dulles agreed, would make it exceedingly difficult to "keep Japan in our orbit." In a snub that boded ill for the conference, the secretary of state not only refused to shake the extended hand of Chinese premier Zhou Enlai, but insisted that he not be seated close to any Communists sitting around the circular table. According to a diplomat present at Geneva, Dulles sat at the conference table "mouth drawn down at the corners, his eyes on the ceiling, sucking his teeth." After a few days of this, he left for home.

To Washington's great surprise, the outcome at Geneva in June 1954 proved far better than Dulles or Eisenhower had predicted. The Soviets and the Chinese suggested a compromise in Vietnam, well short of the outright victory the Viet Minh had anticipated. Still troubled by the prospect of U.S. military intervention in Southeast Asia, and eager to demonstrate China's moderation, Zhou pressed Ho Chi Minh to spin off Laos and Cambodia from Indochina as independent states and to accept a temporary division of Vietnam along the 17th parallel, rather than the 13th parallel as Ho demanded. North of the line, Ho's Democratic Republic of Vietnam could consolidate power. In the south, the French withdrawal would leave in place a weak puppet regime ruled by the playboy emperor, Bao Dai. In 1956, national unification elections would be held. In the absence of any powerful leaders in the south, Ho seemed likely to win control over all Vietnam. These provisions were incorporated in the Geneva Accords approved in June. Although the United States did not sign the agreement, it promised not to "disturb it."

Eisenhower and Dulles considered the 1954–56 grace period a window of opportunity in which to consolidate anti-Communist forces in the southern half of Vietnam. According to Dulles, the measure of success would be successfully preventing the Communist regime in the northern half of Vietnam from "extending communism throughout Southeast Asia and the Southwest Pacific." To achieve this, the Eisenhower administration moved quickly to replace the departing French south of the 17th parallel. U.S. aid, advisers, and support soon flowed to Ngo Dinh Diem, a Vietnamese Catholic politician who had lived briefly in the United States and whom Emperor Bao Dai appointed prime minister in mid-1954. With U.S. encouragement, Diem gradually asserted his authority over competing anti-Communist political and religious groups. In 1956, he cancelled national unity elections and pushed through sham votes removing Bao Dai from power and making himself president of an independent Republic of Vietnam.

The Eisenhower administration promptly recognized and expanded assistance to the new regime, with its capital in Saigon. Between 1956 and 1960, Diem consolidated power, repressed opposition, and continued to receive substantial U.S. assistance. Although a new guerrilla insurgency erupted in 1960, Eisenhower and the American people considered the creation and survival of South Vietnam a real success story in Asia and a key component in the containment of China.

During South Vietnam's gestation period, Dulles constructed other barriers around China. In September 1954, he flew to Manila to convene a security conference. There, Britain, France, Thailand, and the Philippines joined the United States in creating the Southeast Asia Treaty Organization (SEATO), loosely modeled on NATO. Unlike the North Atlantic

Treaty, however, SEATO did not precommit the United States to the defense of member nations. Instead, if any member was attacked, all parties promised to consult and take appropriate action. SEATO members later pledged to defend South Vietnam.

During the next six years, the Soviet Union and China provided modest economic aid to Ho, but did not encourage his effort to unify Vietnam. Ho's allies barely noted the decision by Diem and the Americans to cancel the 1956 election to unite the country.

The Chinese Communist leadership had hoped that its cooperative attitude at Geneva might improve ties with the United States. But Dulles not only snubbed Zhou, but went on to create SEATO, and Mao feared that he was about to offer Taiwan new security guarantees. Thus, while Dulles negotiated the SEATO agreement in Manila during September 1954, Chinese artillery units began shelling several small, Nationalist-held islands off the south China coast. Quemoy (Jinmen) and Matsu (Mazu), the most important of the islands, lay just a few miles off Fujian province. Chiang, who considered these toeholds a critical part of his claim to China, stationed about 50,000 Nationalist troops on the islands. The deployment posed a continual threat to China's coastal shipping and military security. American officials also worried about Chiang's motives. If Chinese forces attacked and overran Quemoy and nearby islands, including the Pescadores (Penghu), which were close to Taiwan, the loss of so many KMT troops might destabilize Taiwan and force the United States to come to its defense.

Mao probably had several motives in shelling Quemoy. He hoped that seizing or forcing the evacuation of some of the offshore islands would reduce the threat to the south China coast. The attack would also show Washington the danger of leaving problems in the region unresolved and, presumably, would force the Eisenhower administration to think twice about signing a formal defense pact with Taiwan.

Mao guessed correctly that Eisenhower and Dulles worried about being pushed by Chiang into an unwanted fight with China. Neither the president nor his secretary of state considered the offshore islands crucial to Taiwan's defense. Chiang's decision to deploy so many troops in an exposed position struck them as a provocative, even foolhardy act. At the same time, both feared a domestic political backlash or encouraging Chinese aggression if U.S. reluctance to defend the offshore islands was mistaken for a step toward abandoning Taiwan.

In December 1954, the administration countered Mao's gamble by offering Taiwan a mutual defense treaty that pledged to defend the island from invasion. However, it did not specifically extend that guarantee to the many small Nationalist-held offshore islands unless the United States decided that an attack on them posed a direct threat to Taiwan. In fact, before offering this assurance to Chiang, Dulles insisted that the Generalissimo agree not to launch a major assault on China without American permission. The secretary defended his policy by telling members of Congress that unless the United States was prepared to risk war with China, then it should "get out" of the Far East and "make our defense in California." In January 1955, at the request of the administration, Congress enacted the so-called Formosa Resolution, giving Eisenhower a blank check to protect the "security of Formosa [Taiwan], the Pescadores [islands], and related positions and territories of that area."

On April 23, 1955, while Zhou Enlai attended a conference of nonaligned Asian and African nations in Bandung, Indonesia, the Chinese foreign minister announced that China would stop shelling Quemoy. In fact, Beijing wanted to negotiate a reduction in tension directly with the United States. Chinese motives for the sudden about-face remain unclear. Dulles claimed that U.S. resolve and veiled threats had scared Mao. Nevertheless, the secretary of state quickly accepted Zhou's proposal to begin ambassadorial talks, first in Geneva, then in Warsaw.

The 1955 talks, the first direct U.S.–PRC contact since 1949, achieved some small but meaningful breakthroughs. For example, since the Korean War, several dozen American citizens, including students and missionaries, had been detained in China. Several hundred Chinese students who specialized in science, had, for security reasons, been kept against their will in the United States. Because they possessed knowledge on subjects such as rockets and nuclear physics, American authorities would only permit their departure to Taiwan, not to the PRC. Arrangements were made to repatriate both groups. (Several of the U.S.-trained scientists contributed to China's development of nuclear weapons and missiles.) Despite a promising start, talks deadlocked on such issues as UN representation for China and the status of Taiwan. Dulles vetoed a Chinese proposal to permit mutual visits by journalists, while Beijing rejected U.S. demands that it renounce the use of force against Taiwan. Chinese hints that progress on other regional disputes would reduce the likelihood that Beijing would use force against Taiwan brought no positive response. Although opinion polls showed that most Americans favored direct talks between Dulles and Zhou Enlai, Washington minimized contact. By the end of 1957, with the two sides talking past each other, the ambassadorial meetings were suspended.

Meanwhile, Chiang Kai-shek expanded deployments to Quemoy and other offshore islands. By 1958, over 100,000 troops, twice the number stationed there in 1954, were in exposed forward positions. Washington privately criticized this as both dangerous and provocative, but did little to make Chiang change course. In fact, during 1957, the United States expanded economic and military aid to Taiwan and stationed nuclear-capable Matador missiles on the island. The end of the ambassadorial talks and the Generalissimo's growing belligerence convinced Mao that efforts at "peaceful co-existence" had yielded nothing and that the time had come to "probe the attitude of the Americans."

In November 1957, Mao visited Moscow, where he praised Soviet technological successes, such as the development of long-range missiles and the Sputnik satellite. The "east wind was prevailing over the west wind," he declared, and announced that the United States was merely a "paper tiger." He asked for and received a Soviet promise to help China develop nuclear energy and weapons, but pledged not to provoke the United States.

Despite signs of public cooperation, Mao harbored growing doubts about Soviet economic and foreign policy. Soviet advisers favored centrally planned development projects. They ridiculed Mao's calls for creation of vast agricultural communes and rural industry. Mao questioned Khrushchev's efforts to reduce tensions with the United States. Moscow delayed giving China nuclear weapons technology, but proposed building radio transmitters for Soviet submarines on Chinese soil. The Soviet Union, Mao complained, was acting cowardly and taking China for granted at a time when its military and technological accomplishments should make it far bolder. Suspicious of the Soviets, fed up with American and Taiwanese behavior, and anxious to initiate his radical Great Leap Forward economic program, Mao decided to provoke another crisis with the United States in the Taiwan Strait. A showdown, he believed, would reveal where the Soviets stood and frustrate any effort by Moscow or Washington to promote a "two-China policy." Also, a foreign crisis could be used to mobilize support within China for the Great Leap.

Without informing the Soviet Union, Mao ordered a massive artillery barrage against Quemoy beginning on August 23, 1958. During the next three days, tens of thousands of shells fell on the island, effectively cutting it off from resupply. When it appeared that the Nationalist garrison might be overrun or forced to surrender, American military planners considered undertaking "nuclear strikes deep into China," possibly causing "millions of noncombatant casualties." During the next two months, China and the United States again came perilously close to a war neither desired.

The Eisenhower administration moved heavy naval reinforcements and 100 nuclear-capable aircraft to the area, but did not immediately pledge to defend Quemoy. The president remained wary of Chiang's desire to "drag us into attacking . . . the whole of China" and believed that even limited strikes could quickly escalate into a major war. The 1954 security treaty with Taiwan called for defending only offshore islands such as Quemoy if an attack on them directly threatened Taiwan. On September 4, Dulles publicly committed the United States to defending Quemoy and soon leaked word that the United States had placed nuclear-capable artillery on the island. Eisenhower, however, struck a more moderate tone, suggesting that China should renounce the use of force against Taiwan and resume ambassadorial talks with the United States. On September 6, Zhou Enlai agreed to negotiations in Warsaw. These began on September 15, while the shelling continued. Meanwhile, U.S. naval vessels began convoying Nationalist supply ships to Quemoy. When Chinese shore batteries refrained from shooting at the escorts, this effectively broke the blockade.

American diplomats told their PRC counterparts in Warsaw that both China and Taiwan should defuse tension by demilitarizing several of the offshore islands. Eisenhower even proposed to Chiang that he voluntarily withdraw Nationalist troops from Quemoy and Matsu, leaving them a buffer zone. As long as KMT forces were not driven out, the president argued, a withdrawal would reduce tensions without compromising Taiwan's security. Both Chiang and Mao rejected these notions. Chiang considered the offshore islands his symbolic steppingstone to China. Mao worried that if Nationalists deserted Quemoy and Matsu and settled down solely on Taiwan, it would create a pretext for the United States and other nations to adopt a "two China policy," treating Taiwan as a sovereign state.

To prevent the Nationalists from abandoning the offshore islands, Mao proposed a compromise. Early in October, PRC officials offered to temporarily cease shelling Quemoy if the U.S. Navy ceased its convoys. Washington agreed, and Nationalist ships were allowed to deliver supplies. Soon the Communists limited shelling to odd-numbered days, then stopped entirely. At one point, a top Chinese commander even offered to send supplies from the mainland to the Nationalist garrison on Quemoy. By late October, the crisis had passed, although the underlying problem remained.

At the end of 1958, Dulles visited Chiang Kai-shek, telling him again that while the United States would defend Taiwan, it would not support a campaign to reconquer China. Chiang issued an ambiguous pledge not to use force to "restore freedom to the mainland." Meanwhile, Chinese diplomats at the Warsaw talks insisted that any improvement of relations required the United States to first withdraw its forces from Taiwan and nearby waters. The contacts in Warsaw again lapsed and the two nations' entrenched positions remained frozen for the next decade.

Sino–Soviet relations slipped further after the Taiwan Strait crisis. In September 1959, Khrushchev flew from a meeting in the United States directly to Beijing. Optimistic about improving relations with Washington, the Soviet visitor called on Mao to "ease international tension" by showing restraint toward Taiwan. Khrushchev criticized Mao's policy toward border disputes with India and labeled as "irresponsible" Mao's claim that China could withstand a nuclear war. Mao dismissed Khrushchev as a "sell-out" and accused his critics within the CCP, who condemned the failure of the Great Leap Forward, of colluding with the Soviets.

THE NEW FRONTIER AND CHINA

Senator John F. Kennedy, Democrat of Massachusetts, challenged Vice-president Richard Nixon's bid to succeed Eisenhower in the 1960 presidential election. In a televised debate that October, Kennedy raised the question of the offshore islands as an example of the "tired thinking" of the outgoing administration. The Democratic nominee opposed a "trigger-happy" defense of specks of land such as Quemoy or Matsu. He would contain China by persuading the Nationalists to withdraw from these outposts and concentrate on the security of Taiwan. Even though Eisenhower had privately urged Chiang to do just this, Nixon dismissed Kennedy's suggestion as "wooly thinking." Kennedy's intention, however, was not to encourage serious debate on China, but to warn Americans that Republicans had overcommitted the United States to the nuclear defense of marginal areas. As president, he would expand conventional military power to resist Communist threats in the Third World.

After his election, Kennedy seldom spoke publicly about China, and when he did, it was usually to describe the threat it posed to peace. Shortly before his death in November 1963, Kennedy told reporters that he was not wedded to a policy of unremitting hostility toward mainland China. If Beijing showed a willingness to coexist peacefully, Kennedy said he would modify American policy. Theodore Sorenson, a close presidential adviser, later wrote that Kennedy "felt dissatisfied with his administration's failure to break new ground" on China and planned to initiate new policies during his second term. Of course, Kennedy's defenders also claimed that once reelected, he intended to withdraw U.S. forces from Vietnam. While no one can know what Kennedy might have done had he lived, his record on China, both before and after becoming president, provided a slim basis for optimism. In fact, Kennedy perceived China, like Cuba, as a direct challenge to his view of world order.

In 1949, while a young member of Congress, Kennedy was one of a handful of Democrats who accused President Truman and the State Department of deserting China, "whose freedom we once fought to preserve." What America's soldiers had saved in war, he lamented, "our diplomats and president have frittered away." As a senator in the late 1950s, Kennedy championed U.S. support for Diem in South Vietnam. He described Diem's regime as "the cornerstone of the Free World in Southeast Asia, the Keystone in the arch, the Finger in the dike." Like Dulles, he viewed a pro-American, anti-Communist South Vietnam as a stopper in the geographic bottle of Southeast Asia, blocking the spread of Chinese influence. Kennedy called Vietnam a showcase of democracy and proof of how the United States could create allies in former colonial areas.

As Kennedy assumed the presidency, the notion that the United States might recognize "two Chinas," or "one China, one Taiwan," had been broached by several influential policy groups. In 1959, studies by the Senate Foreign Relations Committee and by the prestigious Rockefeller Brothers Fund suggested the time had come to discuss a two-China approach. The leading Democratic liberal, two-time presidential nominee, Adlai Stevenson, published similar views in a *Foreign Affairs* article in January 1960. Taiwan, he argued, warranted recognition as an independent state. But before other nations accepted its status, Chiang must give up his claim to represent all China. Despite broad agreement on the need to revisit policy, few politicians were prepared to take the heat from the China Lobby that would follow any call to recognize the People's Republic or seat China in the UN. Organizations such as the "Committee of One Million" pledged to oppose any official who dared to challenge existing policy.

For more than a decade, U.S. policymakers had not only hoped for but had tried to stimulate a split between China and the Soviet Union. By 1961, the Sino–Soviet spit was readily apparent, but it hardly pleased Washington. In fact, the consensus among many of Kennedy's top advisers was that Mao's leadership had proved so reckless and destabilizing that even the Soviet Union found it intolerable. American policymakers who once thought in terms of cooperating with China against the Soviet menace, now speculated whether the United States and U.S.S.R. might link arms against the PRC.

Tension between Beijing and Moscow increased in 1960. Mao ridiculed Khrushchev's timid attitude toward the West, his lack of support for retaking Taiwan, his reluctance to help China obtain nuclear weapons, his sympathy for India, his failure to treat China as a full equal, and his criticism of the Great Leap Forward. These accusations became public denunciations during the summer of 1960. In August, Khrushchev decided to give Mao the chance to practice the "self-reliance" he preached. The Soviets halted most aid projects and began withdrawing technical experts from China. Some limited cooperation continued over the next two years, but for all practical purposes, the Sino–Soviet alliance was finished.

Kennedy and his secretary of state, Dean Rusk, agreed that China threatened peace in a more immediate way than did the Soviet Union. While the Soviets posed a long-term challenge, their policies, especially compared with Mao's, seemed predictable and relatively cautious. Chinese Communist leaders, in contrast, promised support for guerrilla movements throughout the Third World. To Kennedy, this threat could only be met if the United States vastly increased its own military power and developed a "flexible response" capable of countering Chinese-supported "wars of national liberation" in Asia and elsewhere.

The escalating threat to Diem in South Vietnam by Communist Viet Cong guerrillas struck Kennedy as a test case in restraining China's indirect aggression. During his "thousand days" in office, the president increased the number of U.S. military advisers in Vietnam from about 1,000 to almost 16,000 and spent over $1 billion on aid to Saigon. On November 1, 1963, as Diem's violent repression of Buddhists and other dissenting groups in South Vietnam threatened to undermine the war effort completely, Kennedy authorized a coup to replace Diem with more reliable clients. Shortly before his own death later that month, the president repeated his belief in the "domino theory" as a reason why the United States could not abandon the war. If "South Vietnam went," Kennedy told an interviewer, "it would give the impression that the wave of the future in Southeast Asia was China and the Communists."

Some of the president's influential advisers and appointees questioned his hard line. For example, Chester Bowles, a high-ranking diplomat, and UN ambassador Adlai Stevenson, thought Chinese rhetoric was more bark than bite and suggested exploring a compromise with China. Two high-profile Harvard professors whom Kennedy appointed as ambassadors to India and Japan, John Kenneth Galbraith and Edwin O. Reischauer, spoke openly in favor of recognizing the Chinese Communist regime. In part because they feared a Republican backlash to any policy change, the president and Secretary of State Rusk remained unmoved. When Galbraith sent an impassioned cable arguing that Washington should at least not bar the way for Chinese membership in the UN, Rusk replied: "to the extent that your position has any merit it has been fully considered and rejected."

In some ways, Kennedy went beyond Eisenhower in offering support to Taiwan. In the summer of 1961, he promised Chiang that he would exercise a veto if the UN voted to admit China to its ranks. He also gave tacit approval for increased covert operations from Taiwan against the Chinese mainland. A lingering famine, an echo from Mao's Great Leap, had devastated parts of south China in 1961–62. This kindled new hope in Chiang's mind that even a modest invasion of the mainland would trigger an anti-Communist uprising. Kennedy shied away from committing the United States to such a venture, but, given his own fascination with counterinsurgency warfare, he agreed to supply equipment for airdrops and amphibious raids.

By the summer of 1962, Nationalist harassment provoked a Chinese response. Mao redeployed major elements of the People's Liberation Army to the south China coast, opposite Taiwan. Any large-scale Communist attack on the island, Kennedy's aides realized, would draw in the United States. However much he disliked China, even Dean Rusk wanted to avoid a replay of Korea. Rusk reactivated the dormant Warsaw ambassadorial channel in June 1962 to inform Chinese officials that Washington would not support a Nationalist invasion of the mainland. Both Mao and Chiang stepped back from the brink, but the gulf between Beijing and Washington remained unbridged.

During Kennedy's final year in the White House, his administration's view of China grew even bleaker. Two events during October 1962—the Cuban Missile Crisis and the China–India War—convinced the president and many Americans that the PRC threatened global stability. Although Khrushchev had several motives for secretly dispatching medium-range, nuclear armed missiles to Cuba, including a desire to deter a feared U.S. invasion, many American analysts believed he had been pressured into reckless action by Chinese criticism. These analysts suggested that Mao's escalating ridicule of Khrushchev's alleged abandonment of revolutionary leadership forced the Soviet leader to take a dangerous gamble in Cuba. The evidence of this came mostly after the fact, when Mao bitterly criticized Khrushchev's retreat in the face of Kennedy's naval blockade. Whether true or not, it suggested that the Chinese leadership scoffed at the risks of nuclear war.

On October 20, 1962, in the midst of the Cuban Missile Crisis, China launched a month-long military attack along its Himalayan border with India. At that time, and since, many observers noted that Chiang, as well as Mao, considered the disputed border Chinese soil and that the Indians did as much as the Chinese to provoke a fight. These facts, however, changed few minds. Most Americans, including two of China's biggest boosters in the administration, Chester Bowles and Ambassador to India John Kenneth Galbraith, considered democratic India the victim of unprovoked, brutal Chinese aggression. Ignoring the fact that Chinese troops halted operations as soon as they occupied the disputed territory, many Americans believed only the threat of U.S. intervention had blocked a Chinese sweep into India.

In the aftermath of the brief China–India war, Kennedy and Secretary of State Rusk became increasingly fearful of a nuclear-armed China. Once Mao possessed atomic weapons, the president rued, China would become the "greatest menace on earth." After China tested an atomic bomb in 1964 and a hydrogen weapon in 1967, Rusk spoke chillingly of "a billion Chinese armed with nuclear weapons." With or without atomic bombs, the administration blamed China for North Vietnam's growing support for the Viet Cong insurgency in South Vietnam and condemned China's aid to African nations as a plot to export revolution.

These fears prompted Kennedy during early 1963 to push forward with negotiations to achieve a limited nuclear test ban treaty with the Soviets. He hoped that an agreement between Washington and Moscow to control weapons tests would put pressure on Beijing to abandon its effort to build an atomic bomb. As an outside possibility, Kennedy even had his aides explore the feasibility of joining the Soviets in a preemptive strike against Chinese nuclear development facilities. None of this suggests that at the time of his death Kennedy seriously contemplated a new approach toward China.

ALL THE WAY WITH LBJ

In October 1966, almost three years after Lyndon Johnson assumed the presidency, National Security Adviser Walt Rostow sent a reassuring message to his boss. While Johnson's foreign policies had achieved success in Latin America, Africa, and Europe, Rostow boasted, "it is clear that a good part of your Administration's place in history will consist of the reshaping of Asia and our relations in it." Rostow's assessment of the centrality of Asia to Johnson's presidency proved true, but not exactly in the way he imagined. By 1968, after four years of bitter warfare in Southeast Asia, America's national unity, international stature, and Asia policy was in tatters. The disaster in Vietnam buried not only Johnson's Great Society domestic reform program, but dashed any hope for a new departure in Sino–American relations.

Initially, some of the president's foreign policy advisers thought the time had come to speak openly about a change in policy toward China. In December 1963, a month after Kennedy's death, Assistant Secretary of State Roger Hillsman delivered a speech that broached the idea of American recognition of "two Chinas," one on Taiwan, the other on the Chinese mainland. This concept went nowhere, however. A month later, in January 1964, when French president Charles DeGaulle recognized the PRC and severed ties to Taiwan, the Johnson administration condemned the move. Before China was permitted to join the community of nations, the president and Dean Rusk asserted that it must abandon what LBJ called its "doctrine of violence" and cease support for "wars of national liberation."

For the Johnson administration, Vietnam quickly became the test of Chinese intentions. "We will not permit," Johnson declared, the "independent nations of the East to be swallowed up by Communist conquest." As the succession of weak, post-Diem governments in Saigon lost control of rural Vietnam during 1964 and early 1965, Johnson saw the struggle largely as a proxy battle between Washington and Beijing. In his view, Ho Chi Minh and North Vietnam were little more than stand-ins for Mao and China, the tail of the Chinese dog.

Some mid-level policymakers, such as Jim Thomson, a China specialist on the National Security Council, challenged the conventional wisdom about the causes of the Vietnam War. After all, as of 1963, China had provided only advisers, small arms, and food to Hanoi. In a memo to McGeorge Bundy, a top Johnson aide, Thomson questioned whether "this tail (Vietnam) even belongs to that particular dog (China)." He warned against the tendency to "push too far the thesis of Peking's responsibility for the South Vietnam crisis."

In fact, from 1954, when the Geneva agreements led to a "temporary" division of Vietnam, through 1964, neither China nor the Soviet Union had given active support to Ho Chi Minh's effort to unify the two Vietnams. Chinese–Vietnamese hostility had a thousand-year history that only the French and American threats temporarily overcame. Soviet and Chinese aid to Ho seemed partly designed to prevent him from becoming too close to the other Communist power.

The president felt trapped between his commitment to Great Society reforms and a belief that the loss of Vietnam to communism would not only undo the barrier to Chinese expansion but would mobilize his domestic opponents against reform. Reflecting later on his decision early in 1965 to "Americanize" the war in Vietnam by committing large air and ground forces, Johnson told his biographer Doris Kearns, that he expected to be "crucified" either way he moved.

> If I left the woman I really loved, the Great Society, in order to get involved with that bitch of a war on the other side of the world, then I would lose everything at home. All my programs. All my hopes to feed the hungry and

> shelter the homeless. All my dreams to provide education and medical care to the browns and the blacks and the lame and the poor. But if I left that war and let the Communists take over South Vietnam then I would be seen as a coward and my nation would be seen as an appeaser and we would both find it impossible to accomplish anything for anybody on the entire globe.

Johnson reasoned by analogy, comparing Vietnam to the Chinese civil war and the domestic backlash that befell the Truman administration in 1949.

> Everything I knew about history told me that if I got out of Vietnam and let Ho Chi Minh run through the streets of Saigon then I'd be doing exactly what Chamberlain did in W.W. II I'd be giving a big fat reward to aggression. And I knew that if we let Communist aggression succeed in taking over South Vietnam there would follow in this country an endless national debate—a mean and destructive debate—that would shatter my presidency, kill my administration, and damage our democracy. I knew that Harry Truman and Dean Acheson had lost effectiveness from the day the Communists took over China. I believed that the loss of China had played a large role in the rise of Joe McCarthy. And I knew that all those problems, taken together, were chickenshit compared with what might happen if we lost Vietnam.

However inexact the analogy with "who lost China," in Johnson's mind losing Vietnam, or simply being the "first president to lose a war," put at risk everything he hoped to accomplish.

LBJ's linking the war in Vietnam to the Great Society included equal measures of self-serving rationalization, domestic politics, and misinformation about Vietnamese politics and history. In his mind, the United States was half-victim, half-cop, resisting Chinese-inspired aggression against South Vietnam. The fight for Vietnam, in the minds of Johnson and Rusk, was a struggle to preserve the post-WWII order.

Following his huge election victory in November 1964, Johnson began escalating the American presence in Vietnam, first with air power, then with troops. By bombing North Vietnam, Johnson hoped to inhibit Hanoi's ability to produce and transport war materials south. Air and ground attacks against the Viet Cong guerrillas were designed to destroy their fighting ability. According to this strategy, once North Vietnam experienced the pain of losing its industrial base and lacked the strength to resupply the weakened guerrillas in the south, the United States could turn most of the fighting over to the South Vietnamese army. At the war's peak in 1968, over 500,000 American military personnel served in and around Vietnam. U.S. aircraft dropped many more tons of bombs over

Vietnam, Laos, and Cambodia than had been used against Germany and Japan in World War II.

In Johnson's mind, the war often seemed a contest of wills between Beijing and Washington. In April 1965, he declared that "over this war—and all Asia—is another reality: the deepening shadow of Communist China." He believed that "the rulers of Hanoi are urged on by Peking" and that the "contest in Vietnam is part of a wider pattern" of Chinese aggression. China, he asserted a month later, had targeted "not merely South Vietnam, but all Asia." Vice-president Hubert Humphrey agreed, telling Senator George McGovern in 1965 that unless U.S. forces "stopped the Communists in Vietnam . . . they would take all of Asia."

American fears of Chinese expansion were greatly exaggerated. From 1960–65, China actively pursued foreign contacts, mostly among the newly emerging nations of Africa, and in Indonesia. It continued efforts, blocked by the United States, to enter the UN. In October 1964, China finally succeeded in testing an atomic bomb. In the fall of 1965, an article, issued under the name of China's top military leader and Mao's designated successor, Lin Biao, convinced many Americans of Beijing's hostile intent. "Long Live the Victory of the People's War" proclaimed China's support for revolutionary struggles throughout the Third World. Johnson and his top aides described Lin's article as an Asian "Mein Kampf," likening it to Hitler's blueprint for conquest. In fact, the article made clear that while China supported the concept of revolution, the resources, leadership, and bodies to carry it out would have to be found locally.

Besides this questionable reading of history, by 1965, China was about to undergo another violent internal spasm, the Cultural Revolution, which severely limited its power to influence outside events. That September, Mao's hopes for building ties to President Sukarno of Indonesia were dashed when a botched coup by Indonesian Communists provoked a seizure of power by Indonesia's conservative military. This reversal coincided with Mao's effort to revitalize China's revolutionary spirit, as well as his own authority, through his Great Proletarian Cultural Revolution. This chaotic effort to break down bureaucracy and spark a "permanent revolution" provoked conflicts within the Communist party and the government, on factory floors, and in rural communes. Initially, Mao sponsored youthful Red Guards as his vanguard to attack established institutions and push out entrenched bureaucrats. Eventually, Red Guard factions battled each other, and the military intervened to preserve a semblance of order. Foreign relations suffered enormously. Between 1965 and 1968, China recalled all but one of its ambassadors, while the Red Guards sacked the British legation in Beijing, torching the building and beating the chargé d'affairs.

As Mao and his inner circle struggled to keep China from flying apart, they viewed with mounting anxiety the American escalation in Vietnam. To Mao, American troops anywhere near China's borders posed a grave threat. The U.S. build-up in South Vietnam and the threat to the Communist North resembled in some ways the events of 1950 in Korea. In 1965, besides his determination to deter any threat to China, Mao had an additional incentive to assist North Vietnam: his conflict with the Soviet Union. Aiding Hanoi would demonstrate China's support for revolution in the Third World and would expose Soviet timidity.

Mao also felt compelled to respond to Johnson's campaign to recruit allied support for the war. The president actively encouraged military involvement by South Korea, the Philippines, Australia, and New Zealand. Sensing the president's determination to cultivate Asian support for the American war effort, Chiang, in the words of one historian, aggressively tried to link Taiwan's fortunes to those of South Vietnam. The Nationalist leader proposed coordinating attacks in south China with U.S. operations against North Vietnam. Although Washington rejected such a bold approach, it recruited Taiwanese commandos for covert operations in Vietnam, employed many Taiwanese military personnel in technical support roles, and relied heavily on Taiwanese ports, airfields, and repair facilities for use by American aircraft and vessels.

South Korean troops played an even larger supportive role in Vietnam. In 1965, the South Korean president declared it the moral duty of every Korean to "save his drowning friend." During the next several years, a total of nearly 300,000 South Korean soldiers (48,000 at any given time) served in South Vietnam. President Johnson agreed to pay handsomely for this show of support, transferring about $10 billion in cash and military aid to South Korea.

To counter the U.S. build-up in South Vietnam, beginning in 1965, China sent North Vietnam ground to air missiles, anti-aircraft artillery and crews, railroad equipment, mine sweepers, and construction troops. Between 1965 and 1968, a total of 320,000 Chinese troops served in North Vietnam, with up to 170,000 on duty at any given time. Of this total, about 1,100 died in the war, many from American bombs. Even though they did not participate in direct combat against the Americans, the presence of Chinese troops allowed North Vietnam to commit a larger percentage of its own forces to combat. The Soviet Union matched Chinese assistance to Hanoi by increasing its own aid levels, lest Ho move too close to the PRC.

China made little effort to conceal its military assistance to North Vietnam. In fact, PRC officials intentionally communicated it to the United States as a form of deterrence. During 1965, as Johnson made a series of fateful decisions to expand the war, Zhou Enlai and other Chinese officials signaled Washington through third country diplomats that the "Chinese people will not stand idly by" in the face of aggression. The Chinese "message" to Johnson was clear. Beijing did not seek war with America, but it would honor its commitments to Hanoi and would deploy combat troops if the United States either bombed Chinese territory or invaded or threatened the survival of North Vietnam.

The message resonated in Washington. When President Johnson discussed escalation with the JCS in the spring of 1965, he asked whether his sending several hundred thousand troops to South Vietnam "won't cause Russia and China to come in." The Army Chief of Staff, General Harold Johnson, responded that he did not think so. Recalling the events of 1950, the president retorted "MacArthur didn't think they would come into Korea either."

Several times during the next two years, American representatives in Warsaw communicated to Chinese diplomats that the United States had no intention of destroying North Vietnam or attacking China. Chinese officials made it clear that as long as American forces observed these tacit limits, Beijing would restrain its intervention on behalf of North Vietnam. By inducing this concern at the highest level of American policy deliberation, China exercised indirect but critical limits on the escalation of the war in Vietnam.

Even while the Johnson administration expanded the war and tried to divine Chinese intentions, other influential Americans articulated a different view of China. Senator J. William Fulbright, chairman of the Senate Foreign Relations Committee, held hearings in 1964 and again in 1966 that provided a public forum for dissenting views on the PRC. In 1964, Fulbright himself endorsed a policy of "competitive co-existence" with China. Secretary of State Rusk denied the possibility of peacefully coexisting with Maoist China as long as it aided Hanoi and claimed the right to use force against Taiwan. The president, furious at Fulbright for questioning his policy, declared that "it is not we who must examine our view of China. It is the Chinese Communists who must re-examine their view of the world."

Two years later, after Johnson had dispatched several hundred thousand troops to Vietnam, Fulbright convened another round of Senate hearings on China policy. He gave the platform to a group of academic experts, such as A. Doak Barnett and John K. Fairbank, who spoke passionately in favor of positively engaging China. Fulbright characterized their views as "containment without isolation." With so many respected scholars, journalists, and other policy experts calling loudly for a reassessment of policy, Rusk announced that the State Department would permit scientific, cultural, and academic exchanges between private citizens, both American and Chinese. In 1967, the administration announced more liberal rules to permit the export of pharmaceuticals to China. The next year, it offered to give entry visas to Chinese journalists wishing to report on the presidential election.

None of these "atmospheric" moves had much impact. Until the spring of 1968, the war in Vietnam overshadowed everything else U.S. officials said or did regarding China. On the last day of January 1968, after three years of massive American intervention, the Viet Cong launched the surprise Tet Offensive. Although militarily inconclusive, the countrywide attacks dashed all hope of a quick U.S. victory. At the end of March, a despondent President Johnson announced he would cap force levels in Vietnam, seek a negotiated settlement, and not stand for reelection. Without formally saying so, Beijing acknowledged the receding American threat by reducing its own military assistance to North Vietnam.

Even though Mao viewed the Soviet Union as an emerging and primary enemy, the continued presence of half a million American troops on China's southern border represented the greatest external threat faced by the PRC. China dismissed as gimmicks Washington's offers to sell it medical supplies and to validate visas for private visits. In May 1968, declaring that as long as the United States remained allied to Taiwan "there is nothing to talk about," Beijing suspended the periodic Warsaw discussions. Only after Washington changed course in Vietnam and agreed to leave Taiwan—or when China perceived the Soviets as a paramount threat–did there appear to be any likelihood for improved Sino–American relations.

SELECTED ADDITIONAL READINGS

Robert Accinelli, *Crisis and Commitment: United States Policy toward Taiwan, 1950–1955* (Chapel Hill, N.C., 1996); Odd Arne Westad, ed., *Brothers in Arms: The Rise and Fall of the Sino–Soviet Alliance, 1945–1963* (Washington, D.C., 1999); Rosemary Foot, *The Practice of Power: U.S. Relations with China since 1949* (New York, 1995); Thomas Christensen, *Useful Adversaries: Grand Strategy, Domestic Mobilization, and Sino–American Conflict, 1947–1958* (Princeton, N.J., 1996); John W. Garver, *The Sino–American Alliance: Nationalist China and American*

Cold War Strategy in Asia (Armonk, N.Y., 1997); Nancy B. Tucker, ed., *China Confidential: American Diplomats and Sino–American Relations, 1945–1996* (New York, 2001), and, *Taiwan, Hong Kong, and the United States, 1945–1992: Uncertain Friendships* (New York, 1994); Gordon Chang, *Friends and Enemies: The United States, China, and the Soviet Union, 1948–1972* (Stanford, Calif., 1990); Nancy B. Tucker and Warren I. Cohen, eds., *Lyndon Johnson Confronts the World, American Foreign Policy, 1963–68* (New York, 1994); Diane B. Kunz, ed., *Diplomacy of the Crucial Decade: American Foreign Policy during the 1960s* (New York, 1994); Richard Immerman, *John Foster Dulles: Piety, Pragmatism and Power in U.S. Foreign Policy* (Wilmington, Del., 1996); Stanley D. Bachrack, *The Committee of One Million: China Lobby Politics, 1953–71* (New York, 1976); John L. Gaddis, *Strategies of Containment* (New York, 1982); Michael Schaller, *Altered States: The U.S. and Japan Since the Occupation* (New York, 1997); John L. Lewis and Xue Litai, *China Builds the Bomb* (Stanford, Calif., 1988); Qiang Zhai, *China and the Vietnam Wars, 1950–1975* (Chapel Hill, N.C., 2000), and, *The Dragon, The Lion, and the Eagle: Chinese–British–American Relations, 1949–58* (Kent, Ohio, 1990); Chen Jian, *Mao's China and the Cold War* (Chapel Hill, N.C., 2001); Kai Bird, *The Color of Truth: McGeorge Bundy and William Bundy, Brothers in Arms: A Biography* (New York, 1998); Allen Whiting, *The Chinese Calculus of Deterrence: India and Indochina* (Ann Arbor, Mich., 1975); Zhang Shu Guan, *Deterrence and Strategic Culture: Chinese–American Confrontations, 1949–1958* (Ithaca, N.Y., 1992); Robert Schulzinger, *A Time for War: The United States and Vietnam, 1941–1975* (New York, 1997).

NINE

"Only Nixon Could Go to China"

Sino–American Détente, 1969–1974

During 1968, American policy in Asia seemed to hit bottom. The bloody Tet Offensive and its aftermath (more U.S. troops died during 1968 than in any year of the war in Southeast Asia) underlined the failure of the U.S. military to subdue Communist forces in Vietnam. The stalemate fueled dissent among American "hawks" and "doves" alike. After three years of predicting victory, President Johnson had to cap force levels, abandon plans to run for reelection, and seek a negotiated settlement. A war fought to demonstrate America's ability to contain Asian communism had, like the Korean conflict, ended up shattering the Democratic party and enhancing the stature of revolutionary leaders in Asia. By supplying critical support to North Vietnam, China could claim some of the credit for humbling "U.S. imperialism." Mao even urged Ho Chi Minh to reject Johnson's call for peace talks (advice Ho ignored) and to push for quick military victory. The Chinese leader brushed aside a belated call from the Johnson administration to resume diplomatic contact in Warsaw, declaring that the U.S. and PRC had "nothing to talk about."

Richard Nixon's election as president in November 1968 seemed to bode even worse. Although he campaigned on a promise to achieve "peace with honor," since the 1950s, he had called for expanding the military commitment to Vietnam and blamed China for most of Asia's problems. While debating Kennedy in 1960, he had declared: "Now what do the Chinese Communists want? They don't just want Quemoy and Matsu. They don't just want Formosa (Taiwan). They want the world." Nixon later accused both Kennedy and Johnson of not using enough force to prevail in Vietnam or to contain China.

However, Nixon hinted at new thinking in private talks with American diplomats in 1965–66 and in an article he published in October 1967 in the influential policy journal, *Foreign Affairs*. Under the heading "Asia after Vietnam," the future president spoke of the need to give strong support to anti-Communist allies in Asia and reaffirmed his opposition to recognizing or trading with the PRC. Washington must "persuade China that it must change: that it cannot satisfy its imperialistic ambitions." But, he added, in the long run the United States "cannot afford to leave China forever outside the family of nations, there to nurture its fantasies, cherish its hates and threaten its neighbors. There is no place on this small planet for a billion of its potentially most able people to live in angry isolation." Mao Zedong reportedly read a translation of the article and commented to Zhou Enlai that if Nixon became the next U.S. president, he might change policy toward China. Meanwhile, the expanding war in Vietnam dimmed prospects for a new dialogue.

China's major state-controlled newspapers, Renmin ribao (People's Daily) and Hong Qi (Red Flag), ridiculed the new president as the "jittery chieftain" of "U.S. imperialists." In a joint editorial, the two papers described Nixon's inaugural address of January 20, 1969, as a confession that American imperialists were "beset with profound crises both at home and abroad." Despite condemning Nixon and Johnson as "jackals of the same lair," the Communist press did something unprecedented: they published Nixon's speech in its entirety alongside their denunciations. Unknown to the new administration, Mao ordered the papers to print the speech because he liked Nixon's pledge to seek an "open world—open to ideas, open to the exchange of goods and people—a world in which no people, great or small, will live in angry isolation." At the time, however, no one in Washington picked up this signal.

If America's Asian policy lay in tatters as Nixon took office, China's situation, at home and abroad, was scarcely more favorable. The United States, although clearly hoping to exit Vietnam, still had half a million troops on China's southwestern border. To the south, the military standoff between Taiwan and the PRC continued. China's western frontier with India had remained tense since the border war of 1962. To the east, the specter of an increasingly powerful and assertive Japan rekindled fears among Chinese.

But the greatest external challenge came from the Soviet Union, which shared a 4,500-mile-long ill-defined frontier with China. Sino–Soviet hostility had grown steadily worse since 1958. The trend continued unchanged after 1964, when Leonid Brezhnev replaced Khrushchev. By 1965, Beijing and Moscow called each other "traitors" to true communism and began to deploy large military units along their border. Even before large-scale fighting began in March 1969, Mao considered the Soviet Union as the single greatest threat to his own leadership and to China's security.

Although hostility toward the United States had been an underlying theme in Chinese foreign policy since 1949, gradually the fear of what Mao called Soviet "social imperialism" displaced American "capitalist imperialism" as the chief enemy. When Soviet troops invaded Czechoslovakia in August 1968 to depose a liberal Communist regime that rejected Moscow's leadership, Mao considered it a portent of what the Soviet Union had in mind for China.

To make matters worse, if the United States really did negotiate its way out of Vietnam and, as Nixon promised, reduced its future military commitments in Asia, how could China alone possibly contain Soviet social imperialism? To preserve his tattered revolution and China's heritage, Mao saw no alternative but to follow a classic Chinese strategy. "Think about it this way," he told his physician in August 1969. "We have the Soviet Union to the north and the west, India to the south, and Japan to the east." What could China do if these enemies united against it? "Beyond Japan is the United States. Didn't our ancestors counsel negotiating with faraway countries while fighting with those that are near?" In spite of his criticism of old ways, Mao revived the idea of "using barbarians to fight barbarians."

At the same time as these external challenges multiplied, China faced bitter internal divisions. The Great Proletarian Cultural Revolution, launched in 1965–66, not only crushed Mao's domestic rivals, it also wrecked the economy and sowed chaos in cities, factories, the countryside, and on university campuses. By 1968, Mao was using the army to suppress the young Red Guard activists he had mobilized to drive his enemies from power.

The border dispute with the Soviets turned deadly in March 1969. When the "near barbarians" attacked, Mao reached out for help from the "faraway barbarians." Fortunately for Mao, the "faraway barbarians" in Washington had resolved to open a dialogue with China.

THE IMPACT OF SINO-SOVIET BORDER FIGHTING

On March 2, 1969, following shouting matches and fist fights between Chinese and Soviet border guards (as well as incidents in which Chinese troops dropped their trousers and "mooned" the Soviets—only to have their bare bottoms greeted by photos of Chairman Mao displayed by the Russians), a Chinese security unit on tiny Zhenbao Island in the Ussuri River attacked a Soviet patrol, killing thirty soldiers. The Soviets retaliated two weeks later with an artillery barrage that killed about 800 Chinese.

When Soviet Premier Alexi Kosygin tried to place a call to Mao to discuss the violence, a Chinese operator shouted "you are a revisionist and therefore I will not connect you." On August 13, after many small skirmishes, the Soviets escalated the violence with a large-scale attack in Xinjiang, in northwestern China, which destroyed an entire Chinese brigade in an area not far from China's nuclear weapons test site. The PRC leadership pondered whether the Soviet escalation was a pretext for a major attack or, equally dangerous, might simply spiral out of control.

In this context, Mao asked four senior military commanders who had been sidelined during the Cultural Revolution, to undertake a study of the Soviet threat. Marshals Chen Yi, Ye Jiangying, Xu Xiangqian, and Nie Rongzen deliberated from March through September. In a series of reports to Mao, they concluded that the Soviets probably did not intend to wage a full-scale war against China, but stressed the need to be prepared for a worst-case scenario. Unaware that Mao had modified his own views, the marshals apologized for their "unconventional thoughts," especially the idea that to resist the Soviet threat, the PRC should play the "card of the United States." China should consider initiating "Sino–American talks at the ministerial or even higher levels, so that basic . . . problems in Sino–American relations can be solved." Chen Yi believed that Washington would not want to see Beijing either subdued by or re-allied to Moscow. China could, in Marxist terms, intensify the "contradiction" between the U.S.S.R. and the United States by arranging a "breakthrough" in Sino–American relations.

Even before the shooting began, in February 1969, Zhou Enlai seized on these concerns to convince Mao to resume the Warsaw talks between the United States and Chinese diplomats. However, shortly before the first scheduled meeting, a Chinese diplomat in the Netherlands defected to the United States. When the U.S. government refused to return him, Chinese hardliners, including Defense Minister Lin Biao and Mao's wife, Jiang

Qing, persuaded Mao to cancel the talks. The border fighting, however, created a new urgency for dialogue.

In Washington, both President Richard Nixon and his National Security Adviser, Henry Kissinger, were thinking in general ways about improving ties with China. Prior to the Sino–Soviet border clashes of March through August, however, they had not set out actual policy goals. In fact, at least until August 1969, the administration remained wary of China and placed a higher priority on improving relations with Moscow. Nixon and Kissinger believed that by improving ties with the Soviet Union, they could get the Russians to pressure North Vietnam to compromise on a settlement and also achieve nuclear arms control agreements with Moscow. In fact, when Nixon announced plans on March 14, 1969, to deploy a limited antimissile defense system, he justified it with the argument that neither the United States nor the Soviet Union desired to "stand naked against a potential Chinese Communist threat." Since Beijing had no missiles capable of reaching the United States (and would have none for another decade), China's press called this plan evidence of an "evil" conspiracy between the Americans and Soviets aimed at "nuclear blackmail" against the PRC.

U.S. diplomats and intelligence personnel were uncertain of what the Soviets or Chinese were up to along their border. Leaders in both countries, they surmised, might be provoking the border clashes to mobilize their publics for other purposes. American experts speculated that China instigated most of the incidents to deter the Soviets from attacking. But if Chinese "tactics were designed to deter wider conflict," these policymakers worried, they might "in fact bring it on."

Anxiety about a wider war increased during the summer of 1969, when Soviet officials dropped hints of an impending attack and asked whether Washington would tacitly support Moscow. For example, the Soviet ambassador, Anatoly Dobrynin, told a U.S. official that China was everybody's problem, but there was limited time to act jointly against it. The two superpowers "may not have this power much longer," he warned. Another Soviet diplomat asked his American counterpart if Washington "would be pleased if the Soviet Union and China fought one another." In August, following the attack in Xinjiang, another Soviet official asked how the Nixon administration would respond to a strike against China's nuclear weapons complex. He urged U.S. support, since the attack would "eliminate" the Chinese nuclear threat "for decades" and "weaken and discredit the Mao clique." These probes coincided with rumors that Nixon and Kissinger were mulling over a "deal" in which the United States would "allow" or even cooperate with a Soviet attack on Chinese nuclear weapons facilities in return for Soviet help in ending the Vietnam War.

It is difficult to know if high-ranking American policymakers gave serious consideration to backing Soviet moves. At the same time as Moscow sought American support, Nixon took his first positive moves in China's direction. On July 21, the president approved a policy change to allow American scholars, scientists, and journalists to receive passports to travel to China. Although this had little practical value, it marked the first relaxation in travel restrictions in twenty years. A few days later, while traveling in the Pacific, the president spelled out what he called the "Nixon Doctrine." Once the Vietnam War ended, he declared, the United States would not use its own troops to fight in local Asian wars. Although he still considered China a "threat to peace," he noted that China's internal problems made it "less effective in exporting revolution."

As Kissinger later explained, U.S. reconciliation with China would reduce Indochina "to its proper scale—a small peninsula on a major continent." The "drama" of opening ties with the PRC would help "erase for the American people the pain that would inevitably accompany our withdrawal from Southeast Asia." As both Kissinger and Nixon realized, popular excitement over "finding China" might mitigate any political backlash from "losing Vietnam."

By August, Nixon had given up hope that the Soviets would or could pressure North Vietnam into making peace. This led the administration to pursue the "China card" more actively. In an August 1 conversation with Pakistani President Yahya Khan, Kissinger asked Khan (who had an ambassador in Beijing) to inform Zhou Enlai that the United States sought an accommodation with China. In late September, when Soviet Foreign Minister Andrei Gromyko visited the UN, Nixon told Kissinger, "I think while Gromyko is in the country would be a very good time to have another move to China made."

In August, a Chinese Communist official in Hong Kong had mentioned to an American journalist that if Washington really wanted to show its interest in improving relations, it should "withdraw its forces from the Taiwan Strait." In October, Nixon and Kissinger decided to signal Beijing of their serious purpose by ordering an end to U.S. naval patrols in the Taiwan Strait. They sent word to China through Pakistan that the cessation of the patrols was designed to facilitate bilateral talks. Early in December, Ambassador Walter Stoessel in Warsaw literally chased down Chinese diplomat Lei Yang at, of all things, a Yugoslav fashion show, and informed him that Nixon wanted "serious, concrete talks" with Beijing. China responded on December 7 by releasing from captivity two Americans who had accidentally sailed their yacht into Chinese waters in February 1969. Three days later, Lei Yang invited Ambassador Stoessel to visit him for the first of several informal conversations.

Stoessel did most of the talking during the December and January meetings. He explained that Nixon was willing to send a "special representative " to Beijing or to receive a Chinese envoy in Washington. The United States hoped for a peaceful resolution to Taiwan's status and would "oppose any offensive military action from Taiwan against the mainland." The more rapidly the Vietnam War ended and tensions in the region subsided, Stoessel added, the sooner the United States would "reduce those facilities on Taiwan that we now have." These "informal exchanges" led to two formal rounds of ambassadorial talks in January and February 1970. The Chinese announced at the latter meeting that "if the U.S. government wishes to send a representative of ministerial rank or a special envoy of the U.S. president to Beijing for further exploration of questions of fundamental principle between China and the United States, the Chinese government will be willing to receive him."

The Soviets picked up enough information about these exchanges for Ambassador Dobrynin to warn Kissinger that Washington should "not use China as a military threat" against Moscow. Kissinger, of course, took this as proof that the approach toward China was, as hoped, providing the United States with added leverage over the Soviet Union. Although it took more than a year to arrange a visit to Beijing, it seemed that for the first time in twenty years, the United States and China were reading from the same script.

Between March 1970 and the spring of 1971, Sino–American relations seemed to take one step back for every step forward. Through Pakistani and Romanian intermediaries, Nixon proposed that the White House and China's leaders "open a direct channel of communication," which the president would keep secret. Zhou Enlai quickly realized that Nixon intended to "adopt the method of the [American–Vietnamese] negotiations in Paris, and let Kissinger make the contact." In fact, during 1970–71, the White House cut the State Department out of the China policy loop, giving Kissinger full responsibility and sidelining specialists who might outshine the president and his aide.

But just as a breakthrough seemed imminent, external events derailed progress. In April 1970, pro–American elements in Cambodia overthrew Prince Sihanouk, a Chinese ally. In May, American troops invaded Cambodia in a campaign to destroy Communist base areas. Mao responded by postponing further talks in Warsaw and calling for "the people of the world to unite and defeat the U.S. aggressors and all their running dogs." This language so offended Nixon that the president considered sending a U.S. naval flotilla to the China coast—until Kissinger talked him out of it. Despite the ruffled feathers, Mao kept communication lines open through gestures such as the July 10, 1970, release of Bishop James Walsh, an American cleric imprisoned in China as a spy since 1958.

More than the temporary escalation of the Vietnam War, however, slowed the improvement of China's ties with the United States. From the summer of 1970 through September 1971, Mao engaged in a power struggle with Defense Minister Lin Biao, his designated heir. Lin and his followers opposed any reconciliation with the United States, advocating, instead, either a continued hard line toward both superpowers or a compromise with Moscow. Before Mao could push through an alternative policy, he needed time to build a consensus and isolate his erstwhile disciple and rival.

In the fall of 1970, Mao felt confident enough about his position to signal Nixon. In the 1930s, Mao had spoken to the outside world through a young American journalist, Edgar Snow, who passed through the KMT blockade to enter Communist territory. Snow's book, *Red Star Over China*, remains a classic account of the Chinese revolution. Snow had visited China several times after 1949, writing favorable accounts of the PRC. Since 1965, however, Chinese officials had rebuffed his efforts to return. In August, Mao invited Snow, who then lived in Switzerland, to visit China. On October 1, 1970, the journalist stood next to Mao at Tiananmen Square to review the National Day parade in Beijing. A picture of the two standing together appeared on the front page of Chinese newspapers. This was intended as a signal to Nixon, as well as to the Chinese public, of an imminent policy change toward the United States.

According to Mao's physician, the chairman labored under the illusion that Snow sometimes worked for the CIA, guaranteeing that he could serve as a conduit to Nixon. In fact, in 1970, Snow had little influence and few professional connections in the United States. Nevertheless, when they met, Mao told his old biographer that he would welcome a visit by Nixon "as president or as a tourist." He wondered aloud why the president had delayed coming to China. Mao even suggested how Nixon could defuse conservative criticism of such a trip, by "trumpeting his purpose as winning over China so as to fix the Soviet Union."

Although Snow did not publish this interview for several months, Nixon quickly learned of Mao's invitation. Still, the president delayed respond-

Mao Zedong invites his "old friend," American journalist Edgar Snow, to join him on Tiananmen on China's national holiday, October 1, 1970. (Chinese government photograph)

ing. Republicans did poorly in the November 1970 congressional election, and Nixon hesitated to alienate his conservative base. He became especially concerned in December when Zhou Enlai sent word through an intermediary that China would insist that an envoy "discuss the subject" of the vacating "Chinese territory called Taiwan" by U.S. forces. Clearly, differences over Taiwan remained a major impediment to any presidential visit.

During the first months of 1971, Washington and Beijing continued to probe each others' intentions through public statements and messages delivered by intermediaries. Nixon raised the China issue in a speech in March. For the first time since 1949, an American president called China by its formal name, the People's Republic of China, and admitted he hoped to "establish a dialogue" with the PRC. Nixon explained that Washington no longer sought to "impose on China an international position that denies its legitimate national interests." He followed this by lifting some trade and travel restrictions on China dating from the Korean War.

In April, Chinese and American leaders found a serendipitous but effective way to build public support for their dialogue. At a table tennis tournament in Nagoya, Japan, members of the Chinese and American teams spontaneously began speaking and exchanging gifts. When U.S. players mentioned their interest in visiting China, top officials in Beijing decided that the timing was "not yet mature." On April 6, however, Mao suddenly ordered the Foreign Ministry to "invite the American team to visit China." The White House quickly approved the travel plans.

Although the outclassed American players lost their exhibition matches, the Chinese press and public showered the visiting athletes with affection. This genuine enthusiasm convinced Mao and his allies that the Chinese masses would back an opening to the United States. On April 14, at a reception for both teams, Zhou Enlai announced that "your visit has opened a new chapter in the history of the relations between Chinese and American peoples." Just hours later, Nixon ordered termination of additional restrictions on trade with China. So-called Ping-Pong Diplomacy had broken two decades of isolation.

The cascade of favorable publicity provided by American television networks traveling with the ping-pong team convinced Nixon that the American people, too, would support a new China policy. He jokingly asked Kissinger and his aides whether they had "learned to play ping-pong yet." Only Vice-president Spiro Agnew rained on the parade. In a critique that mirrored Lin Biao's opposition to Mao, Agnew complained bitterly to a group of reporters about their favorable coverage of the ping-pong team's visit to China. If Americans had to live in the kind of houses common in China, he snapped, liberals would call it "oppression of the poor." Nixon, who already considered scratching Agnew from the 1972 ticket, complained that the vice-president was too dense to understand "the big picture in this whole Chinese operation, which is, of course, the Russian game. We're using the Chinese thaw to get the Russians shook."

On April 27, the White House received a message from Zhou transmitted via Pakistan. It repeated the invitation to receive Nixon or Kissinger, but dropped the demand that withdrawal of U.S. forces from Taiwan was a precondition and focal point of discussion. Although China insisted that establishing formal diplomatic relations would require the United States to cut ties to Taiwan, the island's status could merely be one of several issues raised. On June 2, Beijing clarified its position further. Zhou sent word through Pakistan that Mao had approved a secret visit, in which Kissinger and Zhou could freely raise "principle issues of concern" to either party. For the Chinese, this would include the "withdrawal of all U.S. armed forces from Taiwan and the Taiwan Strait area." The American side could bring its own issues to the table. Elated, Nixon and Kissinger described this message as "the most important communication that has come to an American president since the end of World War II."

The president characterized the invitation as the result of "fundamental shifts in the world balance of power [that] made it in both [nations'] interest to have relations." In a paraphrase of Mao's remarks to his physician, Nixon asserted that China, "faced by the Soviets on one side, a Soviet-backed India on another," and a resurgent Japan that could "develop [military power] fast because of its industrial base," sought protection from the United States. Mao and Zhou still demanded that "the U.S. should get out of the Pacific" but, Nixon surmised, they really "don't want that."

Nixon predicted that as American military strength in Asia inevitably diminished, Japan would "either go with the Soviets or re-arm," two bad alternatives from China's perspective. Soon after receiving Zhou's invitation (but before Kissinger went to Beijing), Nixon predicted that, with American prodding, Mao and Zhou would agree that a continued U.S. military presence in Japan, Korea, and Southeast Asia was "China's [best] hope for Jap restraint."

On July 9, while visiting Pakistan, Kissinger feigned stomach trouble, dropped out of sight, and flew in a Pakistani airliner to Beijing. As he and his small staff (including John Holdridge and Winston Lord) were driven to a state guest house, veteran diplomat Huang Hua asked Holdridge for assurance that the American envoy would not snub Zhou as John Foster Dulles had at Geneva in 1954. Zhou had nothing to worry about. Kissinger found what he considered a "soulmate" in the urbane prime minister and called him "one of the two or three most impressive men I have ever met." Zhou was more restrained, praising Kissinger as "very intelligent—indeed a Doctor."

The two men conferred for seventeen hours over two and one-half days. In his published account of the talks, Kissinger attributed his success to that fact that he offered Zhou the single thing motivating China—"strategic reassurance, some easing of their nightmare of hostile encirclement." As a gesture of good will, he provided intelligence data on Soviet military deployment along China's border. Zhou, Kissinger reported, made a pro forma demand that the Americans abandon Taiwan, pull out of South Viet-

Nixon's National Security Adviser, Henry Kissinger, meets secretly in Beijing with Chinese Premier Zhou Enlai, July 1971. (National Archives)

nam, and cease assisting a "militaristic Japan." But over lunch, Zhou reportedly assured Kissinger that these were minor irritants.

In fact, the American envoy opened the talks by making several concessions on issues of concern to China. Kissinger declared the United States would reduce its military presence in and around Taiwan as relations with the PRC improved and the Vietnam War ended. Meanwhile, Washington would not support a policy of two Chinas, a one China-one Taiwan policy, or an independent Taiwan. It would also oppose any attack by Taiwan against China. Finally, Kissinger revealed that Nixon intended to formally recognize the PRC, and cut links to Taiwan, following his reelection.

When Zhou briefed Mao on the discussion, the chairman commented that it naturally took time for a monkey to evolve into a human being. The Americans were now at the ape stage, "with a tail, though a much shorter one, in his back." In light of this forward movement, Mao decided, "we are not in a hurry on the Taiwan issue." After some nimble redrafting, the two sides issued a statement for release by the president after Kissinger's return. It declared that: "Knowing of President Nixon's expressed desire to visit" China, Zhou had issued an invitation for him to visit before May

1972, to seek the "normalization of relations" and to "exchange views on questions of concern to the two sides."

When Nixon learned of the agreement, he mused to his chief of staff, H. R. Haldeman, that in politics "everything turns around." The Chinese "made a deal with us" due to "concern regarding the Soviets," their former ally. He (Nixon) had "fought the battle for Chiang" on Taiwan since the 1950s and had always "taken the line that we stand by the South Koreans . . . by the South Vietnamese, etc." How "ironic" that a conservative like himself was the "one to move in the other direction."

Nixon predicted that cooperation between the United States and China would "shatter old alignments." The "pressure on Japan," formerly America's closest Asian ally, might even push it toward an "alliance with the Soviets." Certainly, Moscow would try to redress the balance of power by "moving to Japan and India." Washington would have to "reassure its Pacific allies that we are not changing our policy" nor selling out friends "behind their backs." They, like the American public, must understand that although there was "validity ten years ago to play the free nations of Asia against China," the United States could now "play a more effective role with China rather than without."

Zhou Enlai's geopolitical outlook closely paralleled that voiced by Nixon and Kissinger. Although he rebuffed Kissinger's suggestion that China press North Vietnam to agree to a compromise, immediately after Kissinger left Beijing, the Chinese premier conferred with North Vietnamese leaders. He argued that improved Sino–American relations would stabilize Asia and, ultimately, enhance Hanoi's security. The Vietnamese rejected this notion, complaining that China had "thrown a life buoy to Nixon, who almost had been drowned." Even though a year passed before a tentative peace was agreed to in Vietnam, all sides recognized that China now placed a higher priority on cooperation with Washington than on assisting Hanoi.

Nixon announced the China opening in a televised speech on July 15. The American public, weary of Asian confrontations, responded with great enthusiasm. In private, Democrats brooded about Nixon, the old Cold Warrior who had accused Truman of "losing China," scoring points by rebuilding ties to the PRC. Publicly, however, they could do little more than praise his actions. Conservatives seemed stunned by the turnaround, but focused their attention on protecting Taiwan. Nixon convinced California Governor Ronald Reagan, the rising star of the Republican right, that it made sense to work with the Chinese Communists, since it provided ammunition to use against the more threatening Soviet Communists.

He even persuaded Reagan to travel to Taiwan as his representative to explain matters.

Most politically informed Americans realized that an improvement in relations with Beijing would put pressure on Hanoi to agree to a settlement of the war in Vietnam, would give the United States continued influence in Asia after a withdrawal from Vietnam, and might compel Japan to modify what many Americans saw as its aggressive trade policy.

As the U.S. trade deficit with Japan ballooned in the early 1970s, a member of the Nixon cabinet told journalists that "the Japanese are still fighting the war, only now instead of a shooting war it is an economic war. Their immediate intention is to try to dominate the Pacific and then perhaps the world." The president himself complained at one point that the Japanese were "all over Asia, like a bunch of lice." Nixon and his staff often mentioned that a key benefit of improved ties with China would be less dependence on Japan as a strategic Asian ally and a freer hand to press Japan to limit exports, raise the value of the yen, and reduce trade barriers. Furious at Japan's repeated delays in enacting promised trade reform, Nixon made a point of keeping his China policy secret from Tokyo. He purposely gave Prime Minister Sato Eisaku only a few minutes advance notice of his announcement of his impending trip in order, he claimed, to "stick it to Japan."

China, with its own bitter memories of Japan's wartime aggression and growing anxiety about its neighbor's economic strength and possible designs on Southeast Asia, shared Nixon's sentiments. Beijing saw cooperation with Washington as a way to contain *both* the current Soviet threat and a potential Japanese challenge. Stunned by the sudden change in American China policy, as well as by the president's action a month later to devalue the dollar and impose special taxes on imports, the Japanese described themselves as victims of "Nixon shocks." In the opinion of Japanese leaders, the "Nixon administration was thinking about the possibility of using Communist China as a counterweight to Japan in post-Vietnam Asia." Just as Nixon and Kissinger relied on triangular diplomacy to influence Soviet behavior, the Americans seemed to be "playing a kind of China card to Japan."

During the seven months between Kissinger's initial trip to China in July 1971 and Nixon's arrival there in February 1972, Sino–American détente evolved quickly. In September 1971, after Mao identified Lin Biao as the leader of a "plot," the defense minister's son, Lin Liguo, attempted to assassinate Mao. When the attack failed, both Lins boarded a plane, on September 13, and tried to flee to the Soviet Union. The aircraft crashed in Mongolia, killing all on board. Lin's demise discredited opponents of détente and allowed Zhou Enlai, the foremost advocate of this approach to the United States, to reemerge as Mao's chief deputy.

In October, Kissinger visited China a second time. To build mutual confidence, he provided the Chinese with additional intelligence information on Soviet forces gathered by U.S. satellites. While Kissinger shared secret military data in Beijing, the United Nations disregarded a half-hearted American plea to keep a place for Taiwan in the organization. It voted, instead, to seat the PRC as the sole representative of China.

In other signs of changing Asian alignments, in November 1971, North Vietnamese Premier Pham Van Dong pleaded with Mao Zedong to defer his meeting with Nixon. The Chinese leader, who only three years before had urged Hanoi to spurn peace talks with Washington and push for a military victory, rebuffed the plea. Instead, he told Pham to negotiate the best deal he could with the Americans, even if it meant leaving the South Vietnamese regime in place. At the end of the year, when war erupted on the Indian subcontinent, Washington and Beijing agreed on a "tilt," as Kissinger put it, in support of Pakistan, while Moscow backed India.

THE NIXON VISIT TO CHINA

Both to minimize jet lag and maximize press coverage, Nixon's flight to China was scheduled over a three-day period, with arrival on February 21, 1972. During the lengthy trip, Kissinger suggested several ways the president might "bond" with Mao. Nixon should "treat him as an emperor," but stress that he, like Mao, were both "men of the people" who had "problems with intellectuals." In reality, comparing Nixon's visceral dislike for liberal politicians and journalists to Mao's massive persecution of his critics was preposterous.

In notes to himself, Nixon speculated that the Chinese leadership favored meeting him to "build up their world credentials," speed unification with Taiwan, and "get the U.S. out of Asia." He hoped the summit would speed a settlement in Vietnam and restrain future "Chicom expansion." Both he and Mao wanted a stable Asia and "restraint on U.S.S.R."

On February 21, 1972, Nixon walked down the stairway of his plane at Beijing's airport to shake the hand of Zhou Enlai. Ushered into Mao's presence a few hours later, he spoke eloquently of his own journey from anticommunism to China. What brought him to this meeting was "recognition of a new situation in the world and a recognition on our part that what is important is not a nation's internal political philosophy. What is important

President Richard Nixon meets his old enemy, Chairman Mao Zedong, in Beijing, 1972. (National Archives)

in its policy towards the rest of the world and towards us." Both China and America worried about Soviet behavior and the future of Japan. Why, he asked rhetorically, did the Soviets have "more forces on the border facing you" than facing Western Europe? Sino–American differences over Taiwan, Korea, and Indochina paled in comparison.

In their talks with Zhou Enlai, Nixon and Kissinger stressed a common interest in maintaining a balance of power by "restraining" Russian expansion. The president promised not to make any deals with Moscow aimed at China, to treat China as an equal, and to inform the PRC about any military agreements reached with the Soviets. The Americans would avoid any deals with the Soviet Union in Europe or the Middle East that might "free [Moscow's] hand" for expansion in Asia.

Nixon and Kissinger responded to Chinese criticism of the U.S.–Japan security treaty by asking their hosts to ponder the alternative—a Japan completely uncoupled from its American anchor. "Do we tell the second most prosperous nation to go it alone—or do we provide a shield?" Nixon asked Zhou. Was not a "U.S. Japan policy with a U.S. veto" less dangerous than a "Japan only policy?" If America had no security treaty with Japan (or no military bases in the Philippines and South Korea), Nixon argued, our "remonstrations would be like empty cannon, and the wild horse of Japan would not be controlled." All but calling the U.S.–Japan security treaty a scheme to keep the threatening Japanese genie bottled up, the president told Zhou that the American pact with Japan "is in your interest, not against it."

Nixon referred to Taiwan and Vietnam as minor "irritants" between the United States and China that could be solved gradually, perhaps through some sort of trade-off. He repeated his support for "one China," with Taiwan a part, which he hoped would be peacefully reunited with the mainland. He could not make a "secret deal" that violated the U.S. commitment to Taiwan, but said "I know our interests required normalization" of relations. He promised to establish diplomatic ties, presumably by cutting links to Taiwan, after his expected reelection in 1972.

In banquet toasts on February 27, Nixon and Zhou pledged to oppose efforts by any country (meaning the Soviet Union) to establish hegemony (dominance) in the Asia–Pacific region. Finessing Taiwan's status presented more of a problem. In the original wording of a joint communiqué, Kissinger noted that Washington intended to honor existing commitments to Japan, the Philippines, South Korea, Australia, and New Zealand—but made no reference to Taiwan. State Department officials traveling with Nixon demanded the inclusion of Taiwan. Kissinger reluctantly reopened discussion with the Chinese, who refused to accept such wording. Nixon finally agreed to drop references to all U.S. defense commitments in the Pacific, thereby not singling out Taiwan. The Shanghai Communiqué of February 28, 1972, affirmed America's support for a "peaceful settlement of the Taiwan question by the Chinese themselves" and its promise to "progressively reduce" U.S. forces on the island "as tension in the area diminishes." There was "but one China," Nixon acknowledged and "Taiwan is part of China." The communiqué contained a brief reference to America's chief Asian ally: "The United States places the highest value on its friendly relations with Japan" and would continue to "develop the existing close bonds." The Chinese repeated their opposition to the U.S.–Japan security treaty, condemned "the revival and outward expansion of Japanese militarism" and endorsed "the Japanese people's desire to build an independent, democratic, peaceful and neutral Japan."

In the year that followed Nixon's visit, his China initiative helped the president achieve three major goals: arms control with the Soviets, a cease-fire in Vietnam, and reelection. In May 1972, Nixon traveled to the Soviet Union and signed several accords, including a long sought Strategic Arms Limitation Treaty (SALT). Brezhnev's willingness to host Nixon even while the U.S. Air Force stepped up bombing of North Vietnam revealed Soviet determination to restore their own détente with America.

After the failure of their spring military offensive and signs of diminished Soviet and Chinese support, North Vietnamese and U.S. negotiators concluded a draft cease-fire agreement in October 1972. The terms, not publicly announced, provided for the continued existence of two rival Vietnamese governments. U.S. forces were to depart within 90 days of the agreement, but North Vietnamese and Vietcong troops could remain in South Vietnam. Both Hanoi and Washington could resupply their allies. The rival regimes pledged to discuss a political settlement. As most observers understood, the terms were little more than a cease-fire in place, not the "peace with honor" Nixon had called for. Even though a final accord was not signed until January 1973, this preliminary agreement buried the already troubled candidacy of Democratic presidential nominee George McGovern, whose campaign centered on a pledge to end the war. Nixon won reelection in November with 61 percent of the vote.

In February 1973, following the Vietnam peace settlement, Kissinger returned to Beijing. "The flood gates were opened," he reported to Nixon in describing the warmth with which he was received by Zhou and Mao. Instead of parking Kissinger's aircraft in a dark corner of the airfield, authorities permitted his "plane to taxi right up to the terminal." His photograph graced the "top half of the People's Daily," and "guards saluted" the American delegation "for the first time as we entered the Great Hall and our Guest House."

On earlier trips to Beijing, the Americans thumped the Soviet threat to spur cooperation. This time the situation appeared reversed, as Kissinger found the Chinese "obsessed" by fears of encirclement. "The Soviet Union dominated our conversation," he reported. It was the "centerpiece and completely permeated our talks." Mao and Zhou sounded like their former nemesis, Secretary of State John Foster Dulles, demanding greater American efforts to "counter the Russians everywhere" by forming alliances to "prevent the Soviets filling vacuums." The United States and PRC could "work together to commonly deal with a bastard," Mao declared.

Kissinger raised the issue of Taiwan, repeating Nixon's pledge "to move toward normalization of relations." The American envoy assured Zhou "we would be prepared to move" after the 1974 midterm congressional elections "toward something like the Japanese solution with regard to diplomatic relations." (In 1972, Japanese Prime Minister Tanaka Kakuei opened formal ties with the PRC. Japan closed its Taiwan embassy, but retained an informal liaison office there, staffed by "retired" diplomats. Trade continued unabated. Unlike the United States, however, Japan had no security treaty with Taiwan.) By "mid-1976," Kissinger stressed, "we were prepared to establish full diplomatic relations." In the interim, he and Zhou agreed to establish official liaison offices in Washington and Beijing.

In addition to the strident anti-Soviet tone of the February 1973 talks, Kissinger was struck by the "major turnabout" in the attitude of Mao and Zhou "toward Japan and the U.S." In July 1971, Kissinger recalled, Zhou had described Japan as "fattened economically by the U.S." and about to "expand its militarism throughout" Asia. Throughout the next year, China condemned the U.S.–Japan security treaty. Now "the Chinese . . . clearly consider Japan as an incipient ally" that could help "to counter Soviet and Indian designs." Zhou acknowledged the security treaty as a "brake on Japanese expansionism and militarism" and cautioned the United States against any trade sanctions or other actions that might drive Japan into a "situation where the Soviet Union became its ally instead of the U.S." Mao actually urged Kissinger to spend more time in Japan and to "make sure that trade and other frictions with Tokyo . . . would not mar our fundamental cooperation." Kissinger, suddenly suspicious of China's new warmth toward Japan, cautioned the Chinese to avoid a bidding war with America to "compete for Tokyo's allegiance" as this might encourage "resurgent Japanese nationalism."

By the time he left Beijing, Kissinger's assessment of Chinese foreign policy led him to what even he recognized as a remarkable conclusion. "We are now in the extraordinary position," Kissinger reported to Nixon, that among all nations "with the exception of the United Kingdom, the PRC might well be closest to us in its global perceptions. No other world leaders have the sweep and imagination of Mao and Zhou nor the capacity and will to achieve a long-range policy." The United States and China had become "in plain words . . . tacit allies."

However, the Americans had not given up entirely on détente with the Soviet Union. At the same time that he spoke so glowingly of China, Kissinger told Nixon that with "conscientious attention to both capitals, we should be able to have our mao tai [sic] and drink our vodka, too." In other words, improved ties with China were still considered a spur to cooperation with Moscow, not merely a strategy to contain the Soviets. Despite this hope, during the remainder of Nixon's presidency—just under eighteen months—and that of his four immediate successors, the U.S.–China relationship assumed an increasingly anti-Soviet tinge.

This evolution was influenced by both domestic and foreign developments. In March 1973, Kissinger informed Zhou and Mao that Nixon still planned to normalize diplomatic relations and cut links to Taiwan as soon as possible. Within a month, however, the unraveling Watergate cover-up began to envelop the White House. Although Kissinger had few direct links to the Watergate crimes, his patron, Richard Nixon, possessed diminishing political capital and was hesitant to alienate conservative Republicans who retained affection for Taiwan.

During Nixon's final year in office, relations with the Soviet Union soured. In October 1973, during another round of Arab–Israeli warfare, Brezhnev threatened to send troops to bolster Egypt. Nixon warned of a U.S. military response if he did so. Although a cease-fire averted a superpower confrontation, the resulting Arab oil boycott spiked energy prices and contributed to economic recessions in the United States and Japan.

With the process of normalization and the status of Taiwan put on hold, and with the Watergate crisis hobbling Nixon, dislike of the Soviet Union seemed the main force binding together the United States and China. Trade did not become a significant factor until the late 1980s. Beginning in mid-1973, Washington supplied a growing amount of intelligence on Soviet military matters to the Chinese. When Kissinger met with Mao and Zhou in November 1973, and during conclaves in 1974, both sides swapped tales of Soviet perfidy and discussed ways to contain the Soviet threat against China, South Asia, and the Middle East.

Despite frustrations on both sides, the relationship between the United States and the People's Republic that began in the early 1970s had dramatic, if sometimes unintended, consequences for world politics. Even though both Richard Nixon and Mao Zedong were considered leading ideologues of the cold war, their actions largely stripped that contest of its ideological trappings. After 1972, the cold war in Asia, at least, essentially disappeared. When the North Vietnamese finally swept over South Vietnam in the spring of 1975, few Americans or anyone else considered it a victory for "communism" or a threat to the larger stability of Asia. What passed for the cold war globally during the two decades after Nixon's trip to China was clearly more a rivalry between the Soviet Union and the United States than an ideological struggle or contest for the hearts and minds of the world's people.

Although the Chinese–American relationship from 1973–1989 underwent many small changes, the foundation laid by Nixon and Kissinger and Mao and Zhou proved quite durable. At its core lay a shared belief in the value of strategic cooperation against the Soviet Union. Other issues, such as trade, economic reform, and human rights, took a back seat. While many Americans of varied political viewpoints remained uneasy with China's continued antidemocratic and authoritarian character, they believed that strategic cooperation and economic growth would gradually transform the PRC into a something like a Western nation. The consensus within the Ford, Carter, Reagan, and Bush administrations held that Mao's chief successor, Deng Xiaoping, was committed to economic reform and gradual political liberalization. The cooperative spirit between China and the United States, these presidents believed, had taken deep root and could withstand the vagaries of world politics, including the decline of Soviet power. During the fifteen years following Nixon's resignation in August 1974, this axiom provided a reliable guide.

SELECTED ADDITIONAL READINGS

Richard Nixon, *RN: The Memoirs of Richard Nixon* (New York, 1978); Henry Kissinger, *White House Years* (Boston, 1979), and, *Years of Upheaval* (Boston, 1983); John Holdridge and Marshall Green, *War and Peace with China: First Hand Experiences in the Foreign Service of the United States* (Bethesda, Md., 1994); Jim Mann, *About Face: A History of America's Curious Relationship with China, from Nixon to Clinton* (New York, 1999); Patrick Tyler, *A Great Wall: Six American Presidents and China* (New York, 1999); Nancy Tucker, ed., *China Confidential: American Diplomats and Sino–American Relations, 1945–1996* (New York, 2001); William Burr, ed., *The Kissinger Transcripts: The Top Secret Talks with Beijing and Moscow* (New York, 1998); Robert Schulzinger, *Henry Kissinger: Doctor of Diplomacy* (New York, 1989), and, *A Time for War: The United States and Vietnam, 1941–1975* (New York, 1997); Chen Jian, *Mao's China and the Cold War* (Chapel Hill, N.C., 2001); Rosemary Foot, *The Practice of Power: U.S. Relations with China since 1949* (New York, 1997); William Bundy, *A Tangled Web: The Making of Foreign Policy in the Nixon Presidency* (New York, 1998); Robert S. Ross, *Negotiating Cooperation: The United States and China, 1969–1989* (Stanford, Calif., 1995); Michael Schaller, *Altered States: The U.S. and Japan since the Occupation* (New York, 1997).

TEN

"Tacit Allies" to Tiananmen

China and Presidents Ford, Carter, Reagan, and Bush, 1974–1992

In August 1974, with the Senate poised to convict him of various "high crimes and misdemeanors," Richard Nixon resigned the presidency. The collapse of his popular and political support resulted almost entirely from criminal involvement in the Watergate break-in and cover-up. The triumph of constitutional process over politics and dirty tricks confounded Chinese Communist leaders unfamiliar with checks and balances. Mao and Zhou suspected that a dark conspiracy explained Nixon's fall from power and wondered if opponents of his opening to China had provoked it.

In fact, Nixon's China initiative was one of the most popular and enduring of the controversial president's achievements and bolstered, rather than undermined, his stature. Soon after Vice-president Gerald Ford assumed the presidency, he dispatched now Secretary of State Henry Kissinger to Beijing, where he affirmed that U.S. policy remained steadfast and unchanging. Ford promised to honor Nixon's pledge to soon shift diplomatic recognition from Taiwan to the PRC.

THE FORD PRESIDENCY AND CHINA

Despite the new president's intention to normalize relations with China, as had proved true so often in Sino–American relations, domestic politics intervened. From almost the moment he entered the White House, Ford found himself under attack from conservative Republicans as well as liberal Democrats. His early decision to pardon Nixon for his Watergate crimes, both on compassionate grounds and to put the scandal behind him, enraged a majority of Americans. The increasingly powerful conservative wing of the Republican party, which looked toward California governor Ronald Reagan for leadership, was equally angered by the appointment of moderate Republican and former New York governor Nelson Rockefeller as vice-president. The dramatic collapse of South Vietnam in April 1975, while not blamed on Ford personally, did little to enhance his stature or that of Kissinger. At home, economic stagnation and rising inflation further undermined the administration's popularity.

By the time Nixon resigned, an odd coalition of conservative Republicans and liberal Democrats had begun to criticize the entire basis of détente with the Soviet Union. Moscow, they claimed, used arms control and cooperation with the United States as a fig leaf to hide a military build-up and intervention in Africa and the Middle East. While these critics did not think China posed as great a threat as did the Soviet Union (and some still believed China could be played off against the Soviets), they felt none of the enthusiasm Nixon and Kissinger expressed about ties to Beijing. In fact, critics of détente expressed renewed concern for Taiwan and favored preserving links with the Republic of China even if the United States moved closer to the PRC.

Ford, whom many Americans considered a foreign policy lightweight, attempted to placate these critics by downplaying Kissinger's role and policies. To shore up support among conservative Republicans and counter a nomination challenge by Ronald Reagan in 1976, Ford backtracked on China. Cutting diplomatic ties to Taiwan (whose longtime leader Jiang Jieshi died in April 1975) would anger conservatives, so Ford decided to postpone normalizing relations with China.

When the president traveled to Beijing in December 1975, bringing the bad news, Chinese leaders expressed anger and dismay at his broken promise. To make partial amends, Ford authorized, for the first time, the sale to China of jet engines and advanced computers with military potential. By then the leading Chinese advocate of closer ties to Washington, Zhou Enlai, was terminally ill with cancer (he died the next month), and Mao could barely rise out of a chair to greet the visiting president. Government business was conducted by Vice-premier Deng Xiaoping, a short, spirited, and pragmatic disciple of Zhou's. Deng held a tenuous grasp on power. Radicals, led by Mao's wife, Jiang Qing, who favored preserving Marxist economic and political orthodoxy, challenged Deng's authority.

Ford's reluctance to break ties with Taiwan and recognize the PRC undermined moderates such as Deng, who advocated economic modernization and relaxation of political controls. Moderates argued that closer ties with the West and Japan would bring China important economic and security gains.

In his final years, Mao abandoned many of the so-called Maoist policies favored by the radicals and tried to steer a middle course. Early in 1976, after Zhou's death, he downgraded Deng and reassigned many of his powers to a new premier, Hua Guofeng. A plump and jolly political cipher, Hua was courted by the followers of both Deng and Jiang Qing. When Mao died on September 2, 1976, a power struggle erupted between the factions. In October, Hua cast his lot with the moderates and ordered the arrest of Jiang Qing and her three closest allies, Yao Wenyuan, Zhang Chunqiao, and Wang Hongwen, later derided as the "Gang of Four." Over the next two years, Deng worked his way back into power, gradually displacing Hua. Nominally, Deng occupied a low rank in the CCP hierarchy. He preferred to rule through allies he appointed to top posts, including Communist party Secretary Hu Yaobang and Premier Zhao Ziyang. But from 1978 until he was slowed by old age in the early 1990s, and until his death in 1997, no one doubted that this diminutive veteran of China's revolution wielded ultimate authority.

CARTER AND THE POLITICS OF NORMALIZATION

In spite of his effort to back away from détente, Ford lost his election bid in November 1976. When Democrat Jimmy Carter entered the White House in January 1977, he, too, intended to fulfill Nixon's pledge of 1972. But the new president and his representative in China, former United Automobile Workers head Leonard Woodcock, were also determined to place relations with China on what they considered a more equal footing. They criticized Nixon, Ford, and Kissinger for conceding too much to Beijing and asking too little in return. There would be no more "ass kissing" the Chinese, the new president boasted. But as Carter discovered, it proved harder than he imagined to normalize ties with Beijing or to change the pattern of diplomatic interaction begun under Kissinger.

Carter called for reliance on open, rather than secret diplomacy with China. In practice, he relied heavily on National Security Advisor Zbigniew Brzezinski, who modeled himself on Kissinger and who often kept the State Department and the public in the dark. The Chinese encouraged this, as they preferred dealing with special presidential emissaries rather than routine officials. Not only did Kissinger's imperious "style" persist, so did his indirect policy influence. Several key Kissinger protégés, including Winston Lord, John Holdridge, Brent Scowcroft, Lawrence Eagelburger, Alexander Haig, and Richard Solomon played important policymaking roles in the National Security Council (NSC) and State Department from 1977 until the 1990s. Although Carter took important steps to expand cultural, student, and academic exchanges with China, Sino–American relations continued to be directed by a handful of officials and driven by anti-Soviet motives.

In August 1977, Carter dispatched Secretary of State Cyrus Vance to Beijing. There, Vance suggested that the United States would move quickly to recognize China if it could retain some form of official diplomatic tie with Taiwan. Deng Xiaoping ridiculed this proposal. He noted that Carter offered less than promised by either Nixon or Ford, who had spoken of following the "Japanese model," in which Tokyo severed all formal ties with Taiwan, placing responsibility for trade, travel, and other contact under control of a private organization staffed by retired diplomats. The American proposal to continue government-to-government links with Taiwan looked to Deng much like an unacceptable "two-China policy."

The administration's backward step reflected domestic politics. Carter had negotiated a controversial treaty that gradually transferred control of the Panama Canal to Panama. Conservatives, galvanized by Ronald Reagan, criticized this as abandonment of an American icon and a retreat from glory. Carter desperately needed Republican support to win a two-thirds Senate vote for treaty ratification. To gain the margin for passage, he toughened his stance toward China. If the PRC accepted a modified two-China policy, Carter would probably gain some Republican support for the canal treaty. If the Chinese balked and recognition was deferred a year or two, he would lose nothing. Carter pulled back and waited until the Senate voted on the treaty in the spring of 1978.

While waiting for Washington to make a move, Beijing pursued a more active regional policy, including improving relations with most nations of Southeast Asia. In August 1978, China signed a friendship pact with Japan, setting the stage for greater economic cooperation. Deng then visited Tokyo, where he made a show of meeting Emperor Hirohito, formerly a chief villain in Chinese propaganda. These actions were partly designed to show Carter that China could rely on its Asian neighbors if the United States delayed recognition.

In May, the Chinese government invited surviving members of the wartime Dixie Mission to a reunion in Yenan. Toasts and speeches by Chinese and American participants recalled the spirit of cooperation and the abortive effort in 1944–45 to forge an alliance. As one PRC official lamented, China was still waiting for diplomatic recognition, but could not "wait forever."

That same month, following Senate passage of the Panama Canal Treaty, the president dispatched Zbigniew Brzezinski to Beijing. Carter hoped that sealing a deal with the PRC over recognition would put added pressure on the Soviet Union to conclude a SALT II arms limitation agreement with the United States. Brzezinski, who had a much darker view of Soviet intentions than his boss, had little interest in arms control. Instead, he viewed cooperation with China as an effective way to squeeze the Russians.

The National Security Advisor told Deng that Carter was ready to negotiate the details attendant upon recognizing China and cutting formal links to Taiwan. Washington would cancel its mutual defense pact with Taiwan after giving the year's notice required by the 1954 treaty. During the one-year transition, America would halt arms sales to the island, but it reserved the right to resume sales of defensive weapons thereafter. Future trade, travel, and other contacts between America and Taiwan would be handled by a nongovernmental agency staffed by "retired" diplomats. The target date for an agreement, Brzezinski explained, was December 15, 1978, after mid-term congressional elections but before the Senate took up ratification of the SALT II treaty.

Except for the issue of future U.S. arms sales to Taiwan, the American terms met Chinese expectations. Leonard Woodcock, head of the liaison office in Beijing, took charge of final negotiations. As had been true under Nixon and Kissinger, State Department China experts played almost no part in formulating the policy. Not surprisingly, Deng refused to concede that America was free to sell arms to Taiwan in the future. The Chinese opposed resumption of weapons sales after the one-year moratorium, while the U.S. side reserved the right to continue arms sales after 1979.

Deng tolerated what he considered interference in China's internal affairs because he believed that diplomatic recognition by the United States would speed the flow of Western and Japanese capital, which China desperately needed to foster economic modernization. Also, in a bitter irony, China contemplated invading Vietnam and wanted to secure a deal with Washington before doing so.

During the final stages of U.S.–China negotiations in December 1978, Carter considered extending recognition to Communist-ruled Vietnam as well. Diplomats from both sides had settled many of the issues that had divided Washington and Hanoi since the end of the Vietnam War in 1975.

However, since Vietnam had allied itself with the Soviet Union (it signed a friendship pact with Moscow in November 1978), both Brzezinski and Deng objected to a deal. Vietnam had angered China by expelling several hundred thousand ethnic Chinese and by invading Cambodia in December 1978 to overthrow the brutal but pro-Chinese Khmer Rouge government. China's condemnation of Vietnam as a "Soviet pawn" and Moscow's forward post for Asian conquest sounded as if it had come out of a speech by John Foster Dulles. When Brzezinski warned the president that recognizing Hanoi would be interpreted by Deng as an anti-Chinese, pro-Soviet act, Carter pulled back. Eighteen years passed before President Bill Clinton established relations with Vietnam, in 1996.

On December 15, 1978, without prior notice to Congress or to America's European and Asian allies, President Carter announced that, effective January 1, 1979, the United States would sever ties with Taiwan and recognize the People's Republic of China as the sole, legitimate Chinese government. After a one-year notification period, Washington would cancel its defense pact with Taiwan. The United States, he explained, would temporarily halt weapons sales to Taiwan, but would be free to resume them after one year. Expressing hope for a peaceful solution to the question of Taiwan's future status, Carter announced that Deng Xiaoping would visit the United States.

Even though most Americans applauded the diplomatic breakthrough, questions remained about Carter's lack of prior consultation with Congress and about Washington's future obligations to Taiwan. Republicans, such as senators Barry Goldwater of Arizona and Jesse Helms of North Carolina, were especially critical of Carter, sanctimoniously accusing him of selling out an American ally for empty Communist promises. Goldwater condemned Carter for his "cowardly act" that "stabs in the back the nation of Taiwan." He leveled this charge even though Carter had implemented the terms favored by his two Republican predecessors. Responding to public misgivings, as well as its own concern over the administration's secretiveness, Congress passed the Taiwan Relations Act of 1979. This provided a legislative mandate for future arms sales and asserted that the United States retained a security interest in Taiwan. Any Chinese military action against the island, the act declared, would be of "grave concern to the United States." Despite objections from China that the law interfered with its internal affairs and complaints by Carter that Congress had impinged upon his presidential powers, the bill passed overwhelmingly. To the surprise of Taiwan's friends and enemies in both the United States and China, during the next thirteen years under the rule of Chiang Ching-kuo, the island's economy thrived and it evolved toward political democracy.

Deng Xiaoping tours the United States in 1979. At a Texas barbecue he donned a ten-gallon hat and strapped on a six-shooter. A few weeks later, he ordered Chinese troops to invade Vietnam. (UPI/Bettman Newsphotos)

On January 28, 1979, thirty-four years after Mao and Zhou made their secret, unsuccessful bid to confer with Franklin Roosevelt, Deng Xiaoping arrived in Washington. Exuberantly, he declared that he had always hoped to "visit America before going to see Marx." His week-long cross-country tour captured headlines and won public affection. At a Texas barbecue, for example, the diminutive Deng put on a ten-gallon cowboy hat, picked up a six-shooter, and mugged for photographers. At Disney's Magic Kingdom, he danced with Mickey Mouse. Small wonder that *Time* magazine featured Deng on its cover as 1978's "Man of the Year"—the first Chinese leader so honored since the Communist leader's arch rival, Chiang Kai-shek.

In talks with Carter and other top officials, Deng agreed to permit the United States to establish electronic listening posts in western China. These replaced similar sites lost after the Iranian revolution from which Americans gathered signals intelligence on the Soviet Union. Deng informed Carter of China's plan to stage a limited invasion of Vietnam, justified, he said, by Vietnam's invasion of Cambodia, persecution of ethnic Chinese, and violation of China's border. The president urged "restraint," but made no effort to deter Beijing. Neither leader commented on the fact that barely six years after the last American soldiers quit a war partly designed to contain China, the Chinese were seeking tacit approval from an American president to begin their own war against Vietnam.

On February 17, 1979, two weeks after leaving the United States, Deng sent Chinese troops into Vietnam. The attack, Beijing announced, would teach Vietnam "a lesson." On March 5, after suffering 20,000 casualties during seventeen days of skirmishes with Vietnam's "B team" (its best, "A team" troops were occupying Cambodia), Chinese units withdrew. The major lesson of the conflict seemed to be that the People's Liberation Army could not fight well beyond its own borders.

Following the normalization of relations and the brief China–Vietnam war, Carter tried to build a stronger foundation for Sino–American diplomacy. He vigorously promoted student and cultural exchange programs. Within a decade, more than 80,000 Chinese graduate students and other professionals had come to the United States for advanced training. A few thousand American students and many more tourists traveled in the other direction. This people-to-people contact brought ordinary Chinese and American citizens into proximity for the first time since the Second World War.

Although two-way trade remained modest during Carter's presidency, he laid the groundwork for a dramatic expansion. In the summer of 1979, the president recommended, and Congress approved, granting China provisional Most Favored Nation (MFN) status. This meant that Chinese exports to the United States would be taxed at the lowest (most favorable) rate granted to other countries. Without MFN status, Chinese products would be priced out of the market. For over a century, Americans had waited for trade with China to boom. The provisional grant of MFN, along with China's economic modernization, set the stage for the nation's entry into the world economy. Annual two-way trade between the United States and China increased from practically zero in 1971 to almost $13 billion in 1988. In later years, it grew even more rapidly.

Under Deng, Communist authorities began relaxing the many constraints Mao had imposed on daily life. Deng spoke of "seeking truth from facts," rather than from ideology. He promoted economic modernization, foreign investment, creation of small-scale private enterprise, and the return of individual farm plots to peasants. Deng vaguely praised democracy, but had little tolerance for political dissent.

Beginning in December 1978, student activists and urban intellectuals in several Chinese cities created the "Democracy Wall movement." They displayed political posters on public walls to spark debate on issues ignored by the official press. Initially, the Chinese leadership tolerated this challenge. But by March 1979, when wall posters questioned the Communist party's monopoly of power, authorities swiftly suppressed the dialogue. Offending posters were torn down and new ones banned. Dozens of activists, including Wei Jingshen, author of a famous poster called "The Fifth Modernization—Democracy," were arrested and given stiff prison terms. Wei spent much of the next seventeen years in and out of prison, before being allowed to emigrate to the United States in 1997.

President Carter had made U.S. support for human rights a major diplomatic initiative. He criticized political repression in countries as varied as the Philippines and the Soviet Union. Yet the Carter administration turned a blind eye toward Chinese mistreatment of the regime's critics. Washington avoided picking a fight with the Chinese government, especially given the rapid deterioration of U.S.–Soviet relations.

In December 1979, Soviet troops invaded Afghanistan in an effort to save a tottering Afghan Communist regime that had taken power several years earlier. If their clients were deposed, the Soviets feared losing influence in South Asia and facing a fundamentalist Islamic regime on their border. The Carter administration interpreted the invasion as a threatening Soviet move toward the oil-rich Persian Gulf. In response, the president postponed Senate ratification of the SALT II arms treaty, canceled grain sales to the Soviet Union, imposed a boycott on U.S. participation in the 1980 Moscow Olympics, and vowed to protect the Persian Gulf region against Soviet encroachment. Carter also sent Defense Secretary Harold Brown to China, where he informed Deng that the United States was prepared to sell "non-lethal" defense equipment to China, including air defense radar, computers, communication equipment, and transport helicopters.

By 1980, American anger at Soviet actions in Afghanistan and its meddling in Africa outweighed concerns over China's human rights record. Carter had hoped to broaden the cultural and economic scope of Sino–American relations, placing less emphasis on its military aspects. He did, in fact, lay important groundwork for this. But the deterioration of relations with the Soviet Union pushed the Chinese–American relationship back into an anti-Soviet posture, where it had begun in 1971. In addition to rising tension with the Soviet Union, high energy prices, gasoline shortages, inflation, and the prolonged detention of U.S. hostages in Iran paved the way for the election in November 1980 of the most anti-Communist president since World War II, Ronald Reagan.

REAGAN AND THE EVIL EMPIRE(S)

In April 1978, a few months before the United States normalized relations with China, Ronald Reagan (then a private citizen) delivered a speech in

Taiwan. "It is hard for me to believe," he declared, that "any sensible American who believes in individual liberty and self-determination would stand by and let his government abandon an ally whose only 'sins' are that it is small and loves freedom." Two years later, as the Republican nominee for president, he denounced Carter's "betrayal" of Taiwan, which he called an "American ally." If he were elected, Reagan promised to consider a "two-China policy" in which the United States restored "official relations" with Taiwan. When asked if he would recognize Taiwan as an independent nation should it declare itself separate from China, Reagan answered "Yes, just like a lot of countries recognized the thirteen colonies when they became part of the United States." In a tart reply, Beijing warned that Reagan's position, including his stated intent to sell arms to Taiwan, "if carried into practice would wreck the very foundations of Sino–U.S. relations."

Shortly after Reagan ignited these fireworks, vice-presidential nominee George Bush, foreign policy adviser Richard Allen, and veteran CIA China specialist James Lilley carried a far more conciliatory message from the Reagan campaign to China. They reassured the Beijing leadership that if elected, Reagan would not backtrack on Taiwan. At first the candidate refused to acknowledge this pledge, but did so later, after convincing himself that the Taiwan Relations Act already conferred a form of American recognition and protection to the island. This provocative flip-flop foreshadowed the conflict over China policy that beset the president and his advisers during the first Reagan administration.

In addition to the president, National Security Adviser Richard Allen, NSC China expert James Lilley, and Defense Secretary Caspar Weinberger voiced strong sympathy for upgrading the U.S. relationship with Taiwan. Secretary of State Alexander Haig, a Kissinger-Nixon protégé, favored closer ties with the People's Republic, especially as a way of neutralizing the Soviet Union. This internal bickering, and conflict with China, quickly erupted over the issue of arms sales to Taiwan.

Shortly after taking office, Reagan received a request from Taiwan, which sought to purchase advanced fighter jets, specifically the FX model, from the United States. Beijing and Washington had not resolved their differences on the question of arms sales to Taiwan, and this issue threatened to derail Sino-American relations just as the United States was gearing up to challenge the Soviet Union. Haig proposed to solve the dilemma by offering to sell advanced weapons to *both* China and Taiwan. Although Reagan and his inner circle were skeptical of this plan, they authorized Haig to broach the idea quietly and informally to Chinese officials during meetings in Beijing in June 1981.

Ignoring these instructions, Haig boasted at a news conference upon his arrival in China that the Reagan administration was prepared to sell the PRC advanced weapons systems, including planes and missiles. This infuriated the president, who promptly told reporters he had "not changed his feelings about Taiwan" and intended to sell it, not the PRC, weapons. The Chinese disliked having the bait of arms sales dangled in front of them, and they ridiculed Haig's approach as "doomed to failure." Chinese officials turned up the heat by condemning not only the possible sale of advanced fighter aircraft to Taiwan, but also the transfer of ordinary weapons. If Washington did not stop all arms sales within a short time, China hinted, it might downgrade relations with the United States.

Angry exchanges continued until the summer of 1982. Ultimately, the Reagan administration agreed not to sell the FX fighter; instead, it permitted Taiwan to acquire American technology to produce by itself an older plane, the F-5e, already flown by the Taiwan airforce. China grumbled and demanded the United States set a date for cessation of all arms sales to Taiwan. In June 1982, Haig resigned as secretary of state. (He soon went to work for United Technologies as a highly paid arms dealer, selling weapons systems to China, Taiwan, and other countries.) Haig's departure set the stage for a compromise. On August 17, 1982, the United States and the PRC issued a joint communiqué in which the American government declared it would reduce and eventually terminate arms sales to Taiwan, but only as conditions in the region permitted. The PRC got the U.S. government on record as accepting the principle of an arms sales cut-off, while Reagan got the PRC to tolerate an indefinite period during which the United States could supply weapons to Taiwan. In a memorandum he wrote for internal use, Reagan insisted that arms sales to Taiwan should reflect the balance of power between China and Taiwan. If China grew militarily stronger, arms sales to Taiwan should increase.

Reagan's support for Taiwan was not merely a personal quirk. Many of his advisers, including Haig's successor as secretary of state, George Shultz, believed that policymakers since 1971 had overstated China's geostrategic importance. China, in this view, was a useful but not a vital ally. It provided the United States with some leverage against the Soviet Union and could play an important role in stabilizing Asia. But the PRC, Shultz believed, was not a world-class power to whom the United States need make fundamental concessions. American interests in Asia, Shultz declared in a speech delivered early in 1983, should remain centered on Japan, whose strong economy, democratic system, and global heft were much more important in the short and medium run.

The Chinese, too, reassessed their relationship with the United States during the early years of the Reagan administration. Besides the dispute over arms sales to Taiwan, China had misgivings about Reagan's agenda. Since 1971, the PRC had looked to the United States as a counterweight to the Soviet Union. But Reagan's huge arms build-up and challenge to Soviet influence in Asia, Africa, the Middle East, and Latin America scared Chinese leaders, who were wary of being swept into an unwanted conflict between the two superpowers. At the end of 1982, Communist party Secretary Hu Yaobang told a Party Congress that henceforth China would follow a more independent foreign policy, distinct from that of either the United States or the Soviet Union.

These developments suggested that Sino–American tensions were likely to increase. In fact, following the joint communiqué of August 1982, relations between China and the United States quickly improved and remained close through the end of the Reagan presidency.

Several factors accounted for this. Deng's modernization program required a steady flow of European, Japanese, and American capital and technology, as well as export markets for China. Deng's chief aides, Communist party leader Hu Yaobang and Premier Zhao Ziyang, were, if anything, even more pro-Western than their boss. Both men enjoyed traveling abroad, admired foreign culture, and wore Western fashions. They often spoke of China's need to emulate aspects of Western and Japanese society.

In addition to material and cultural incentives for cooperation, China shared America's dismay at Soviet intervention in Afghanistan. Throughout the 1980s, China worked closely with the CIA to assist the anti-Soviet Moujeheddin rebels. With funding from the CIA, China provided a fleet of sturdy mules to deliver U.S.-financed weapons and supplies to these Afghani guerrillas. This cooperation stymied the Soviets and enhanced ties between Beijing and Washington. It also prompted Reagan to approve sales of additional weapons technology to China.

Unfortunately, the president's frequent unscripted remarks about China and Taiwan drove Beijing's leadership to distraction. Several times during 1982–83, Reagan referred to the government of Taiwan as an "American ally." His language contradicted a series of U.S.–China understandings. Reagan's remarks also jeopardized his trip to China, scheduled for early 1984. Chinese leaders pleaded with U.S. diplomats and private American visitors to China during 1983 to get Reagan to cease talking about a U.S. "alliance" with Taiwan. For example, in a December 1983 discussion with this author, then a Fulbright exchange scholar teaching in Beijing, Communist party leader Hu Yaobang asked for assistance in sending a "per-

Author Michael Schaller presents a copy of an earlier edition of this book to Chinese Communist party General Secretary Hu Yaobang, Beijing, 1983. Shortly after this meeting, Hu was removed from power by Deng, allegedly for pushing democratization too rapidly. (Author's Collection)

sonal" message to the White House. "Tell Reagan," Hu asserted, that "if he wants a successful trip to China he can use to boost his reelection, he should keep his big mouth shut about Taiwan." After receiving similar warnings from several sources, Reagan dropped the subject.

In April 1984, the president traveled to the People's Republic of China, a Communist nation he had criticized since entering political life. He made the usual tourist rounds, visiting the Great Wall, the terra cotta soldiers in Sian, and the giant pandas in the Beijing Zoo. Reagan made several public speeches in which he criticized the Soviet Union, praised democracy, but said nothing provocative about Taiwan. He justified his inconsistent judgments of the Soviet Union and China—at least in his own mind—by telling American journalists that he visited "so-called communist China," rather than a real "evil empire."

President Reagan, who found China to be a useful ally against the Soviet Union, enjoys himself amidst the "buried army" of ancient Chinese clay soldiers near the city of Sian, 1984. (Ronald Reagan Presidential Library)

During the final four years of the Reagan administration, relations with China remained positive and low key. Britain's 1984 agreement with China to return Hong Kong when the colony's ninety-nine-year lease expired in 1997 eliminated a major headache. Portugal made a similar deal to return Macao.

Within China, student discontent over political constraints resulted in a series of demonstrations during 1985–86. Only in retrospect were these protests understood as the forerunner to the much larger movement that erupted in May 1989. In January 1987, Communist party chief Hu Yaobang, who sympathized with student demands for political reform, became the chief victim of the protests when Deng Xiaoping removed him from office and installed Zhao Ziyang as party leader.

American officials displayed little interest in or concern about these internal events. They did object vigorously to China's entry into the international arms market. Although the United States was then, and still remains, the world's largest arms merchant, Washington took a dim view of other nations selling weapons to what it considered unstable regions or unfriendly states. As Chinese technology improved, it began marketing several types of short- and medium-range guided missiles. Among its clients were Iran, Pakistan, and several other Middle Eastern nations. The Reagan administration, and its successors, vigorously opposed these sales and threatened sanctions if China continued its exports. Beijing alternately denied selling such weapons and promised not to do so again. As China's technical capacity improved and its desire for lucrative exports grew, the issue of missile and weapons technology sales to less developed nations arose periodically over the next two decades.

GEORGE BUSH AND THE TIANANMEN MASSACRE

Although China was a "nonissue" in the presidential election of 1988, George Bush would have been happy if it had been. He enjoyed giving people the impression that because of his service as head of the U.S. liaison office in Beijing in 1974–75, he should be considered a "China expert." In fact, Bush had no special understanding of China and was happy to return to Washington from his brief assignment in Beijing. As Reagan's vice-president, he remained outside the circle of those shaping the president's China policy. Bush did, however, value stability and the status quo. All things considered, Chinese relations with the United States were thriving in 1988–89. Two-way trade had increased to $13 billion, cooperation in Afghanistan had forced a Soviet retreat, and China's modernization ap-

President George Bush exchanges a toast with Deng Xiaoping in Beijing, 1989. (George Bush Presidential Library)

peared to be going well. Like most Americans, the president believed that economic growth would contribute to political democratization and that China would gradually become "more like us." When he assumed the presidency in January 1989, Bush hoped to preserve the policy and situation he inherited. In spite of this, China policy changed around him in dramatic and unpredictable ways.

In February 1989, after attending the funeral in Tokyo of Japanese Emperor Hirohito, Bush decided to make a good will visit to China. The president hosted a banquet at a hotel in Beijing for Chinese political leaders and prominent intellectuals. Among those on the guest list drawn up by the U.S. embassy was Fang Lizhi, a prominent astrophysicist, university president, and crusader for democratic reform. The Chinese government objected, but seemingly agreed to a deal in which the scholar would be seated at a rear table, out of the spotlight. However, when Fang and his wife arrived at the banquet, Chinese police barred their entry. As word of this incident spread quickly among the foreign press, Bush's aides blamed Ambassador Winston Lord for embarrassing the president by inviting Fang; Lord was soon fired.

While in itself a minor ripple, the episode revealed dangerous trends. These included Bush's tendency to accommodate Chinese leaders whatever the cost, the Chinese government's extreme fear of even mild political dissent, and the cauldron of resentment bubbling beneath the surface of Chinese life. The Bush administration, along with most Americans, was unprepared for the political upheaval of May–June 1989.

Student resentment over the Communist party's monopoly on power had led to small demonstrations in 1985 and 1986. Dissent exploded after April 15, 1989, following the death and funeral of former Communist party chief Hu Yaobang, a belated hero to those favoring democracy. During April and May, rallies protesting government corruption and repression occurred in about eighty cities. Gradually, disgruntled students and workers throughout China focused their activity in Beijing's Tiananmen Square. The massive plaza, fronting the imperial Forbidden City, Mao Zedong's tomb, and several major government buildings, symbolized central authority in China. Zhongnanhai, the compound where top Communist party and government officials lived, lay less than a mile away.

Those protesting at Tiananmen had varying goals. Many simply wanted the Communist party to loosen its grip on public life and allow greater freedom of expression. Others demanded immediate creation of a pluralist, Western-style democracy. Factory workers called attention to low pay and primitive working conditions. At least a few hoped to spark a revolt against the regime. First tens and then hundreds of thousands of students, workers, and civil servants camped out in the square. Chinese leaders seemed stunned, and the outside world was fascinated by the drama.

The presence of many foreign journalists and T.V. crews, as well as tourists, in Beijing turned the demonstration into a global video event. As the crowd grew, President Bush and many of his China policy advisers focused on the impending visit to China of Mikhail Gorbachev, the reformist Soviet leader. They worried that improved Soviet relations with China might complicate Washington's dealings with Beijing. Rather than criticizing Chinese handling of the street protests, the Bush administration concentrated on reassuring China of America's good intentions.

By the time Gorbachev arrived in Beijing on May 15, 1989, at least a half million people had occupied Tiananmen Square, and within a few days the crowd swelled to an estimated one million. Students intoxicated by a taste of freedom and attention from the world press erected a replica of the Statue of Liberty, which they dubbed the "Goddess of Democracy." Citing Gandhi and Martin Luther King, Jr., as their models, they held up posters declaring "Give Us Democracy or Give Us Death." These words and symbols had a special potency for millions of American television viewers. Chinese students, workers, intellectuals, and civil servants seemed

Students and workers demonstrating at Tiananmen Square in late May of 1989, captured the attention and affection of Americans by displaying a mock-up of the Statue of Liberty, dubbed the "Goddess of Democracy," in front of Mao's somber portrait. A few days later, the demonstration was brutally suppressed. (Corbis)

to demand the rights Americans took for granted. China was, after all, moving in a progressive direction. Surely, American journalists on the scene reported, Communist authorities would submit to the will of the people.

Senior Chinese officials, including Communist party chief Zhao Ziyang and Premier Li Peng, visited Tiananmen several times to discuss a compromise that would end the protests. But the movement's loosely organized leadership had no clear agenda or authority to speak for anyone. The more radical elements among the students refused to consider anything short of fundamental political change. By about May 17, "hardliners" in the Communist hierarchy convinced themselves and Deng Xiaoping that the students were counterrevolutionaries, perhaps under foreign control. They even claimed to see in the demonstration a lingering plot by John Foster Dulles, the American secretary of state in the 1950s, to restore capitalism! When Zhao defended the student protestors' goals, if not their methods, Deng stripped him of authority and promoted Jiang Zemin, a leader from Shanghai, as head of the party. Warning that a rush into multiparty democracy would kindle a civil war worse than the Cultural Revolution and would retard economic progress, Deng entrusted Premier Li Peng, the head of government, to restore order. Between May 17 and 20, Li received Deng's backing for a declaration of martial law, charging that the demonstrators were counterrevolutionaries influenced by Western "spiritual pollution." When local police and troops hesitated to use force to disperse the crowd, the central government brought in special units from outside the capital.

Late on the night of June 3, after government authorities issued a final ultimatum to clear Tiananmen, military units and tanks assaulted the 20,000 or so people who remained in the square. In the ensuing chaos, somewhere between 700 and 2,500 Chinese civilians were killed as they fled into surrounding streets. Scientist Fang Lizhi, a leading critic of the government, fled with his wife to the sanctuary of the American embassy in Beijing. An estimated 10,000 students, workers, and civil servants who had participated in the protests were soon arrested, while thousands of others fled the country.

Reporters seeking George Bush's response to the tragic events in China caught up (literally) to the president as he jogged on June 4 near his vacation home in Maine. "Not while I'm running," the winded chief executive replied to shouted questions. This seemingly flippant reaction to the slaughter of Chinese civilians dogged Bush for the remainder of his presidency. Although he was neither callous nor unconcerned with what had happened at Tiananmen, he hoped to avoid saying or doing anything that would anger China's leaders and further reduce American influence over events. At the urging of the state and defense departments, the president suspended arms sales to the PRC—a ban that ultimately lasted five years. In mid-June, the White House announced suspension of high-level official contact with Chinese leaders, and in July, the United States, Japan, and Western Europe suspended economic aid and loans to China.

The American public, the media, and members of Congress found the president's cautious demeanor inappropriate to the scale of violence. Since Nixon's opening to China in 1971, the public and legislators had pretty much deferred to presidential initiatives on China. With the exception of the Taiwan Relations Act in 1979, the executive branch had defined and carried out China policy with minimal input from Congress or other interest groups. China's image in the United States had been quite positive, with the press and public accepting the argument that economic modernization would promote political pluralism. As McDonald's and Kentucky Fried Chicken outlets proliferated in Beijing, Americans naturally assumed China was becoming "more like us."

In fact, the "massacre" at Tiananmen, as American journalists called it, was neither the largest nor most brutal repression of dissent by Chinese

Communist authorities. Far more people were jailed, brutalized, or died as a result of the anti-Rightist movement of the 1950s, the famine caused by the Great Leap Forward, and the chaos of the Cultural Revolution. In fact, Deng and his military allies were relatively patient and cautious in their actions in June 1989. What had changed was the heightened visibility of events at Tiananmen, the display of Western symbols such as the Goddess of Democracy, and the American assumption that the Chinese leadership would bow before the forces of progress. When Deng ordered the People's Liberation Army to attack the defiant protestors and arrest their sympathizers, he shattered American optimism, and the public blamed the Bush administration as well as China's leaders for its disappointment.

In Congress, Senate Majority Leader George Mitchell, Democrat of Maine, along with a broad spectrum of Democrats and Republicans, condemned China's government for what it had done and Bush for seeming to do nothing. Many of the 43,000 Chinese graduate students studying on American campuses led rallies in support of their fallen comrades and appealed for permission to remain in the United States indefinitely. In response, Congress quickly passed legislation drafted by Representative Nancy Pelosi, Democrat of California, granting Chinese students automatic visa extensions so they need not return to China. Bush vetoed the bill, but authorized the Immigration and Naturalization Service to grant visa extensions on request. Critics saw his action as one more concession to the "butchers of Beijing."

Voices at the left, right, and center of American politics seemed united in their condemnation of China. Conservative journalist and sometime presidential candidate Patrick Buchanan proclaimed that "Mr. Deng and his comrades have declared war on the Chinese people; and America must stand with the people as allies against Mr. Deng." A group of leading China scholars at Harvard University's Fairbank Center for East Asian Studies signed a petition asserting nearly the same thing.

Even as Bush announced an end to high-level contact with Chinese officials, he secretly ordered two top aides, National Security Adviser Brent Scowcroft and Deputy Secretary of State Lawrence Eagelburger, to travel to China on June 30 for a secret meeting with Deng Xiaoping. The emissaries carried a plea from Bush to reduce the level of violence and to open a direct communication channel to the White House. Chinese leaders, however, interpreted the move as a signal from Bush that they need not take seriously American criticism and sanctions.

In December 1989, Bush sent Scowcroft back to China on a second secret mission to discuss with Deng Fang Lizhi's release, relaxation of political repression, and, incredibly, the sale of American aircraft and satellites, which could not be completed while the crackdown on dissidents remained in effect. Not only did Scowcroft fail to achieve these objectives, but word of both his past and current trip to Beijing leaked out while he was in China. Members of Congress, the media, and the American public expressed outrage upon learning that only a few weeks after the Tiananmen incident, and in defiance of his pledge to shun Chinese leaders, Bush had sent top aides to confer with Deng—and had done so again six months later. In a widely reported opinion piece that appeared in the *Washington Post* on December 19, 1989, former ambassador to China Winston Lord accused Bush of sending "misguided missions to China" via "fawning emissaries." By the end of the year, U.S. China policy seemed adrift. Congress, the press, and the public complained that the president's main concern appeared to be restoring the status quo and resuming arms sales.

In fact, important voices inside and outside the administration saw Tiananmen as merely an inconvenient speed bump on the path of Chinese–American cooperation. Barely two months after the slaughter in Beijing, Henry Kissinger, now a private consultant, spoke out forcefully in defense of close cooperation with China. The "United States," he asserted, "needs China as a possible counterweight to Soviet aspirations in Asia." Former President Richard Nixon urged Bush to "ignore extremist voices" of the human rights advocates and "stay the prudent course" of close ties to Beijing. Only this, Nixon cautioned, would permit the United States to "maintain the balance among China, Japan, and the Soviet Union."

By the beginning of 1990, however, this "geostrategic/balance of power" argument lacked much vigor. Under Gorbachev's leadership, the Soviet Union was transforming itself into a more democratic state, rapidly unburdening itself of Eastern European satellites and reducing commitments to communist regimes from Cuba to Afghanistan to Vietnam. Nixon and Kissinger seemed alone in not recognizing that Soviet power was shrinking, not expanding. Kissinger then floated the idea, which Bush endorsed in a news conference in January 1990, that close cooperation between the United States and China could counterbalance growing Japanese power. Needless to say, American allies in Tokyo were not reassured by this explanation, which portrayed Japan as a threat.

The next month, Deputy Secretary of State Eagelburger testified before Congress that unless China remained closely tied to the United States, it might sell missiles, nuclear weapons technology, or other weapons of mass destruction to rogue states in Asia and the Middle East. Whether true or not, this suggested that even China's friends in the U.S. government held a pretty dismal view of its motives. None of these rationales for easing restrictions impressed the American public or congressional critics.

Nevertheless, during 1990, President Bush relaxed many of the trade and loan sanctions he had imposed on China immediately after the events of June 1989, and he authorized the resumption of contacts with Chinese officials. On June 25, 1990, the two governments arranged a deal for Fang Lizhi and his wife, Li Shuxian, to leave the American embassy for an academic position at the University of Arizona. Bush's press aide, Marlin Fitzwater, described this move as a "far sighted, significant step that will improve the atmosphere for progress in our bilateral relations." In effect, the White House used Fang's release as a fig leaf to cover the desire of the United States and its allies to restore international loans and trade with China. Over the next few months, the Japanese and Europeans resumed a nearly normal trade relationship with the PRC. In November 1990, Bush received the Chinese foreign minister in the White House, effectively ending restrictions on high-level contacts. In January 1992, Bush even met with Chinese Prime Minister Li Peng, a chief "villain" of the Tiananmen incident, during a visit to the United Nations headquarters in New York. For all intents and purposes, the administration had put the events of June 1989 behind it.

By the summer of 1992, as Bush campaigned for reelection, the issues of arms sales to Taiwan and his alleged "appeasement" of China became part of the domestic political contest. With the glow of the 1990–91 Gulf War victory fading, and the economy in decline, the president faced a barrage of criticism on China from both the right and left. Conservatives such as Patrick Buchanan condemned Bush for not restoring diplomatic recognition to Taiwan and offering it firm security guarantees. Democratic presidential nominee Bill Clinton attacked Bush for ignoring ongoing Chinese human rights violations and called for stripping China of Most Favored Nation trade status.

Since Reagan's 1982 compromise with Beijing on U.S. arms sales to Taiwan, the island's status had receded as an issue. Chinese leaders occasionally grumbled about the sale of American weapons to Taiwan and what they called U.S. interference in China's "internal affairs," but generally, they downplayed the problem. Then, in the midst of the president's lackluster reelection campaign, Bush suddenly announced his intention to sell Taiwan advanced F-16 fighter planes. Acquisition of these planes would give Taiwan an edge over China's airforce.

Bush's decision reflected both political and strategic concerns. In March 1992, China had purchased twenty-four Russian Sukho-27 advanced jet fighters. Unable to buy similar aircraft from the United States, Taiwan moved to purchase French Mirage jet fighters. Late in July, the General Dynamics company announced it would lay off nearly 6,000 workers from its Fort Worth plant because it could not sell planes to Taiwan. Leading Democrats, including Senator Lloyd Bentsen and Governor Ann Richards, both of Texas, blamed Bush for the layoffs. "I don't know what deals have been made between George Bush and Communist China," Richards complained, but "when it means the loss of [almost 6,000] jobs in Fort Worth, Texas, it's time to wake up and smell the coffee." On September 2, Bush visited the General Dynamics plant in Fort Worth to announce the impending sale of 150 F-16s to Taiwan, valued at $6 billion.

The president's sudden reversal stunned the Chinese. But rather than attack his decision, Beijing said little publicly. Deng, in fact, much preferred Bush to Clinton and avoided any criticism that might hurt the incumbent's reelection. Unfortunately for Bush, neither his arms sales decision nor China's grin-and-bear-it response revitalized his campaign. Republican conservatives still complained he did too little to help Taiwan, while Clinton ridiculed Bush as China's lapdog. In his speech accepting the Democratic presidential nomination, Clinton promised "an America that will not coddle tyrants from Baghdad to Beijing." On the campaign trail, he promised to settle accounts with those whom many Americans considered the "butchers of Beijing." When the election results were tabulated in November 1992, Bill Clinton had defeated George Bush and informed observers braced themselves for yet another twist in Sino–American relations.

SUGGESTED ADDITIONAL READINGS

Richard Madsen, *China and the American Dream* (Berkeley, Calif., 1995); Jim Mann, *About Face: A History of America's Curious Relationship with China, from Nixon to Clinton* (New York, 1999); Patrick Tyler, *A Great Wall: Six American Presidents and China* (New York, 1999); Robert S. Ross, *Negotiating Cooperation: The United States and China, 1969–1989* (Stanford, Calif., 1995); David Shambaugh, *Beautiful Imperialist: China Perceives America, 1972–1980* (Princeton, N.J., 1991); Robert G. Sutter, *The China Quandary: Domestic Determinants of U.S. China Policy, 1972–1982* (Boulder, Colo., 1983); Alan G. Gorowitz, ed., *The Taiwan Relations Act: Twenty-Five Years After and a Look Ahead* (Atlanta, 1999); Nancy B. Tucker, *China Confidential: American Diplomats and Sino–American Relations, 1945–1996* (New York, 2001); Jimmy Carter, *Keeping Faith: Memoirs of a President* (New York, 1982); Zbigniew

Brzezinski, *Power and Principle, Memoirs of the National Security Adviser, 1977–1981* (New York, 1983); James A. Baker, III, *The Politics of Diplomacy—Revolution, War, and Peace* (New York, 1995); Harry Harding, *A Fragile Relationship: The U.S. and China since 1972* (Washington, D.C., 1992); Liang Zhang, comp., and Andrew J. Nathan, et al., ed., *The Tiananmen Papers: The Chinese Leadership's Decision to Use Force Against Their Own People—In Their Own Words* (New York, 2001); Jan Taylor, *The Generalissimo's Son: Chiang Ching-kuo and the Revolutions in China and Taiwan* (Cambridge, Mass., 2000).

ELEVEN

Into the Twenty-First Century

At the onset of the new millennium, it seemed the best and worst of times for U.S.–China relations. The two nations had become economically enmeshed to a degree no one had predicted a decade earlier. In 2000, near the end of the Clinton presidency, Congress acknowledged China's emergence as a major economic power by finally granting "permanent, normal, trade relations" (PNTR) status to the PRC. In place of annual arguments over whether or not to approve "most favored nation" trade status, China would receive the same low tariff treatment as America's other major trading partners. However, implementing PNTR required that China join the World Trade Organization (WTO), a group that monitors international trading rules. This required additional negotiation. The fact that China was even poised to enter the WTO was a measure of how far down the road it had already traveled from Marxism to a market economy.

In addition to the decade-long debate over whether and under what terms to grant China preferential trade status, the two countries remained divided, even hostile, on a wide range of issues. These included American concern with the treatment of political and religious dissidents within China, the security of Taiwan and the sale of advanced U.S. weapons to the island, China's military build-up, and its alleged espionage against the United States. Soon after President George W. Bush took office in 2001, his aides began describing China as a "strategic competitor," a rival rather than a partner of the United States. In April 2001, Democrats and Republicans in the House of Representatives voted 406 to 6 to condemn China for violating the human rights of political dissidents and religious minorities. The PRC also had a card to play in response to this criticism. In July, China Russia signed a new treaty of "friendship and cooperation," pledging to boost trade and work to resist efforts by any power (i.e., the United States) to impose a unilateral security framework on Asia. One Russian commentator described the treaty as an "act of friendship against America." As one policy observer put it, the process of economic and political globalization had moved China and the United States continually closer without necessarily making them more cooperative. In the words of a Chinese proverb, they shared the same bed but had different dreams.

For almost twenty years after Nixon's visit to Beijing, Chinese–American trade remained quite modest. At the time of the Tiananmen incident, for example, two-way trade totaled about $13 billion a year. Beginning in the early 1990s, however, commerce exploded. After a century of deferred expectation, China became one of America's top four trading partners (behind Canada, Mexico, and Japan), with two-way trade in 2000 totaling about $116 billion. The fabled "China market" appeared to have finally arrived, but in an unexpected form: The United States sold China goods worth about $16 billion, while Chinese exports to the United States totaled nearly $100 billion, creating an $84 billion trade gap in Beijing's favor!

As the new century began, growing numbers of ordinary Chinese and Americans interacted. Unprecedented numbers of Chinese and American tourists, students, business representatives, academics, and performing artists visited each others' countries. Between 1990 and 2000, the Asian population of the United States doubled, from 2 percent to 4 percent. Almost 54,000 students from the PRC, more than from any other nation, attended American universities. Annually, about 250,000 Asian immigrants, most ethnic Chinese, came to the United States. Immigrants from Asia comprised 40 percent of total annual immigration. These new Americans ran the gamut from scientists and engineers to unskilled laborers. Hollywood "action adventure" films (usually in the form of "pirated" video cassettes) reached mass audiences in China, while Americans flocked to view a new wave of Chinese cinema from both Taiwan and the PRC. These films explored topics as varied as martial arts, the pattern of rural life, and the impact of rapid modernization on families.

In barely twenty-five years, China and the United States had moved from positions of nearly complete military, cultural, political, and economic hostility and isolation to something like "normality." This contact, many Americans hoped, would accelerate China's evolution toward Western-style democracy. Secular Americans held this faith as firmly as nineteenth century missionaries believed Christianity would transform China.

Even as trade, tourism, and immigration increased dramatically, China again became a contentious issue in American politics. Mainstream Democrats as well as Republicans voiced similar concern over human rights issues. Conservatives such as presidential hopeful Pat Buchanan voiced the same criticism of Chinese labor practices as the liberal leadership of American labor unions. These critics of China raised serious issues that needed to be addressed. However, in the late 1990s, certain Republican politicians, joined by some journalists, sounded uncannily like the China Lobby of the early cold war. The Clinton administration, they claimed, had taken illegal campaign funds from groups linked to the PRC and, in return, had ignored China's violations of trade pacts and even turned a blind eye to its nuclear espionage in the United States. Armed with pilfered technology, these doomsayers argued, China literally targeted the United States for attack.

Representative Dan Burton of Indiana and Senator Fred Thomson of Tennessee, Republicans who led congressional investigations, charged that Chinese government money had "subverted our electoral process" and "affected the [outcome] of the 1996 presidential race." The arrest in 1999 of an ethnic Chinese scientist, Wen Ho Lee, for allegedly passing American nuclear weapons secrets to Beijing, rekindled images of China as a hostile nation. Not even the violence at Tiananmen in 1989 had so shaken American faith. After all, Chinese mistreatment of other Chinese was one thing, threatening the United States was quite another. Against all odds, at the start of the twenty-first century, influential Americans tossed around allegations about Chinese espionage, dirty campaign money, and unfair trade, which echoed the shrill language of the cold war or, still worse, the "yellow peril."

Upon his election as president in 1992, Bill Clinton, like many state governors, had visited Taiwan four times on trade missions, but had never been to the People's Republic of China. As a candidate, Clinton minimized the importance of foreign policy and charged that Bush's focus on international affairs had led him to ignore and mismanage the economy. The Democratic challenger had also criticized Bush for "coddling" the "butchers of Beijing" and pledged to make China's continued MFN trade status contingent on an improvement in its human rights record. Clinton's criticism of China closely matched views expressed in public opinion polls. Before the violence of 1989, the American public overwhelmingly perceived China as a friendly country. In the years after 1989, a majority of Americans voiced concerns about Beijing's treatment of its own citizens and its intentions toward the United States.

When he took office in January 1993, Clinton announced that he hoped he would not have to revoke China's temporary MFN status "if we can achieve continued progress" on the human rights front. Reversing Nixon's dictum of 1972, that it did not matter how China treated its own people, only how its external interests affected the United States, Clinton insisted that it was vital to "stick up for ourselves and for the things we believe in and how these people are treated in that country." With dubious economic logic, the new president claimed that China's 1992 trade surplus of $15 billion with the United States provided Washington with great leverage over Beijing, since it showed the PRC's dependence on exports to America.

Clinton's views of China were both shaped by and reflected in the attitudes of his top foreign policy advisers, Secretary of State Warren Christopher, Assistant Secretary of State for East Asia Winston Lord, and National Security Adviser Anthony Lake. At his confirmation hearings, Christopher declared that the administration's policy "will be to seek to facilitate a broad, peaceful evolution in China from communism to democracy" by "encouraging the forces of economic and political liberalization in that great and highly important country." Lord, an aide to Kissinger during the secret 1971 trip to China, favored linking trade liberalization to human rights. At his confirmation he promised to seek "cooperation from China on a range of issues." But, he added, "Americans cannot forget Tiananmen Square." These remarks prompted Chinese Foreign Minister Wu Jianmin to respond that the United States should not meddle in his country's internal affairs.

The new administration's hope that trade would prod China to improve its treatment of dissidents did not indicate hostility toward the PRC. In fact, the president and his aides hinted to Chinese officials that an improvement in their human rights record would lead to more trade and would also fortify the president's ability to resist pressure from congressional Republicans who agitated to restore formal ties to Taiwan.

But the Clinton administration sent mixed signals. Early in 1993, Clinton sidelined efforts by prominent congressional Democrats to make annual renewal of China's MFN status conditional on a major improvement in its human rights performance. Hedging his earlier threat, on May 28, 1993, he issued a flexible Executive Order that gave China one additional year to "shape up" before facing a possible loss of MFN trade privileges.

While U.S. policymakers debated whether and how to press for changes in Chinese domestic politics, China entered a period of accelerated economic growth. In 1992–93, Deng Xiaoping pushed through a host of new economic reforms that encouraged private enterprise and foreign trade and investments. As China became the world's fastest growing economy in the 1990s, American business executives beat a path to Beijing in hope of selling airplanes, computers, and satellites. U.S. business interests joined the Chinese in pressing Clinton to act flexibly on MFN.

In November 1993, during a conference in Seattle attended by leaders of Pacific nations, presidents Clinton and Jiang Zemin of China met briefly. Each did little more than read position papers to each other, reasserting their respective views on why trade should or should not be linked to domestic behavior. Jiang visited local U.S. factories and families to generate Americans' support for abandonment of the human rights criterion. At a gathering of 1,000 Boeing aircraft workers, Jiang urged business and labor leaders to remove "all the negative factors and artificially imposed factors" that limit trade. At the home of one Boeing employee, Cary Qualls, the Chinese president gave a stuffed panda to the Qualls children, ate chocolate chip cookies baked by Melanie Qualls, and declared that "every country's families have different characteristics."

Over the next several months, Jiang and other PRC officials made a great public show of courting European and Japanese business and political leaders, demonstrating that they could turn to other suppliers of goods and capital if the United States continued pressing for change in China's human rights policies. Early in 1994, two influential Clinton economic advisers, Treasury Secretary Lloyd Bentsen and Commerce Secretary Ron Brown, urged the president to abandon his and the State Department's effort to link MFN status to human rights. They told Clinton that pressure on the PRC impeded American exports without advancing Chinese democracy. The president wavered between these two conflicting positions.

In March 1994, Clinton sent Secretary of State Christopher to Beijing. In the days before his arrival, Chinese security officials arrested several prominent dissidents, including Wei Jingshen. This prompted Christopher to declare "you can be sure that human rights will be at the top of my agenda when I get to Beijing." Responding to what they considered a challenge, Chinese officials got into a shoving match with U.S. embassy staff waiting for the arrival of the secretary's plane.

The airport fray foreshadowed the tone of Prime Minister Li Peng's private discussions with Christopher. Li, one of the architects of the Tiananmen crackdown, declared that "China will never accept the United States' concept of human rights." Confident that the Clinton administration would ultimately extend China's MFN status regardless of how it treated political dissidents, Li urged Christopher to drop the subject completely. When the American envoy repeated his condemnation of political repression, the prime minister shot back with a reference to Christopher's role in the investigation of the riots in Los Angeles that followed the acquittal of police officers who beat suspect Rodney King a few years before. "You've got racism and human rights problems in the United States. The Rodney King beating was a human rights problem. So don't come over here and talk to us about our human rights problems."

American business representatives in Beijing supported Li Peng's remarks. They complained that the Clinton administration's persistent effort to use MFN status to influence China's human rights performance sacrificed lucrative trade and investment opportunities without speeding political change. Criticism of Christopher by the U.S. business community further reinforced the Chinese belief that they could defy Clinton's demands. As a sop to Washington, PRC officials announced the release of a handful of students arrested at the time of the Tiananmen incident.

In the face of a united front between Chinese officials and American business interests, Clinton caved in. In May 1994, he announced that henceforth China's MFN trade status would continue to be extended annually without consideration of its human rights record. To put a brave face on this full retreat, the president ordered a ban on the importation of certain Chinese automatic weapons popular among gun owners. In reality, this was more a gun control measure than a rebuke of China. Without quite saying so, the administration acknowledged that even though the Chinese government might sometimes behave ruthlessly toward its own people, for both strategic and economic reasons, the United States had to do business with it. China had called the American bluff over the threat to impose trade sanctions, and the Clinton administration had folded.

Many Democratic liberals and human rights activists criticized this reversal, but Republican leaders and their corporate allies had always opposed the MFN–human rights link. Thus, while they ridiculed Clinton's waffling, they supported his ultimate decision as a boost to business. Problems over Taiwan, however, proved far more divisive.

At roughly the same time as Clinton dropped threats of trade sanctions against China, Taiwan's president, Lee Teng-hui, popped up at the Honolulu airport. As one of a new generation of KMT politicians, Lee was the first president of Taiwan born on the island. His aircraft, en route to South Africa, had been cleared to make a refueling stop in Hawaii. In deference to Beijing, the State Department had rejected Lee's request for an entry visa, which would have permitted him to get off the plane and walk around. (Ordinary travelers from Taiwan freely entered the United States. Restrictions applied only to high-level officials.) The Taiwanese president's appearance in Honolulu was part of an orchestrated campaign to raise his own profile in the run-up to presidential elections on the island. He also hoped to mobilize support for Taiwan among congressional Republicans, Clinton-haters, and others who sympathized with his complaint about not being permitted to leave his plane.

This tactic worked, for the next month, in June 1994, the U.S. Senate passed a resolution by a vote of 94–0 calling on the State Department to grant entry visas to Taiwanese officials. The Senate acted despite Beijing's objection that such a move would constitute an indirect form of diplomatic recognition of what China considered a renegade province. In addition to the Republicans, who savored the opportunity to embarrass the president, the Senate action reflected a changing attitude among Americans.

Since U.S. "de-recognition" of the Republic of China in 1979, Taiwan had become far more democratic. The process began following the death of Chiang Kai-shek in 1975. The Generalissimo's son and successor, Chiang Ching-kuo, relaxed the harsh rule imposed by his father in 1949 and emphasized building a modern economic base. By the time the younger Chiang died in 1988, Taiwan had entered the ranks of modern industrial, exporting nations. His successor, Lee Teng-hui, a native Taiwanese rather than a post-1949 mainland arrival, with a Ph.D. in agricultural economics from Cornell University, sped the pace of political liberalization and economic development. Although only a tiny fraction the size of the PRC, Taiwan, in 1993, purchased $16 billion worth of American exports, more than all of China. (By the end of the decade, two-way trade with Taiwan totaled $54 billion, and the island continued to buy more American exports than the mainland.) As an emerging democracy and a valued trading partner, Taiwan recaptured much of the political goodwill within the United States that it had lost at the time America normalized relations with the PRC.

Congressional expressions of support for Taiwan were not, however, purely idealistic. As in the past, the Kuomintang party operated well-funded lobbying arms in the United States and other nations that promoted the island's interests. Republican politicians, journalists, state and local officials and others were frequently invited on "VIP" tours of the island. Retired members of Congress sometimes received lucrative jobs as consultants to Taiwanese companies. Taiwanese investments and purchases in the United States were often strategically placed to boost influence. Bill Clinton, as noted earlier, had, as governor of Arkansas, traveled to Taiwan four times on trade missions. Taiwan bought good will without violating American laws.

Efforts to cultivate Republicans paid off handsomely after November 1994 when, behind the leadership of Georgia Congressman Newt Gingrich, the GOP won control of the House of Representatives for the first time in decades. In early 1995, upon his selection as Speaker, Gingrich acted as Taiwan's top booster in Washington. He called on the Clinton administration to invite President Lee to visit the United States as an official guest. The Speaker also urged the readmission of Taiwan to the United Nations. "Frankly," Gingrich declared after meeting with top KMT officials in Taipei, "Taiwan does deserve to be treated with respect."

Seizing the opportunity to raise his own status as well as that of his government, in the spring of 1995, President Lee formally requested permission to visit the United States. He used, as a pretext, an invitation to attend commencement ceremonies at Cornell University where, in 1968, he had earned a Ph.D. Lee's friends had endowed a professorship in his name, and he described the trip as a sentimental, private visit.

The State Department knew that China would denounce any visit to the United States by Lee and refused to issue a travel visa. Prodded by Gingrich and the GOP majority, the House, by a vote of 396 to 0, and the Senate, with only one dissent, called upon the administration to grant Lee entry. The State Department countered with a silly offer to permit Lee to visit Honolulu and play a round of golf! Encouraged by Congress and strong support from the American press, Lee held out for Cornell.

Although most China specialists in the State Department opposed the visit, the president personally sympathized with Lee's request. Clinton shared with many Americans an admiration for Taiwan's progress toward democratic rule and greater economic equality. Taiwan provided a positive example of an Asian nation combining economic progress with personal freedom. Like many Americans, Clinton thought China would do well to follow at least part of Taiwan's lead.

The president and his political advisers had an additional motive for approving Lee's request. They worried that rejecting it might give congressional Republicans an excuse to modify the Taiwan Relations Act of 1979. Given half a chance, Clinton feared, Gingrich and the GOP might try to restore formal ties with the island and provoke a crisis with Beijing. At the same time, Clinton and other leading Democrats viewed Taiwan as a potential source of campaign funds. If Democrats were seen as Taiwan's "enemy," financial aid from the island might flow exclusively into Republican pockets. A more flexible policy on visits could break the GOP monopoly on access to Taiwan's wealth.

Beyond these political concerns, President Clinton genuinely resented China's effort to dictate who could and could not visit the United States.

"Just as the Chinese demand to be respected in their way," he told aides, "they have to respect our way." Just as "we are supposed to be sensitive to their traditions and history, they need to be sensitive to ours." American values with respect to Lee Teng-hui's visit, he declared, "are reflected in the congressional majorities" that supported it.

In 1992, President Bush had decided to sell F-16 fighter planes to Taiwan, in part to demonstrate he was not guilty of "coddling dictators" in Beijing. In 1995, Clinton approved a visa for Taiwan's president, in part to prove he was not a "wimp" who granted China continued MFN status without an improvement in its human rights policy. In June 1995, Lee Teng-hui spoke at Cornell's commencement and proclaimed that Taiwan remained a member of the "family of nations" and was "here to stay."

The PRC responded on July 19, 1995 by announcing a series of air, sea, and ground military exercises, including plans to fire missiles, near Taiwan. This muscle flexing signaled to the government and people of Taiwan that China would react forcefully if the island's rulers formally declared independence from the mainland. Beijing let both Washington and Taipei know that it would use all means necessary, including nuclear weapons, to prevent Taiwan from asserting formal independence. Clinton hastened to assure PRC president Jiang Zemin that the United States did not support Taiwanese independence or its readmission to the UN. While this temporarily calmed the situation, China's blunt threats angered many Americans.

Why, ordinary Americans asked, did China make such a fuss about Taiwan's status. After all, the island had been separated from the mainland since 1949. Following Nixon's visit to Beijing, Washington had maintained good trade and political relations with both regimes. This situation continued even after 1979, when the United States recognized the PRC as the sole government of China and downgraded ties with Taiwan.

In spite of their nominal, ongoing civil war, China had become a major tourist destination for Taiwanese, as well as an investment partner. By the late 1990s, for example, Taiwanese had invested about $50 billion on the mainland, including joint business ventures involving individuals connected to the PRC and Taiwan leadership. Tens of thousands of mainlanders worked on Taiwan, some legally and others without documents. Americans wondered why Beijing risked upsetting arrangements that appeared to profit everyone. Did it indicate that China was led by irrational expansionists?

The answer had as much to do with internal Chinese politics as it did with international relations. Since the death of Mao and the decline of Marxist orthodoxy, the Chinese Communist party faced a stiff challenge to its identity and legitimacy. Most Chinese relished the greater personal, if not political, freedom they enjoyed. Materially, life had improved dramatically for hundreds of millions of workers and peasants since 1976. But that begged the question of what, in this new age, the Communist party actually stood for. Maoist dogma about permanent revolution and class struggle had been supplanted by Deng Xiaoping's proclamation that "getting rich is glorious." While many Chinese found this appealing, it did little to justify the party's monopoly of power.

As China's ruling elite decentralized the national economy, encouraged private enterprise and farming, and relaxed cultural controls, it searched for ways to justify its continued political monopoly. Confronted by complaints about official corruption and by angry workers and farmers whose livelihood was sometimes threatened by new domestic and foreign competition, the Communist oligarchy celebrated its role as the champion of Chinese nationalism. Defense of the nation, then, justified one-party, authoritarian rule. Only a strong Communist party could prevent regional tensions and provincial rivalries from tearing China apart. Only the party could assure the return of lost Chinese territories such as Hong Kong, Macao, and Taiwan—and prevent foreign powers such as Japan and the United States from dominating Asia, or, as in the nineteenth century, slicing up the homeland.

Communist officials encouraged a sense of nationalism that verged on "victimhood." Stoking resentments against a supposedly U.S.-supported Taiwan independence movement mobilized millions of Chinese behind a Communist party leadership that portrayed itself as the ultimate defender of national unity and honor. This pattern showed itself in May 1999, during the air attacks launched by NATO and the United States against Yugoslavia. When American aircraft accidentally bombed the Chinese embassy in Belgrade, PRC authorities accused Washington of deliberate, "criminal aggression," a charge widely accepted within China, but nowhere else. In Beijing, police stood by as mobs sacked part of the U.S. embassy and ransacked several McDonald's restaurants, another symbol of American influence. In April 2001, both government officials and ordinary Chinese expressed outrage when an American reconnaissance plane on a routine mission in international air space collided with a Chinese air force jet tailing it near Hainan Island. The Chinese plane and pilot were lost, and the American aircraft made an emergency landing on Hainan. Most observers blamed the Chinese pilot for the incident, but Beijing demanded a U.S. apology and detained the twenty-four-person crew for eleven days. Many Chinese criticized their own leadership for not acting tough enough.

Ironically, advocates of greater democracy in China had not counted on the power of aroused nationalism.

Early in 1996, Chinese and Taiwanese leaders both found it useful to provoke a crisis. President Lee Teng-hui, planning to stand for reelection in Taiwan's first true open and democratic vote, verged on declaring Taiwan independent of the mainland. The PRC responded by carrying out provocative military maneuvers in waters around Taiwan. It even fired missiles over the island. Washington warned Beijing that any armed attack on the island would have "grave consequences" for China, and Clinton deployed a large naval flotilla in the area. The crisis subsided after March 23, when Lee won reelection, but refrained from declaring independence.

As tensions flared between China and the United States, American officials placed renewed emphasis on the semi-dormant security alliance with Japan. Since Nixon's opening to China and the end of the Vietnam War, American military forces based in Japan and Okinawa had seemed almost superfluous. During the 1980s, when Reagan challenged Soviet influence globally, the United States tried, with only modest success, to enlist Japan as a more active cold war partner. This effort faded, along with the Soviet Union, in the early 1990s.

In April 1996, with one eye on China, President Clinton visited Japan. Clinton and Japanese Prime Minister Hashimoto Ryutaro agreed to extend and revitalize the U.S.–Japan mutual security pact. Americans pledged to assist Japan in developing a regional antimissile defense system. Although nominally designed to counter a potential North Korean threat, American plans to build missile defenses in Asia and within the United States seemed directed against China's small but growing rocket arsenal.

China's muscle flexing, although not aimed directly at the United States, provoked politicians and the press to voice the most strident anti-Chinese rhetoric since the Nixon visit of 1972. In the run-up to the 1996 U.S. presidential election, Republican nominee Bob Dole bitterly attacked Clinton's China policy, even though the Democratic incumbent had stood by Taiwan and criticized Chinese behavior. Dole and other Republicans demanded that the president provide increased military assistance to Taiwan and China's other neighbors.

Congressional Republicans also tapped into a growing popular fascination with Tibet, an ethnically and religiously distinct area controlled by China. This vast, sparsely populated area had long been dominated by a form of Buddhism that looked to successive Dalai Lamas as spiritual and political heads of state. Tibet had been part of the Qing empire until 1911, when it broke away from China. Communist forces re-annexed Tibet to the

PRC in 1950 and imposed a treaty in 1951 that promised a degree of cultural and religious autonomy. In 1959, Tibetans, aided by the CIA, revolted against Chinese rule. When the rebellion collapsed, Tibet's religious leader, the Dalai Lama fled into exile in India.

Over the subsequent decades, the Dalai Lama won a Nobel Prize for peace and also proved a media-savvy advocate for the cause of Tibetan autonomy. He conducted seminars for wealthy Americans in expensive resorts and even appeared on television commercials. His popular appeal, as well as China's continued heavy-handed rule, that included cultural repression and settling large numbers of non-Tibetans in the province, created genuine sympathy among Americans for Tibet's plight. Several Hollywood films produced during the 1990s, such as *Seven Years in Tibet, Little Buddah,* and *Kundun* presented Tibet in glowing images that recalled "Shangri-La," the heaven-on-earth of the 1937 film *Lost Horizon.* These films brought the plight of Tibet before a larger public and prompted congressional Republicans to pass resolutions condemning China's occupation policies.

Until Dole and his GOP colleagues launched these attacks, Chinese officials had not shown much enthusiasm for President Clinton. But the pro-Taiwan, anti-China Republican rhetoric made the Democratic incumbent more appealing to Beijing. To avoid making trouble for Clinton, China resolved several small issues dividing the two countries and suggested an exchange of presidential visits following the American election. Clinton's reelection eased China's immediate concern, but soon Beijing's alleged effort to buy political influence in the United States exploded, along with the Whitewater and Monica Lewinsky scandals, as one of issues dogging Clinton during his second term.

In the run-up to the 1996 election, Clinton and Vice-President Al Gore had aggressively raised campaign funds. They eagerly tapped donors among the growing Asian-American community. The lax laws governing political donations stipulated that only U.S. citizens or legal residents could make contributions. Shortly before the 1996 vote, evidence surfaced that some foreign nationals and Chinese-owned businesses had given funds to the Democratic party, as well as to individual candidates. When this came to light, the Democratic National Committee returned the money to the questionable donors. This failed to mollify Republicans, who retained control of both houses of Congress, despite Clinton's reelection. For most of the next four years, Representative Dan Burton and Senator Fred Thomson conducted highly partisan probes into Clinton's fundraising.

At the center of the controversy were two Chinese-Americans, Charlie Trie and John Huang. Trie, an obscure restaurant owner from Little Rock,

Arkansas, was a self-described Clinton "groupie." In return for gathering donations valued at about $645,000, Trie was permitted to take visiting Chinese businessmen on tours of the White House.

John Huang also attracted Republican attention. Before serving in the Clinton Commerce Department, Huang had worked as the U.S. representative of the Indonesian Lippo Group, a banking conglomerate owned by the Riady family. While working as a Democratic fundraiser in 1996, Huang brought in nearly $3.5 million and treated donors to White House tours.

Whether or not, as Republicans charged but never proved, the Riady family had made illegal campaign contributions and received special treatment, they certainly had done a favor for Hillary Clinton's friend and former law partner, Webster Hubbell. After resigning from the Justice Department under a cloud (he was later convicted of illegally billing clients while a private attorney), Hubbell was hired by Lippo. Clinton's critics claimed the job was actually a form of "hush money" paid to Hubbell to buy his silence about unspecified misdeeds by the Clintons.

These murky relationships revealed more about the muddled nature of campaign fundraising in the United States than about any organized Chinese effort to manipulate American politics. Congressional investigators failed to uncover any evidence of collusion between the president and Chinese officials. Many of the Chinese-Americans, Chinese nationals, and Chinese-owned businesses linked to questionable donations to the Clinton reelection campaign were actually associated with Taiwan or Chinese communities in Southeast Asia, not with the PRC. For example, Republicans ridiculed Vice-president Al Gore for accepting donations from Buddhist monks during a brief stop in 1996 at a temple in Los Angeles. Besides the fact that Gore probably did not know that local Chinese-American business groups had used the monks as a cover for their contributions, the religious sect and its adherents were based in Taiwan. Republicans showed no interest in tracking down Taiwan-based donations to GOP candidates.

As soon as serious questions were raised about these Chinese-linked donations, Democratic party officials returned all the money raised by Trie and most of that channeled through Huang. This only convinced Republican critics they were on to something and they promised to show that Clinton and Gore colluded in a plot by China to "pour illegal money into American political campaigns" and to "subvert our electoral process." Ultimately, investigators found a few, minor figures who may have channeled small amounts of money from Chinese nationals with links to the PRC. But all "Chinese money" comprised chump change compared to the $2 billion or more raised and spent by the Democratic and Republican parties in 1996.

These persistent attacks put Clinton's policy on the defensive. Diplomats and academic "China experts" generally agreed that the best way to insure that China respected international trade and copyright practices and treated its own labor force more fairly was to grant Beijing "permanent, normal trade relations" (PNTR) and speed its entry into the WTO. But Clinton hesitated until nearly the end of his second term before taking any actions that might be construed by his opponents or the American public as too "pro-Chinese." Meanwhile, the president's critics, largely, but not exclusively, on the religious right, blamed him for tolerating China's crackdown on Christian religious groups and indigenous spiritual movements, such as the Falun Gong sect.

Perhaps nothing exemplified the quasi-racist criticism of the Clinton administration as much as the March 24, 1997 cover of the conservative Republican journal, *National Review*. Dubbing the president the "Manchurian Candidate" (an allusion to the 1963 film depicting a Chinese Communist "sleeper agent" and assassin), the cover portrayed Bill and Hillary Clinton and Vice President Al Gore in "yellow face." The president, shown as a buck-toothed, squinty-eyed house boy wearing a straw hat, serves coffee. The first lady, similarly buck-toothed and squinting, is dressed as a Maoist Red Guard and waves a "Little Red Book." The hapless vice president wears Buddhist robes and carries a begging bowl stuffed with cash. The *National Review* repeated the mantra that China had bought the 1996 election and "owned" the president, ignoring the fact that well over 99 percent of contributions to both parties came from sources other than China or its friends.

In February 1997, after three years out of public view, Deng Xiaoping died at age 92. In power almost as long as Mao, Deng had left nearly as dramatic an imprint on China as had the PRC's founder. President Jiang Zemin , a Deng protégé, stepped up to fill his mentor's place. On June 30, 1997, in an act portrayed as finally erasing ignominious defeat in the first Opium War, Jiang presided over the return of Hong Kong to China. Portuguese Macao followed in 1999, after 442 years as a colony. This left only Taiwan separated from the "motherland."

As agreed to before the American presidential election, Jiang Zemin visited Washington in October 1997. Clinton and Jiang failed to soften the hard edges dividing their two countries. The American president refused to cease U.S. military sales to Taiwan; Jiang rejected calls for China to adopt American human rights standards. Clinton chided Jiang by telling him that China stood on the "wrong side of history" by refusing to expand political freedom for its people.

President Bill Clinton, with Chinese President Jiang Zemin, reviews Chinese troops near Tiananmen Square, June 1998. (Corbis)

But soon after Jiang left the United States, a State Department spokesman reassured China that the United States firmly opposed Taiwanese independence, any sort of "two-China" policy, or Taiwan's reentry into the United Nations. China responded by releasing democracy rights crusader Wei Jingsheng, who had spent most of the previous fourteen years in jail. Wei was exiled from China and given asylum in the United States. He accepted an invitation to the White House and took a job at Columbia University.

Unfortunately, Wei proved a more inspiring symbol of democracy while in China than in exile. He found it difficult to adjust to life in the United States and soon alienated most of his American supporters. Nearly as unhappy in the "free world" as in China, Wei adopted a nomadic lifestyle, claiming that enemies continued to pursue him.

In June 1998, amidst the furor of the Monica Lewinsky sex scandal, a politically wounded President Clinton traveled to China. There he spoke forcefully about the misgivings many Americans felt toward the Chinese government. In an unprecedented, live, televised press conference held with Jiang in Beijing, Clinton said of the Tiananmen incident, "I believe and the American people believe that the use of force and the tragic loss of life was wrong." Picking up the cudgels, Jiang replied that "had the Chinese government not taken the resolute measures, we could not have enjoyed the stability that we are enjoying today."

Although these assertions covered familiar ground, Clinton and Jiang then engaged in a lively and thoughtful discussion about the nature of democracy, the treatment of dissidents in both countries, and American concern about Chinese misrule in Tibet. This was probably the most wide-ranging political debate aired publicly in China since 1949. In a speech he delivered in Shanghai a few days later, Clinton showed his appreciation for the open forum by publicly endorsing the "Three No" policy near and dear to the Chinese leadership. The United States would not support an independent Taiwan, would not recognize two Chinas, and would not support UN membership for Taiwan. This reassured Beijing that, at least for the time being, Washington would not challenge its self-image as the sole government of all China and all Chinese. But just as the roller coaster of U.S.–China relations seemed to level off, new crises threatened to spin out of control.

In 1997–98, the Asian "economic miracle" came to an abrupt halt. After two decades of rapid growth, Thailand, South Korea, and Indonesia were rocked by severe financial problems linked to excess debt and corruption. Even though the panic did not directly affect Asia's biggest industrial economy, Japan, that nation remained mired in a chronic recession that began in the early 1990s. The prospect of stalled Chinese economic development left American officials shuddering. Fortunately, the sustained growth of the U.S. economy during the second Clinton administration provided an outlet that helped several Asian nations export their way back to solvency by 2000. Nevertheless, these events stressed the link between Asia's stability and prosperity and the key balancing role played by the American economy. It seemed all the more important to integrate China more fully into the world economy.

While financial analysts pondered the impact of the Asian economic crisis, new questions arose over the status of Taiwan. Facing an election the next year, in the summer of 1999, Lee Teng-hui began speaking of Taiwan as a sovereign nation that China should deal with on a "state-to-state" basis. This appeal to a segment of the island's population that preferred separatism to any link with Beijing outraged the PRC. Lee's rhetoric alienated as many voters as it attracted. In March 2000, in a three-way race, Chen Shui-bian won election as Taiwan's first president from outside the Kuomintang. PRC leaders took no pleasure in Lee's defeat, since Chen came from the Democratic Progressive party, an advocate of Taiwan independence.

In 1999–2000, the Clinton administration felt whipsawed by Taiwan's leaders, who toyed with declaring independence, China's strident opposition to any such move, and accusations from congressional Republicans and journalists that in return for financial support the president had ignored China's growing threat to U.S. and Asian security. For example, in May 1999, Representative Christopher Cox, a California Republican, released a 700-page portion of a larger classified report (commissioned by Speaker Newt Gingrich, who hoped to show a link between Chinese campaign money and Clinton's actions) that accused China of engaging in a massive espionage scheme. According to Cox, China had spent years secretly collecting computer codes and design information from the nuclear weapons laboratory at Los Alamos, New Mexico, and from other facilities. From these sources, it learned how to build seven of America's most advanced nuclear warheads that could be placed on long-range missiles. As a result, the report asserted, China posed a "credible direct threat against the United States."

According to the authors of this study, Chinese espionage stretched back to the early 1950s. Then, a Chinese-born scientist, Qian Xuesen, working on jet and rocket propulsion, played a key role in developing some of America's first missiles. But when he attempted to return to China, he was stripped of his security clearance and kept in the United States against his will for several years. After 1955, when Qian and several other Chinese scientists were finally permitted to leave, they pioneered the development of China's first ballistic missiles and nuclear weapons. Now, as in the cold war, the Cox report implied, every Chinese exchange student, scholar, permanent resident, or Chinese-American citizen might be a potential spy prepared to carry out an act of treachery. These allegations were accepted at face value by most of the press. Even *The New York Times* praised the Cox Committee for performing an "invaluable service with its unsparing investigation."

China, like the United States and most other nations, certainly gathered military and technological secrets from abroad. Security at American weapons laboratories and in private defense facilities had been lax and probably had resulted in the loss of classified information. But most nonpartisan specialists believed that China's efforts to acquire military technology exploited a combination of open sources, accidental disclosures, and pumping scientists for useful data at international conferences. Outright theft of secret data by Chinese agents was a small part of the operation. In fact, some of those who most harshly accused China of espionage based their conclusion on a handbook published openly by the PRC that suggested ways in which Chinese scientists could gather information from foreign books, articles, conference papers, and the Internet. A certain amount of espionage would always be necessary, the manual acknowledged, but a massive amount of information could be gleaned from open sources.

China's critics seemed equally enraged by Beijing's admission that it trolled for foreign information and by America's porous security. Yet most experts argued that the very openness of American society, with its free exchange of information, assured its scientific and technological strength, not its weakness.

Despite exaggerated talk of a Chinese nuclear threat to the United States, Taiwan, and other parts of Asia, the fact remained that at the beginning of the millennium, the PRC had a tiny navy, an obsolete air force, and about twenty missiles with nuclear warheads capable of reaching U.S. territory. (It had several hundred short-range missiles able to reach Taiwan.) In comparison, the United States could hit China with as many as 8,000 nuclear weapons. China's military capacity would, inevitably, increase with its economic development. But greater power need not make it a greater threat. Skillful diplomacy was designed to manage change and avert arms races.

In an atmosphere that sometimes approached hysteria, the FBI identified and eventually arrested a prime suspect in China's alleged espionage plot. Wen Ho Lee, a Taiwan-born physicist and weapons designer at the Los Alamos laboratory, was suspected of downloading a vast amount of top secret data from a secure computer and passing the copied computer tapes to China. Off the record, federal officials claimed that Lee had stolen the "crown jewels" of American nuclear weapons secrets and his betrayal threatened to tip the global balance of power in China's favor.

Lee was held in solitary confinement for a year and threatened with execution unless he confessed. Yet the FBI, and the departments of Energy and Justice failed to uncover evidence of Lee's espionage. Officials belatedly admitted that they had ignored other leads because of a mindset that targeted ethnic Chinese. Ultimately, Lee was permitted to plead guilty to a single count of unauthorized copying of classified data. He admitted copying the files, but insisted it was for his own use. After the plea bargain, investigators suggested that Lee may have hoped to trade the tapes for jobs with institutions in Australia, Switzerland, or Taiwan, rather than China.

In July 2000, just as serious doubts emerged about the Wen Ho Lee case, Representative Cox released a follow-up report highlighting the North Korean "threat" to American security. Cox declared that North Korea was not only a "monstrous tyranny," but also posed "one of the greatest threats to American and allied interests anywhere around the globe." The Clinton administration, he suggested, had largely ignored evidence of a North Korean effort to build atomic weapons and a missile system.

Whatever North Korea's pretensions, by 2000, the reclusive, hard-line Communist regime was so beset by famine and poverty that it extended a hand of friendship to its arch rival, South Korea. After an exchange of visits between Korean presidents Kim Jong Il and Kim Dai Jong, tensions on the peninsula eased considerably. Cox's accusations fell largely on deaf ears. However, since the PRC remained North Korea's only patron, the report served as an indirect way to demonize China. As some cynics have noted, both Cox reports, on the Chinese and North Korean nuclear missile threats, coincided with Republican congressional efforts to revive the expensive but faltering antiballistic missile program (ABM) begun during the Reagan administration. Before leaving office, President Clinton hesitated to approve ABM deployment, which appeared costly, unreliable, and unpopular among both America's allies and potential adversaries.

Republicans countered that China already posed a threat and that so-called rogue states such as North Korea, Iran, and Iraq might, with China's help, soon deploy nuclear-armed rockets. China's admission, in 2000, that it had sold missile technology to Iran and Pakistan during the 1990s raised troubling questions, even though Beijing pledged to cease future transfers. President George W. Bush's determination to build a missile shield seemed likely to provoke renewed tension between China and the United States.

ANOTHER WALK THROUGH TIANANMEN

After a century of often topsy-turvy relations, China and the United States seemed, in some ways, to have revived the mutually hostile images and relations that thrived in the late nineteenth century and during the cold war. During the "thaw" of 1971–89, Chinese and American leaders found a common interest in restraining the Soviet Union. As Mao put it bluntly, "we can cooperate against a bastard!" But the Soviet threat began fading under Gorbachev and largely disappeared with the collapse of the Soviet Union in 1991. This alleviated Beijing's dependence on Washington for security, as well as Washington's need for Chinese leverage against Russia. In 1989, the Tiananmen incident revived among Americans some of their worst fears about Chinese government values and behavior. Even though most Chinese live today in a more free and materially abundant society than at any time in the past century, China still falls well short of American human rights and democratic standards.

Chinese leaders, for both cynical and sincere reasons, questioned U.S. motives. From the perspective of the government in Beijing, China had moved toward the goal of greater democracy and respect for human rights. They feared that more rapid reform and loosening of controls might lead to the kinds of chaos that engulfed post-Communist Russia. Also, as China moved toward WTO membership, it would have to phase out subsidies for state-run industry and open its credit, agricultural, and consumer markets to foreign competition. However positive this change proved to be in the long run, it would almost certainly displace millions of workers and peasants who depended on the state-run economy. This, the PRC leadership argued, required a strong government hand to assure an orderly transformation.

China also questioned U.S. motives on Taiwan, as well as its efforts to enhance the security treaty with Japan. Whatever other reasons existed for playing the nationalism card, China's rulers really do consider Taiwan a renegade province, and they bitterly resent its being treated as a sovereign state. U.S. assertions of interest in the island's security, along with continuation of the security treaty with Japan, strike many Chinese as thinly veiled efforts to "contain" China.

The large Chinese trade surplus with the United States (about $84 billion in 2000) also looked different from each side of the Pacific. American politicians, labor unions, and manufacturers complain that China floods America with cheap products, but seals itself off from foreign competition. By one calculation, at least 28 percent of all Chinese exports go to the United States, while, proportionately, a much smaller fraction of U.S. exports are sold to China. In fact, the trade pattern followed the rule of comparative advantage. China sells the United States mostly textiles, shoes, toys, and other light consumer goods. Few of these products have been produced in American factories since the 1960s, when their production shifted to Japan, then to Taiwan, Southeast Asia, and Latin America. Thus, the big Chinese surplus did not directly undermine manufacturing jobs in the United States, but came at the expense of Asian and Latin American exporters. The United States sells China computers, civilian aircraft, automobiles, scientific equipment, and foodstuffs—all products that American industry produces competitively.

Since American immigration law dropped racial and ethnic quotas in 1965, the number of Asians entering the United States has increased dramatically. During the 1990s, the number of ethnic Asians living in this country increased from 2 to 4 percent of the population. Ethnic Chinese comprise a large portion of this group. In the 1990s, a few sensational cases of immigrant smuggling, organized prostitution rings, and drug cartels revived images of Chinatown gang wars and opium dens in San Francisco and New York. The Wen Ho Lee "spy" case similarly revealed how quickly American officials and journalists assumed that Chinese-American "group loyalty" made even respected professionals predisposed to betray the United States in favor of their ancestral homeland. In fact, ethnic Chinese and other Asian immigrants are generally well-educated, highly motivated, and law-abiding citizens. Far from undermining America, Chinese, like Latin American immigrants, have helped revive inner cities and have economically and socially enriched the fabric of American life.

In spite of mutual suspicion between China and the United States at the beginning of the new millennium, the process of economic and cultural globalization may be greater than the power of sovereign governments. For example, the five million Chinese and numerous foreign tourists who visit the Forbidden City each year still pass through the portal of Tiananmen, capped by its giant photograph of Mao Zedong. As they walk across acres of gray cobblestones and past the vermilion pavilions topped by orange glazed tiles, they finally approach the Palace of Heavenly Purity. Here, the Ming and Qing emperors once resided, and the palace remains the symbolic center of the Chinese universe. Starting in October 2000, visitors encounter another powerful symbol, the forest green logo of Starbuck's Coffee, which recently opened a shop beside the palace.

In June 2001, China's central government and the Beijing municipal administration sponsored a concert in the Forbidden City as part of their eventually successful effort to attract the 2008 Summer Olympics. Nearly 30,000 Chinese each paid between $30 and $2,000 to sip a latte while listening to the "Three Tenors" perform Italian opera arias in the immense courtyards through which Boxers and Red Guards had not so long before chased foreigners and bourgeois revisionists. It seems a fair guess that during the twenty-first century, separately and together, the United States and China will pursue paths that will amaze us.

SELECTED ADDITIONAL READINGS

David M. Lampton, *Same Bed, Different Dreams: Managing U.S.–China Relations, 1989–2000* (Berkeley, Calif., 2001); Jim Mann, *About Face: A History of America's Curious Relationship with China, from Nixon to Clinton* (New York, 1999); Patrick Tyler, *A Great Wall: Six American Presidents and China* (New York, 1999); Robert Ross, ed., *After the Cold War: Domestic Factors and U.S.–China Relations* (New York, 1998); Robert G.

Sutter, *U.S. Policy toward China: An Introduction to the Role of Interest Groups* (Lanham, Md., 1998); John W. Garver, *Face Off: China, the United States, and Taiwan's Democratization* (Seattle, Wash., 1997); Ezra F. Vogel, ed., *Living with China: U.S.–China Relations in the Twenty-First Century* (New York, 1997); Richard Bernstein and Ross H. Munro, *Coming Conflict with China* (New York, 1998); Bruce Cumings, *Parallax Visions: Making Sense of American–East Asian Relations at the End of the Century* (Raleigh-Durham, N.C., 1999); James L. Watson, *Golden Arches East: McDonald's in East Asia* (Stanford, Calif., 1997); Ko-Lin Chin, *Smuggled Chinese: Clandestine Immigration to the United States* (Philadelphia, 2000); As distinct from thoughtful criticism of China and U.S. policy, the following examples more closely resemble the "yellow peril" tracts of earlier times: *Report of the Select Committee on U.S. National Security and Military/Commercial Concerns with the People's Republic of China* ["Cox Report"] (Washington, D.C., 1999); Bill Geertz, *The China Threat: How the People's Republic Targets America* (Chicago, 2000); Steven W. Mosher, *Hegemon: The Chinese Plan to Dominate Asia and the World* (San Francisco, 2000); Edward Timperlake and William C. Triplett II, *Red Dragon Rising: Communist China's Military Threat to America* (Chicago, 1999), and, *Year of the Rat: How Bill Clinton Compromised U.S. Security for Cash* (Chicago, 1998). A far more balanced discussion of likely events can be found in Gordon Chang, *The Coming Collapse of China* (New York, 2001).

Index